RECEPTIONS AND TRANSFORMATIONS OF THE BIBLE

RELIGION AND NORMATIVITY
VOLUME 2

RECEPTIONS AND TRANSFORMATIONS OF THE BIBLE

Edited by Kirsten Nielsen

Acta Jutlandica
Theological Series

Aarhus University Press |

Receptions and transformations of the Bible
Religion and normativity vol. 2
© Aarhus University Press and the authors 2009

Cover, design and typesetting by Jørgen Sparre
Printed by Narayana Press, Gylling
Printed in Denmark 2009

ISBN 978 87 7934 426 7
ISSN 0065 1354 – Acta Jutlandica
ISSN 0106 0945 – Theological Series

Published with the financial support of
Aarhus University Research Foundation
The Learned Society in Aarhus
The Theological Faculty at Aarhus University

Aarhus University Press
Langelandsgade 177
DK-8200 Aarhus N
www.unipress.dk

INTERNATIONAL DISTRIBUTORS:
Gazelle Book Services Ltd.
White Cross Mills
Hightown, Lancaster, LA1 4XS
United Kingdom
www.gazellebookservices.co.uk

The David Brown Book Company
Box 511
Oakville, CT 06779
USA
www.oxbowbooks.com

TABLE OF CONTENTS

PREFACE

In 2005 the Faculty of Theology, Aarhus University, chose as its research priority area *Religion and normativity*. This research priority area builds on existing research on topics covered by the faculty's strengths, and is divided into three themes:

Theme 1: The discursive fight over religious texts
Theme 2: Bible and literature – receptions and transformations of the Bible
Theme 3: Religion, politics, and law.

The research priority area has contributed to a deeper understanding of the role played by religion in defining past and present cultures and societies. Its participants have compared Judaism, Christianity, Islam and antique religions in the light of exegetical, historical and systematic perspectives. In a contemporary context, they have explored whether religion is still normative.

The result of their research is presented in a three-volume work entitled:

The discursive fight over religious texts in antiquity, Religion and normativity, Vol. 1, ed. by Anders-Christian Jacobsen.

Receptions and transformations of the Bible, Religion and normativity, Vol. 2, ed. by Kirsten Nielsen,

Religion, politics, and law, Religion and normativity, Vol. 3, ed. by Peter Lodberg.

The three editors wish to express their sincere thanks to the participants in the research area for many stimulating discussions during the research period, and for their contributions to these three volumes.

The Faculty of Theology, Aarhus University, has provided excellent working conditions and financial support, for which we are most grateful.

Thanks are also due to Aarhus University Press for taking care of the publishing in a very professional way.

Finally we wish to thank the University Research Foundation and Det Lærde Selskab (the Learned Society) Aarhus for financial support.

Anders-Christian Jacobsen, Peter Lodberg, Kirsten Nielsen
Aarhus, April, 2009

INTRODUCTION[1]

Kirsten Nielsen

Religion and normativity. Receptions and transformations of the Bible is the second volume in a 3-volume work, the result of inter-disciplinary studies at the Faculty of Theology, Aarhus University from 2005 to 2008. During this period a large number of faculty members worked on the subject of "Religion and Normativity" as a specific research priority area involving three themes. The first was "The discursive struggle over religious texts in antiquity" (Volume I), which focuses on the construction of normative texts in early Christianity and Judaism and is followed by a discussion of the authoritative interpretation of the canon and the rewriting of normative texts in new situations. The subject for the second group was "The Bible and literature: Reception and Transformation" (Volume II), with the sub-title "Receptions and transformations of the Bible". With the Bible as their common starting-point, partly in the Jewish and partly in the Christian tradition, some contributors to this volume have worked on the reception and transformation that takes place in and through literature, while others have concentrated on the role that the Bible has played in both philosophical thought and religious practice. The third group, "Religion, politics and law" (Volume III), has focused on the question of religious authority in a broader social context, and in particular on a fundamental philosophical appraisal of our current understanding of democracy in the relationship between state, church and religion in a multi-cultural society.

Normativity

In the course of the research project the three groups drew up a working definition of the concept of *normativity*: 'A (religious) norm is a precept/model concerned with an interpretation of life and/or practice whose binding character is built on a socially accepted authority.' This working definition has provided the focus for the studies and thereby served to raise such questions as: How does a religious norm come to be experienced as binding for individuals or groups? What is it that defines it as 'binding'? Does the Bible still have a normative function, or has literature, for example, taken over as the setter of norms and the creator of identity?

---

1   This introduction has been translated by Edward Broadbridge.

General Reflections. Receptions and transformations of the Bible

The working group behind the present book, Volume II, has concentrated on the *Bible* as normative. As a canon the Bible has a normative function in Christianity, just as the written and oral Torah is normative for Jewish communities. But it is not only in religious practice that the Bible plays an important role. It is reflected in various ways in historical and modern literature and in philosophical thought on the nature of life. How then can the Bible be understood as 'normative' today? Is it still normative as a historical account? Is its worldview in any sense normative? Or its conception of God? Is the Bible in a sense 'normative' when used as a source of inspiration for a more authentic life?

It is questions such as these that are treated in the various articles on the 'reception and transformation of the Bible'.

Volume II consists of three sections dealing with receptions and transformations of the Bible in (1) literature, (2) philosophy, and (3) the Jewish and the Christian communities' respective use of the Bible. Each of the three sections has its specific focus and is therefore introduced with some general reflections on how reception and transformation take place. The section on the Bible in literature is introduced by David Bugge under the title *The Bible in literature: a typology*, p. 20-27. Marie Vejrup Nielsen's article, *Wrestling with the text*, presents the central premises behind articles on the Bible in philosophy and science, p. 88-92 while Marianne Schleicher's contribution, *Addressed by scripture*, p. 136-140, introduces the reader to the use of the Bible in Jewish and Christian practice.

That reception and transformation are closely linked is demonstrated by *David Bugge*, who formulates his main thesis thus: 'True, any reception includes a construction and so, to some extent, a transformation, just as every transformation implies a reception. This is but a hermeneutical truism. In our everyday language, however, there is a difference of degree between the two concepts in question, of great use when forming a general view of the varied constellations of the Bible in literature. While *reception* simply indicates the pure act of receiving a certain text, *transformation* points to the change or metamorphosis that takes place.'

On this basis David Bugge distinguishes between five different forms of reception and transformation of the Bible in literature. The first is *retelling*, which is close to being a pure translation of a text. Next comes *further writing*, in which the biblical figures retain their names but the author supplies a high degree of *gap-filling*. The third form is *rewriting*, which is characterised by a wider degree of scene change in that the context is often no longer the Bible but the present day. A further form is *counter writing*, in which the biblical narrative is changed so that the point or the moral is turned 180 degrees. The fifth and final form is defined through the concept of *writing as such*, where the focus is the writing process itself. As an example of this David Bugge cites the figure of Cain as depicted by the Danish writer Martin A. Hansen (1909-55). Cain, Bugge says, 'is not only a literary character; he becomes the symbol of the writer himself *in his capacity as a writer*' (cf. p. 26).

David Bugge applies this typology to the reception and transformation of the Bible in literature, but behind the whole question of reworking the original lies the fundamental condition for all engagement with the Bible: the difference in time and culture between the biblical world and ours. How to receive texts written in another culture and addressed to readers very different from ourselves? This subject, which continues to occupy theologians and philosophers, is the starting point for *Marie Vejrup Nielsen's* reflections. For is it possible at all to overcome the distance in time between the biblical texts and the present day? And is it defensible to insist that texts by writers from antiquity can still be normative today? A common denominator in the three articles in this section, argues Marie Vejrup Nielsen, is 'a critical attitude towards the Bible, ranging from a dismissal of the text altogether, to a position more concerned with reaching its deeper meaning and bringing it to light through new ways of reading.' p. 89. The need to keep wrestling with these ancient texts and to both receive and transform them arises because they 'are texts about what it means to be human. In short, they matter to us, irrespective of whether we engage with them in order to find truth or, alternatively, to examine them critically and maybe even finally discard them' p. 92.

Reception and transformation are further illuminated in *Marianne Schleicher's* introduction. In Jewish and Christian tradition the Bible is understood as a form of address by God to mankind. The address exists in written form and is therefore set free from its original situation. Since scripture is no longer limited to its original audience, it is possible for the community to read it as a recurrently present address and thus to overcome the time lapse between then and now. Marianne Schleicher summarises the aim of her introduction thus: 'The general reflections in this section on the reception and transformation of the Bible in religious communities will suggest how the ritual setting and human psychology enable this transformation.' p. 136. How this transformation can take place is explained through Julia Kristeva's concept of intertextuality, which she defines as 'a transposition of one (or several) sign system(s) into another.' Or to put it another way: 'a dialogue among several writings: that of the writer, the addressee (or the character), and the contemporary or earlier context.' p. 137. Employing Kristeva's theory, Marianne Schleicher demonstrates how the text acquires a mediating function between three contexts: the author, the text and the addressee. Further application of Kristeva's psychoanalytical theories serves to amplify how the individual can experience the texts as a personal address during a service of worship.

Receptions and transformations of the Bible in literature

These general reflections are followed by the relevant articles in each section. Those on reception and transformation in literature discuss the following modern writers: Torgny Lindgren from Sweden, Philip Pullman from England, the Czech-French writer Milan Kundera and the Danish Martin A. Hansen.

Kirsten M. Andersen shows how time and again Torgny Lindgren's novel *Doré's Bible* refers to the Bible with Doré's illustrations, but as a great humorist Lindgren knows how to exploit the biblical references in surprising ways. The main character is steeped in biblical ideas, having pored over the Bible often as a child. But he gradually drifts away from it, first when he is sent away from home, and later when his Bible is lost in a fire. He then attempts to re-create what has been lost. In an important scene before the fire the narrator, back home on a brief visit, has the opportunity to kneel and touch the Bible in its resting-place in a safe. The scene is imbued with a sardonic feeling of awe. The father stands to attention and commands the boy. The whole scene has a biblical tinge, even though it takes place in a world devoid of liturgical practice and with no religious or divine authority. The protagonist's childhood meeting with Doré's illustrations comes to determine his understanding of existence. He sees everything around him in the light of these pictures. So when the Bible is finally lost, he makes every effort to recreate it through memory.

The novel deals with the universal realisation that every individual inherits the world into which he or she is born – in this case as a prisoner of Doré's powerful illustrations, which become his mentor. Simultaneously the boy experiences other forms of authority in his home, notably through two contrasting versions of paternal authority. His father and grandfather represent science and art respectively, the father being the rationalist who applies mathematics and logic even when imagining God and eternity, the grandfather being a former professor of literature who retells the great literary classics to the boy. The novel is full of such contrasts, forcing the reader to a renewed consideration of what influences a person, including what authority lies within the ideas we inherit. We are all late-born children in relation to previous generations. Kirsten M. Andersen describes *Doré's Bible* as a novel that raises the question of the 'existential meaning of authority: of what it means to hand down tradition, instruct and educate.' p. 29.

Laura Feldt's article is concerned with a topical example of fantasy literature, Philip Pullman's trilogy *His Dark Materials*. By way of introduction Laura Feldt points out that all reception and transformation of the Bible in modern literature, positive as well as negative, may be said to participate in the perpetuation of the earlier work in the cultural memory, and as such always contributes to confirming the authority of the Bible.

With this in mind she demonstrates how the Bible still plays a normative role even in Pullman's fantasy trilogy. Despite the fact that his work is often labelled anti-Christian because of its extremely critical attitude towards the church as an institution, Laura Feldt argues that the author is in fact deeply indebted to the myth of the Fall of Man in Genesis 3, which is introduced directly no fewer than three times in the trilogy, and not just in its original but also in its transformed form. Moreover, the very narrative form that Pullman employs in the story of Lyra and Will reflects the myth of Adam and Eve in Genesis. The use of the myth of the Fall as an intertext also explains why there is no happy ending to the trilogy. Furthermore, Pullman develops his anthropology in direct continuation of the Old Testament. In consequence, man's lot can be described as the passage from community and blessedness to hard work, pain, and separation. In defining the human condition in terms of toil, pain, separation, sex, and the search for love and wisdom *His Dark Materials* also echoes Old Testament anthropology.

Laura Feldt therefore concludes that 'Biblical texts continue to shape, and be re-interpreted by, not only high culture but popular cultural products such as fantasy fiction. Indeed, it appears that fantasy literature is able to re-enact central biblical stories in a modern context in a way that reaches out to a greater public than the Bible itself.' p. 60-61.

In his article on Milan Kundera *David Bugge* elects not to point out particular motifs in Kundera's work but rather to discuss in principle the question: 'How does literature and its particular way of exploring human existence relate to the Gospel?' p. 65. His thesis is that there is 'a striking parallel between the Christian Gospel and Milan Kundera's meta-literary reflections on the art of the novel.' p. 65. For when Kundera characterises the novel as the imaginary paradise of individuals, the question is whether this paradise is so different from the kingdom of God of which Christianity speaks.

Kundera is not a Christian writer. On the contrary, in his opinion a writer must avoid all forms of identification with religion or ideology. For far too long art has been employed in the service of the church. He insists that '...putting a novel to the service of any authority, however noble, would be impossible for a true novelist.' p. 67. Literature must create *new* insight into human life; that is its raison d'être. The many truths of modernity thereby challenge the one and only truth. And yet, an analysis of Kundera's novel *The Farewell Party* reveals that the plot itself is an expression of 'a straight reception and transformation of the Gospel's "paradise" theme', showing how 'a radical all-including condemnation' has been replaced by 'a radical all-embracing love.' p. 76.

The Danish author Martin A. Hansen offers an example of a modern writer who has struggled with his relationship to Christianity and with the question of how far one can combine a Christian interpretation of life with being a writer. In his article *Jakob Nissen* describes how the writer to begin with sought inspiration from the Bible. But the conventional way of reading the Bible was a barrier to new understanding. Not until he met one of the great contemporary critics, Georg Brandes, who read the Bible like any other work of literature, could Martin A. Hansen himself re-read the biblical narratives. And his new insight meant that he could see that the gospel was *not* an expression of bourgeois norms, as he had been led to believe, but something quite different: 'The Gospel is strange, violent, terrifying at times, horrible to those who only have a taste for decency.' p. 80.

For Martin A. Hansen it was important to see the Bible as a source of inspiration for art but at the same time to underline that, precisely in its encounter with art, Christianity 'would be safeguarded against the pitfalls of inflexibility and rigidity, and be constantly renewed.' p. 82.

Receptions and transformations of the Bible in philosophy

The section on literary reworkings of the Bible is followed by three articles on the Bible's role in philosophy. Iben Damgaard has chosen to look at Søren Kierkegaard in this respect, while Maria Møller deals with the Danish theologian K.E. Løgstrup (1905-81) who, like Kierkegaard, has played a crucial role in Danish philosophy and theology. In the third article Marie Vejrup Nielsen looks at modern thought on evolution and at the ways in which scholars of evolution have used the Bible both in researching their field and in communicating their results.

The starting point for *Iben Damgaard* is the reader's role and the reader's freedom, both of which are important to Søren Kierkegaard, who adopts a relatively free attitude when reworking biblical texts and themes. However, this does not prevent him from believing that the Bible enjoys a particular authority. In what, then, does this authority consist? For Kierkegaard it is crucial that the reader does not just *read* the texts but repeats them in his own life. '*Reception* involves *transformation*, since the meaning to be understood in the text is only fully realised in the reader's actualization of it in his own existence. The reader is expected to transform the text into action, and this is stressed throughout the discourse when Kierkegaard reminds the reader of the task of responsible decision and self-appropriation.' p. 101. Kierkegaard argues that the biblical texts have become such an integral part of our culture that we have ceased to be aware of their challenging potential, and he therefore sets out to deconstruct this 'domestication' of scripture. The article explores this by focusing on Kierkegaard's reception and transformation of the Book of Job. Kierkegaard recontextualises Job's questions about the meaning of life and suffering in his fictional story of a 19th century young poet in the midst of a life crisis. The young poet identifies passionately with Job and uses Job to legitimise himself, but he lacks the capacity for earnest self-examination that, for Kierkegaard, is crucial to the art of being a good reader.

Through his works Kierkegaard seeks 'to produce an alienating distance to the biblical text that forces us to see it anew on the one hand, and proximity and contemporaneity with the biblical text on the other since we are constantly encouraged to ask ourselves how *we* would react if *our* existence lay like broken pottery around us.' p. 105.

While philosophers and theologians have in various ways discussed the Bible as a norm for human existence, the question of normativity also arises in the process of research on the Bible. In her contribution *Maria Louise Odgaard Møller* shows that, for the theologian and priest K.E. Løgstrup, work on the biblical texts in preparation for the Sunday sermon was subject to a norm, namely, the requirement to speak the truth. Embarking from a historical-critical approach to the Bible, Løgstrup identified truth with historicity in the biblical accounts of Jesus of Nazareth, and this had consequences for his sermons. The form of reception and transformation that Løgstrup undertakes consists of a clear reduction of the message, in that significant features of the gospel (e.g. the resurrection) are toned down to such a degree that Jesus' life is equated with ordinary earthly life: 'only when there is a historical truth to be found in what the texts tell us can they be valid and applicable to people today. And this is precisely how the normative can be defined: that which has and retains validity because its content can be defined as "true". p. 106.

In response to this Maria Louise Odgaard Møller draws on Ricoeur's conception of what truth is, showing how poetic truth, in contrast to the truth embodied by Løgstrup's reductive Jesus figure, is precisely what may serve as normative for people today. It should be added, however, that Løgstrup's wish to place Jesus' humanity at the centre of his approach to the Bible accords with a common view of the role of literature: namely, that its purpose is to explore human existence (cf. Kundera's view of the novel, p. 66).

The fact that the biblical message is mediated over time becomes especially clear when the message and the world picture to which it originally belonged are confronted with modern scientific research. In the light of our current understanding of the history of mankind's development, the biblical narratives cease to be credible. But do they also cease to be meaningful in an existential sense? And how is it that even scientists studying evolution include biblical motifs in their descriptions of it? Does the Bible still retain a certain authority that scholars can indirectly make use of when, for example, they speak of 'Mitochondrial Eve'? *Marie Vejrup Nielsen* deals with such questions in her article on reception and transformation in evolutionary theory, and on the role that the narrative form as such plays in modern research into evolution.

One of the leading scholars in this area, E.O. Wilson, is well aware that, in contrast to traditional religion, the theory of evolution has the disadvantage of being unable to refer to a form of divine authority. But then it has other advantages, the prime one being that it builds on a true, scientific foundation. However, if man is to live by this truth, science must become more conscious of the language it uses: 'If science is not in itself able to tell stories, it must transform its language in order to do so. It must become narrative, otherwise religion will win.' p. 127. Nevertheless, as Marie Vejrup demonstrates, it is not random forms of narrative but, time and again, specifically *biblical material* that the scientists draw on to tell the new story of mankind. For the biblical material both creates a familiarity and yet makes room for the incomprehensible. At the same time, however, the continued inclusion of the Bible as a point of reference in scientific accounts of evolution has meant that the great controversy over the respective explanatory claims of religion and modern science remains both highly topical and highly charged.

Receptions and transformations of the Bible in religious communities

The third section of the book is concerned with the use of the Bible by Jews and Christians respectively. The use of the Torah as an artefact is examined as a specific aspect of Jewish culture, while Bible-reading as a performative act, and hymn writers' deployment of the Bible as intertext, are discussed as examples of Christian usage of the Bible.

In her article on the reception and transformation of the Torah *Marianne Schleicher* argues that in Jewish tradition the artefactual use of scripture plays a far more prominent role than actual textual usage. Most often the texts are used not for exposition but as 'a symbol that can be manipulated to signify whatever individuals, collectives and institutions project into it.' p. 141. She demonstrates this by showing how the Torah represents a holy object in Judaism and how its usage as such creates a link between the Torah and the lives of the individual congregations. This theme is developed further in her interview with the former Chief Rabbi in Copenhagen, Bent Melchior.

At the same time, Marianne Schleicher observes a twilight zone where the use of Torah can be called neither artefactual nor interpretative. As an example of the latter she includes a poem by the Israeli poet Yehuda Amichai in which the story of the sacrifice of Isaac (Gen 22) is transformed to such a degree that the poem ends with the words: 'But the true hero of the binding / Is the ram.' p. 155.

Her conclusion is that the scroll has served primarily as *the* holy object in Jewish tradition. As such it has been able to create a link between the individual, the community and the holy, and conversely to confer authority on the Jewish community's faith and practice. By contrast, *exegesis* of the Torah is first and foremost the domain of the elite, though this has significant consequences: 'In other words, reception and moderate transformation of religious normativity, sanctioned by scripture, requires only manipulative artefactual use of scripture; whereas significant change within the historical and cultural context requires radical reception and transformation of scripture-based normativity through a textual approach.' p. 156-157.

A main theme of *Johannes Nissen*'s article on reading the Bible in church is that reception and transformation should lead to a change in one's life. His point of departure is the question of what purpose the church actually serves, formulated as follows:

In churches, the Bible is often "used" practically and ethically as a compendium of rules, as a prescriptive and proscriptive blueprint for pastoral practice and moral behaviour. In this context the word "used" points to the underlying assumption that Scripture is seen as a source book at our disposal rather than a means of God's grace through which we are formed and moulded (Colwell 2005, 212-213). But the Bible is not just a series of rules and propositions. Rather, it is a series of stories. Overwhelmingly, Scripture takes the form of narrative. p. 163.

It is not enough to read the Bible merely as narrative, however. A new category must be introduced: that of *performing* the text. Here it is the lived human life that is being brought into focus, opening the way for a critical reading of the biblical writings and for the question of the Bible's authority. The experiences of the reader and the church acquire a critical function in relation to the Bible and the traditional interpretation of it. For authority can never be imposed on others by force; authority is an offer. It is the reader who must decide to what degree he or she will accept biblical authority.

Johannes Nissen thus operates with three steps in the reader's reception and transformation of the text: listening, learning and living. The first involves not only listening attentively to the text as such, but listening to the text of life as well. And in doing so one must learn what God's will is in the concrete situation. Johannes Nissen therefore concludes: 'Christians read and perform the text in the hope that their lives will be transformed. When this occurs, they as readers become disciples.' p. 170.

The third section is concerned with the church's use of the Bible. But whereas the first two articles relate to the Bible itself, *Kirsten Nielsen* looks more closely at the use which the church itself indirectly makes of the Bible through hymn-singing in the Danish Lutheran church. Her analysis of the images of God in modern Danish hymns reveals that the hymn-writers utilise the Bible to a high degree as an intertext for their hymns, giving them a share of the authority that the church ascribes to the Bible. However, this acquired authority – allowing the hymns to function as a norm for the church's faith and practice – does not imply that they take over an inflexible set of dogma lock, stock and barrel. Since a very large amount of biblical material takes the form of imagery and is thus open to new interpretation, the new context of both the hymn itself and the reader's life involves both reception and transformation. The Bible's use of many and various images of God sets the norm for the modern poet, namely that hymns should be formulated in an open language that allows for many new interpretations.

The conclusion is that the norm that the Bible sets for speaking of God is: *multiplicity, interpretation and innovation*. Both the Bible and the Danish Hymn Book are thus in agreement with the Old Testament prohibition on imagery: 'For the norm which the prohibition on imagery asserted must be defined for the church's way of speaking about God as follows: 'You must not make any fixed, limited image of God'. To live up to the biblical norm it must therefore be required of the theologian and the hymn writer alike that their reading of the biblical message takes place not only as a repetition of the biblical words, but also as a reception and transformation of them.' p. 186.

Reception as pure repetition is inadequate; the biblical message must be transformed in such a way as to retain its actuality and relevance. A large number of modern Danish hymns show that this is possible – and in so doing, like all good literature, they represent a challenge to every theology that stiffens into rigid forms and refuses to yield to the necessary transformation.

The Bible as norm, the Bible as inspiration

The publication of *Religion and normativity. Receptions and transformations of the Bible* represents the latest scholarship in theology at Aarhus University. Each of the contributors offers his/her own distinctive insights, but they are all agreed on the fundamental view that normativity and authority are created in the meeting between the biblical texts and those who make use of them. Normativity presupposes man's acceptance. This acceptance may be deeply personal, or it may be a more or less unconscious consequence of the cultural environment one has grown up in. The acceptance of the Bible as a religious authority means that it functions as a determining factor in the ongoing attempt by the individual or the community to come to a satisfactory interpretation of life – theoretically as well as practically.

It is no surprise that the Bible continues to serve as a norm-giver. Classic Christian theology sees it as an inspired text, in particular 2 Tim 3:16, which has been used as an argument for this doctrine of inspiration: 'All Scripture is inspired by God and is useful for teaching, rebuking, correcting and training in righteousness.' This passage has often been interpreted to mean that the Bible is an infallible guide – not just in religious matters but also in temporal questions. If we compare this view with that of the contributors to this book, it will become clear that the latter on the whole depart from this traditional understanding of the relationship between inspiration and the Bible. The Bible is not regarded as inspired in the sense of being an infallible work whose content and form must therefore simply be reproduced. The surprise is that the Bible continues to serve as a *source of inspiration*. Normativity therefore reveals itself in the fact that, despite the great distance in time and culture between then and now, writers, religious specialists, laypeople and philosophers continue to use the Bible as a recurrent intertext in their struggle with life's great questions.

When the writer, the philosopher, the specialist or the layman rework the biblical motifs and narratives, and thereby pass on their interpretations, the Bible functions as an intertext for the new text. The reader is invited to enter into dialogue with both the biblical intertext and the new work – be it novel, poem, philosophical essay, prayer or hymn. In the Western world the introduction of the biblical intertext will in most cases remain a genuine possibility, since the majority will recognise it. Nor will it merely be one among many. Because of its cultural and personally accepted authority it will be a significant partner in the conversation about the meaning of life – including the reader's own life. The reworking of the Bible helps to create identity, but in the meeting with collective and individual experiences there is a potential for a change in both attitude and practice.

Modern scholarship emphasises the Bible's many faces, its various genres and theologies. Moreover the Bible itself has come into being through a lengthy process of reception and transformation. This too can contribute to its acquiring a normative function in inspiring new interpretations of the biblical message. The great precursor still challenges readers to receive and transform anew. As a norm the Bible is an inexhaustible source of inspiration with which to research human existence. And with its many voices it challenges all forms of conventionality and rigidified Judaism or Christianity – as well as every kind of totalitarian ideology.

PART I

Receptions and transformations of the Bible in literature

GENERAL REFLECTIONS
RECEPTIONS AND TRANSFORMATIONS
OF THE BIBLE IN LITERATURE

David Bugge

The Bible in literature: a typology

Every attempt to put forward a typology as to what part the Bible plays in fictional literature involves an element of arbitrariness. Where to draw the boundaries between various types of literary texts that have been influenced by biblical narratives? And on what criteria should they be drawn? The following proposal is no exception.

As the title suggests, the approach here involves the double notion of the *reception and transformation* of the Bible in later literary texts. True, any reception includes a construction and so, to some extent, a transformation, just as every transformation implies a reception. This is but a hermeneutical truism. In our everyday language, however, there is a difference of degree between the two concepts in question, of great use when forming a general view of the varied constellations of the Bible in literature. While *reception* simply indicates the pure act of receiving a certain text, *transformation* points to the change or metamorphosis that takes place.

So the typology below will classify the literary reception of the Bible in accordance with the degree of transformation of the biblical narratives concerned. By this criterion a scale is outlined, ascending from the mere *retelling* of the Bible, via *further writing*, and *rewriting*, to *counter writing*, and completed by an account of the relationship between fictional *writing as such*, i.e. the very writing process, and a given biblical theme. The terminology (retelling, further writing, etc.) should be understood as just a proposal that is by no means bound to the classification itself. Having outlined the typology, I will show how all the various types distinguished can be applied to the literary reception and transformation of one and the same biblical narrative, using the story of Cain by way of example.[1]

Retelling

The literary type that is nearest to the biblical text itself may be called a *retelling*. There is only a gradual transition from the pure translation of the Bible to this type, for of course every translation is also, in a way, a retelling (*traduttore traditore*).

---

1 For the benefit of German and Scandinavian readers, I list here the German/Danish equivalents of the terms proposed: Nachdicthung/gendigtning (retelling); Weiterdichtung/videredigtning (further writing); Umdichtung/omdigtning (rewriting); Gegendichtung/moddigtning (counter writing); Dichtung als solche/digtning som sådan (writing as such).

Still, it makes sense to treat retelling as a separate entity, since the reteller enjoys greater literary freedom than the translator, and for that reason is regarded as an author in his/her own right. While a translator (even one who translates the Bible into everyday language) remains relatively bound to the wording of the original (*so treu wie möglich, so frei wie nötig*), the reteller is free to leave out passages or to present them in a different order. And to a considerable extent, he/she is permitted to play with the language, e.g. by putting prose into verse.

Retelling is best known from the various Children's Bibles that flood the book market, often with a softening or omission of the harsher passages. In recent years, however, we have seen an increasing supply of books containing retellings of the biblical stories for adults – an attempt to redress the growing alienation of modern societies from the biblical universe.

Further writing

In retelling, transformation is at its lowest. The next literary type to be considered leaves much greater scope for the writer; we may well call it *further writing*. It is related to retelling in so far as the biblical figures still appear by their original names and in their original contexts. Adam is still Adam, coupled with Eve, living in Eden, etc.

Unlike retelling, however, further writing does not stop here, but adds new information that elucidates the biblical story in some respect or other. So, compared to retelling, this type of transformation may go further in at least two ways: by filling in gaps *within* the biblical narrative in question or by elaborating what happened *later on*. Further writing was practised widely in the early Church (the Apocryphal Gospels), and it has played an important part in rabbinic tradition (Haggadah). Later famous examples are the *Christ Legends* by Selma Lagerlöf and Thomas Mann's *Joseph and His Brothers*.

On an inner level, further writing often supplies a more explicit psychological dimension to the original tale, e.g. by introducing inner monologues by the various characters. Moreover, a number of modern existential problems are frequently inserted into the old story, fruitfully imbuing the familiar, traditional text with a modern sensibility, though here there is an obvious danger of (or opportunity for) anachronism.

Rewriting

As we approach the next stage in the relationship between the Bible and literature, we see a shift towards genuine transformation. We may call this type of literature *rewriting*. Rewriting, as opposed to re*telling*, denotes a genuinely literary text that has acquired a considerable degree of imaginative independence from the original story; and compared to *further* writing, *rewriting* involves a more thorough change of scene with regard to names, locations, time, etc.

In rewriting, a biblical narrative and its meaning are placed in an entirely different, usually modern, context. Well known examples are Graham Greene's *The Third Man* (the Prater scene), Camus' *The Fall*, the works of Dostoevsky, and the narratives of the Inklings (Tolkien, Lewis). Sometimes the focus is on a larger biblical event that prefigures the plot of the literary work, e.g. the myth of the Fall of Man, the accounts of the Temptation and of the Last Supper, the Passion Story, and the Eschatological Drama. At other times the focus is on a biblical figure and on a certain concept or problem that he/she represents, e.g. Jacob and deceit or blessing, Moses and the law, Job and the problem of suffering, Mary and maternity, Judas and betrayal. In these cases, the link is often indicated simply by a typical attribute, e.g. limping (Jacob), ashes (Job), a blue veil (Mary).

The relationship between a biblical narrative and a rewritten literary story varies. The backdrop to the biblical story may come to the fore in the rewritten version, with the literary text verging on an allegorical rebus and the process of the reading reduced almost to deciphering a code. In more successful cases, however, an interaction occurs so that the biblical intertext creates a fruitful sounding board for the literary work, while the contemporary story, in turn, is able to revitalise the ancient book.

Counter writing

The most thorough type of literary transformation of the Bible can be characterised as *counter writing*. Here, the setting of the original biblical text may be retained, as in further writing, or the story may be cast in a totally different universe. In either case, however, counter writing differs from the two previous types. Denoting a conversion of the original narrative, it turns the biblical point or moral upside down. In the process, the familiar and the surprising form a synthesis, creating a powerful and often humorous literary effect that arises from the contrast between the solemn aura of the sacred text and the shape it has been given.

So, on the one hand, counter writing is indebted to the biblical text, the latter providing the matrix, so to speak, for the former. On the other hand, this debt is of a purely negative kind, since the matrix is used for the express purpose of replacing the point by its diametrical opposite. Structurally, counter writing leads a parasite's life, feeding on the Bible, but frequently a parasite's life with a very original outcome.

This sort of transformation assumes various literary forms. Sometimes a whole narrative is counter written, as in the case of André Gide's short story 'The Return of the Prodigal Son' and Isak Dinesen's 'Babette's Feast' (though the latter might be considered rewriting). Sometimes a single biblical expression is turned 180 degrees, as happens when (once more) Isak Dinesen turns the Double Love Commandment into an aesthetic ideal: 'Thou shalt love thy art with all thy heart, and with all thy soul, and with all thy mind. And thou shalt love thy public as thyself' ('A Consolatory Tale', Dinesen 1942, 291); or when she rewords a line from the Lord's Prayer: 'Thy will be done, William Shakespeare, as on the stage so also in the drawing-room' ('Tempests', Dinesen 1958, 101).

Writing as such

In all the types mentioned above, the reception and transformation of the Bible take place *within* the literary texts. Before turning to my main example, however, it is worth examining a final way in which the Bible and literature can be conjoined, i.e. when *writing as such* is seen to involve the reception and transformation of a certain biblical point or theme. Here, the focus shifts from the plot of the fictional text to the writing process itself, although such meta-literary reflections may well be made within a novel, a poem, or a drama.

The process of writing as such has been likened to various biblical themes; and the figure of the writer, in his capacity as a writer, has been variously compared with that of an apostle or of Satan himself. Of particular interest in the Jewish-Christian context is the notion of aesthetic messianism in, for example, the works of Walter Benjamin. And in his autobiographical book *De profundis*, Oscar Wilde relates an episode from his imprisonment when he was rereading the New Testament. It struck him that the very essence of Christ's nature was that of the artist: an intense imaginative sympathy that is the basis of all artistic creation. Christ himself is considered the artist of all artists, and thus this radical transformation ends with a sort of identification.

Main example: the Cain figure in literature

Time and again, the story of Cain and Abel in Genesis (Gen 4:1-24) has attracted the attention of writers: Dante, Shakespeare, Byron, Baudelaire, Ibsen, Conrad, and Steinbeck, to mention but a few, have all been inspired by the fundamental existential themes that the myth deals with: jealousy, fratricide, expulsion. In addition, the form and the plot are so compact that they invite artistic supplementing. The biblical account offers no psychological elaborations, such as inner monologues; and the text contains a good many loose ends that call for explanation: Why did the Lord look with favour only on Abel's sacrifice? How did Adam and Eve live on after the loss of their sons? And how did Cain's future life turn out?

Already in the New Testament, authors were inspired by the story (Mt 23:35; Heb 11:4, 12:24; 1 John 3:12; Jud 11), seeing the righteous Abel as a pre-figuring of the crucified Christ. Theological interpretations lasted throughout the Middle Ages and into Reformatory and post-Reformatory times. In modern times, however, the reception of the myth has changed, with theological interest in the story being supplemented, or replaced, by a psychological approach. And in contemporary literature, Cain often becomes the central figure in the narrative.[2]

---

2   For thorough investigations of the Cain figure in literature, in which some of the following examples are also dealt with, cf. Bjørnvig 1964; Illies (ed.) 1975; Quinones 1991; Wright 2007.

Retelling (Cain)

As an example of *retelling* we may take Selina Hastings' *Children's Illustrated Bible*. The language, though very close to the biblical original, is modernised in various ways, and difficult sentences are left out, e.g. those that involve a Hebrew play on words ('Cain' sounding like the Hebrew for 'brought forth', Gen 4:1) or those that contain non-traditional imagery (the ground opening its mouth to receive Abel's blood, Gen 4:11).

In addition, Eric Thomas' several illustrations are accompanied by Hastings' interpretative explanations. The picture of the fratricide, for example, is captioned as follows: 'Cain killed Abel because God preferred his offering' (Hastings 2004, 22), an interpretation that is only implicit in the Genesis text. Hastings goes even further in the caption that accompanies a drawing of the various crops that Cain would have grown (wheat, grapes, figs, etc.): 'God rejected Cain's offering for he did not give the best of his produce' (p. 22). The statement is Hastings' attempt to give logical (or moral) grounds for God's reaction, for which there is actually no substance in the original text. Finally, the illustrations themselves sometimes contain interpretative additions, e.g. placing the mark of Cain upon his forehead (p. 23), in accordance with a later iconographic tradition.

In Hastings' Children's Bible, the retelling aspect still dominates. The instances above, however, suggest that the more interpretative elements are contained in the retelling, the closer it comes to further writing.

Further writing (Cain)

Fresh evidence that the biblical myth of Cain still inspires *further writing* can be found in the American author David Maine's novel *Fallen* (2005). Proceeding in reverse chronological order, the novel tells the story of the first family of mankind. Embarking with Cain as an old, marked man, and continuing by way of flashbacks, the author fills out the narrative, taking it right back to Adam and Eve's exile from the Garden of Eden. Loose ends from the Genesis account are tied up, and by inserting into the story a modern psychological sensibility, the novelist revitalises the ancient myth, turning it into a timeless portrait of typical patterns in family life. In the very opening of the first chapter, the novelist already goes beyond the original text:

The mark burns upon him all the time now. Its hurt is open and shameful like a scab picked until it bleeds. In years past he could find ways to forget it or at least misplace his awareness for a while; it was never easy but he managed. These days he cannot. There is nothing to fill Cain's time so the mark does this for him (Maine 2005, 3).

By learning what happened *later on*, we have already moved far beyond the original account in Genesis. In referring to the notion of 'filling one's time' the passage quoted adds a modern psychological dimension to the account of Cain's experience, but at the same time the novel remains faithful to the ancient universe with regard to details of names, food, housing, etc. The setting of the story is thus familiar from the Bible.

Rewriting (Cain)

There are numerous examples of playwrights and novelists *rewriting* the story of Cain. To illustrate this type of transformation, however, let us take a lyrical example. The English poet Edith Sitwell places the fratricide in the very title of one of her collections, *The Shadow of Cain* (1947). Whereas David Maine adopts a modern attitude to the ancient narrative, Sitwell situates the original character within a modern context. For this reason it is appropriate to classify her account as rewriting, even though the names have not actually been transformed in her fluid poetic universe.

In the aftermath of the Second World War, Sitwell levels the charge of fratricide against those guilty of bombing Hiroshima and Nagasaki:

There are no thunders, there are no fires, no suns, no earthquakes
Left in our blood … But yet like the rolling thunders of all the fires in the world, we cry
To Dives: "You are the shadow of Cain. Your shade is the primal Hunger".
"I lie under what condemnation?"
"The same as Adam, the same as Cain, the same as Sodom, the same as Judas"
(Sitwell 1947, 17-18).

Again, the blood of Cain's brother cries out from the ground, but the addressee is now the Allies. *The biblical point, however, is intact*: in other words, Cain is still the essence of sin, the representation of human failure. A landscape devastated by the ravages of an atomic bomb is associated with names from the Old Testament. The addition of Judas makes clear that the questioner's point of view is that of the present, or at least post-biblical, since otherwise Dives (the rich man in Luke 16:19-31) could not be compared to Judas. Despite Dives' attempt to escape his guilt, there is no understanding or mercy for him as the shadow of Cain. The verdict is unequivocal. There is room only for the hungering Lazarus in Abraham's bosom.

Counter writing (Cain)

In Sitwell's poem, Cain is no longer considered simply a historical figure of the past, but rather a representative of contemporary man. Yet the biblical point remains: Cain is guilty and deserves condemnation. In modern times, however, another form of transformation can be found, in which an attempt is made to defend Cain and relieve him of guilt, the charge being levelled against Destiny or God instead. Such accounts represent *counter writing* in the sense that they turn the biblical point upside down.

In some of these works, Cain is the pitiable creature suffering from a destiny he never asked for. In others, he even becomes the *rebellious hero*, representing the self-assertion of mankind against an unreasonable and high-handed God, as happens in Baudelaire's poem 'Abel et Caïn' in *Les fleurs du mal* (1857). The first half of the poem depicts Cain's miserable condition and God's privileging of Abel, but in the second half this description is replaced by another vision, here rendered in Francis Scarfe's translation:

Tribe of Abel, one day your carcass will manure the fetid soil.
Tribe of Cain, your task is not yet done.
Tribe of Abel, your shame will come when the sword is shattered by the peasants' stake.
Tribe of Cain, ascend to heaven, and throw God down to earth (Baudelaire 1986, 230).

The vision assumes an almost eschatological character. A despotic God is to taste his own damnation. The poet's counter-writing intention is evident here, despite the fact that there is no transformation of the very logic of the original narrative; rather, what we see is a reversal of the characters' positions. Repudiation is still the case. For the artist, standing outside the bourgeois community, it seems obvious to side with Cain, the outcast, or even to identify with him, justifying his crime as a heroic, promethean deed.

Writing as such (Cain)

An original way of receiving and transforming the figure of Cain through literature can be found in the work of the great mid-20th century Danish novelist Martin A. Hansen. In Hansen's works, Cain is not only a literary character; he becomes the symbol of the writer himself *in his capacity as a writer*. But what leads Hansen to make this unusual and rather sombre comparison?

A quite literal relationship between Cain and the figure of the artist is suggested in the biblical narrative itself. Cain became the ancestor of Jubal, 'the father of all who play the harp and flute' (Gen 4:21); in Hansen's own words, he gave birth to 'an artistically gifted family'. In addition, one can note a connection between Cain and the peasant's son Hansen himself, each of them having left the cultivated land to become 'a restless wanderer on the earth' (Gen 4:12).

However important these suggestions of exterior relationship may be, they do not by themselves get to the heart of Hansen's use of the Cain symbol: his interpretation of the fratricide as a metaphor for the interpersonal costs involved in the very act of fictional writing. From his own experience Hansen sees the writer as a spider, a parasite, a vampire, sucking the blood of his fellow human beings, on false pretences of involvement, in pursuit of material for his books. As Hansen puts it in one of the stanzas of his poem 'Human' (Danish: 'Menneske'):

Step down here into the smithy where he is forging,
the brother murderer Cain, the ingenious,
the writer's mind, crying for the sufferers
like the crocodile (Hansen 1948, 363; my translation).

The smith Cain (the Hebrew name simply means 'smith') is not only a biblical figure transposed to the writer's poetic universe: Cain is the writer himself, the reception of the biblical text implying a double transformation, in time as well as profession. But whereas Baudelaire's counter writing contains an element of artistic identification, the original negative value is here intact.

In Hansen's opinion, the writer is incapable of changing himself. In the words of the writing schoolmaster in Hansen's novel *The Liar*: 'I cannot turn back, but that we all know. Only the button-molder can remold' (Hansen 1986, 200). So, in an Ibsen-inspired image, the suggestion is made that only a greater artist, i.e. the refining silver-smith (cf. Mal 3:3) can make up for the writer's fratricide, by receiving the crocodilian Cain into *His* story, which neither Bible nor literature will ever be able to comprehend in its complete, ingenious transformation.

Bibliography

Baudelaire, Charles 1986. *The Complete Verse*. London: Anvil Press.

Bjørnvig, Thorkild 1964. *Kains Alter. Martin A. Hansens Digtning og Tænkning*. Copenhagen: Gyldendal.

Dinesen, Isak 1942. *Winter's Tales*. New York: Random House.

Dinesen, Isak 1958. *Anecdotes of Destiny*. London: Michael Joseph.

Hansen, Martin A. 1948. 'Menneske I-III'. *Heretica*, 5, Copenhagen: Wivels Forlag, 356-64.

Hansen, Martin A. 1986. *The Liar* (Danish: *Løgneren* 1950). London: Quartet.

Hastings, Selina 2004. *Children's Illustrated Bible*. New York: Dorling Kindersley.

Illies, Joachim (ed.) 1975. *Brudermord. Zum Mythos von Kain und Abel*. München: Kösel-Verlag.

Maine, David 2005. *Fallen*. New York: St. Martin's Press.

Quinones, Ricardo J. 1991. *The Changes of Cain. Violence and the Lost Brother in Cain and Abel Literature*. Princeton, N.J.: Princeton University Press.

Sitwell, Edith 1947. *The Shadow of Cain*. London: John Lehmann.

Wright, Terry R. 2007. *The Genesis of Fiction. Modern Novelists as Biblical Interpreters*. Aldershot, England, Burlington, VT: Ashgate.

NECESSARY FICTION

INVESTIGATING POWERS OF DEPICTION RECEPTION AND TRANSFORMATION IN THE NOVEL *DORÉ'S BIBLE* BY TORGNY LINDGREN

Kirsten M. Andersen

> *To a certain extent, maybe it was my grandfather's fault as he*
> *stuffed my childhood with words and literature. He never*
> *realised that the world cannot be described, but only depicted.*
> Torgny Lindgren: *Doré's Bible*

> *Our art is a state of being blinded by the truth:*
> *The light on the recoiling distorted face is true, nothing else.*
> Franz Kafka: *Aphorisms*

Throughout his work, the Swedish author Torgny Lindgren (1938) makes constant use of biblical figures and vocabulary. Lindgren demonstrates a rare poetic license in relation to the biblical universe; there is no foreseeable pattern – rather, the universe is configured in all sorts of different ways. In the short stories the frequent use of subtle associations and phrases may serve to disrupt the discourse or, on the contrary, weave the entire story together. In the novels the biblical language is one among several poetic elements that serve to reinvent the genre in a very particular style. Lindgren is a highly distinctive novelist and humorist.

The different ways of handling and bending the biblical universe serve the overall structure of the novel *Doré's Bible* in a manner that is both effective and puzzling, and which contributes significantly to the field of literature and theology. The dialectic of irony constitutes one of Lindgren's main literary tools.[1] Rhetorically, irony involves saying one thing but meaning something else. In Lindgren's case the use of irony is complex and sophisticated. It manifests itself in his creation of a profound texture, both ambiguous and polysemantic that matches a dual vision of the world. Good and evil, God and the devil, life and death may be distinguished, but cannot be separated.

In the novel, Paul Gustave Doré's popular illustrated Bible plays a crucial role in creating this dual vision of life. In a clear instance of irony, the Bible has quite literally been locked in the Lindgren cupboard (Lindgren 2005, 87). There is a particular scene in the novel in which the illustrated Bible is placed at the bottom of a cupboard

---

1   This theme is the focus of Magnus Nilsson's analysis of Lindgren's works (Magnus Nilsson 2004).

manufactured by the Lindgren wood workshop. For a short time the main character of the novel is allowed to kneel down to see and touch this family copy of Doré's Bible, while his father stands upright beside him. But the kneeling son is not given sufficient time to take the Bible out and look at it, or even to leaf through it (Lindgren 2005, 102-103). The scene is imbued with a sardonic feeling of awe.

Throughout the novel figures and phrases from the biblical universe are employed extensively in a world that is nevertheless devoid of liturgical practice and of religious or divine authority. The Bible is seen purely as literature, and together with other literary works constitutes a cultural norm of questionable validity. The Bible's function as a kind of matrix or code is less important than the questioning of what is normative. The authority of parents and of tradition is a historical fact – a complex burden, but an unavoidable condition of life. In *Doré's Bible* Lindgren presents a character with a rich cultural background but no education; a master of undigested *Bildung,* naïve, satisfied, and with no feeling of guilt.

Among other issues *Doré's Bible* raises the question of the existential meaning of authority: of what it means to hand down tradition, instruct and educate. To create his metaphorical framework, Lindgren uses a number of binary expressions with opposite meanings or values: depiction/description, word/letter, spirit/letter, original/copy, true/false, truth/lies. Alongside the story itself there is a constant reflection on the meaning of literature as such, with particular emphasis on the question of selfhood, truth, trust and credibility.

Doré's Bible is the third novel in what Lindgren has defined as a triptych, the first two being *Sweetness* (1995) and *Hash* (2002). Characters from the two first novels also appear in the last, though not in the main roles. In what follows, the focus is on *Doré's Bible* alone as an example of the way in which biblical narratives, characters and language are transformed in Lindgren's work.

The art of the novel

In an interview given in 1984 immediately after the novel *Bathsheba* was published, Torgny Lindgren was asked why he had chosen to turn the old biblical story of Bathsheba into a novel. Lindgren emphasised at the time that the novel should in fact be seen as quite separate from and independent of its biblical original in 2 Samuel - 1 Kings. His intention in the novel was not to preserve an oral tradition – to retell or revitalise a good story. He does pay tribute, however, to the fact that he grew up in Västerbotten, northern Sweden, which had a lively oral tradition consisting both of biblical narratives and of all kinds of stories about strange incidents and great people from the village remembered from long ago, and he admits that the early experience of storytelling played an important role in his formation as a writer. But the reason he gives for detaching the novel from its biblical source indicates what lies behind his poetic concern and his experience with the genre of the novel. His interest is not in fiction for fiction's sake, but in producing a body of reality created by and articulated in language (Schueler 1984, 18; Nils Gunnar Nilsson 2004, 10). Lindgren is an existentialist author, concerned with all that man is heir to – with the worlds that men are initiated into. In this poetic endeavour biblical language constitutes an indispensable tool.

Unlike the short story, the novel does not have to rely on plot to organise the sequence of events so as to keep the reader in suspense and maintain flow and energy.[2] A novel depends on more than its storyline. Referring to Thomas Mann, Torgny Lindgren claims that there are no other criteria for constructing a novel than what the author finds poetically applicable (Schueler 1984, 13). In drawing this distinction between the art of storytelling and the art of the novel, Lindgren highlights a distinctive trait of the twentieth-century novel, in which the poetic endeavour is distanced from the traditional, Aristotelian theory of mimesis: the notion that the plot (*mythos*) is an imitation or representation of actions that happen in a more or less fixed succession and are of a more or less fixed nature (Aristotle VI 19; VIII 4). 'In the case of a novel you can't leave it there; as a writer you may add precisely whatever you want, everything that belongs to the subject. There is in fact only one criterion for what may be included, and that is what the author's impulse finds is poetically productive' (Schueler 1984, 13). Consequently, Lindgren's poetic use of biblical figures, phrases, and stories belongs exclusively to its own fictional context; the poetic work, in his view, belongs to its own historical time and would be unthinkable without current knowledge, modern science, contemporary worldviews and philosophical ideas. It is in the light of this that Lindgren argues that the point of writing a novel such as *Bathsheba* is not simply to retell an old story.

From his work and experience Lindgren offers a twofold definition of the novel. On the one hand it is a product of the writer's inner vision, his imagination, and on the other it represents an investigation. He tells us how he often finds himself borrowing terminology from other art forms: music, painting and so on in order to challenge the genre:

I always spend a very long time reading. I read everything I happen to come across and then when I am bursting at the seams with material, I put all the written sources away. Then I know how the landscape must appear. I hear how it must be heard and I experience a multitude of sensations and write according to a vision from within. Then I believe in what I write, the novel is a product of systematised insights.

A novel is an investigation. We imagine that there is a kind of truth and we believe that there is a truth beyond the investigation. In the body of the work there is probably no truth, just the investigation (Schueler 1984, 14).

---

2   Lindgren is an excellent storyteller, a master of plot construction, and this is particularly evident in his short stories. Ex: Lindgren *Merabs Skönhet* and his early novel *The Way of the Serpent*.

Given Lindgren's genre distinction between the story and the novel, it is crucial that the novel *Bathsheba* is seen as belonging to its own world, just as the biblical version belongs to its. As *figura* however they both belong to the human sphere. Literature that makes use of biblical characters and themes reflects the Bible as literature, as fiction, and invites self-criticism and reflection.

Most noteworthy of all, perhaps, is the close connection between Lindgren's articulation of his general thoughts on the genre, and his actual work on the language of the novel he is currently engaged in and the fictional universe that is being developed; the thoughts on genre are incorporated into the endeavour itself, and vice versa. It is obvious, for example, that the experience of writing *Hash* – the composition, material, and framework of the novel – fed directly into Lindgren's terminology in his subsequent efforts to define the genre. *Hash* turns out to be – at least in part – about two men setting out to find the best 'pölsan', a characteristic local dish similar to the Scottish haggis. At the time of writing Lindgren defined the novel itself as a haggis, and explained how he had an idea for the theme from the start, while at the same time being preoccupied by the question of form, more particularly the form of formlessness. The same could be said of 'pölsan', haggis. As Lindgren says:

I am very fascinated by Mahler's symphonic works. There is a lack of structure, they seem not to be thoroughly composed the same way as – let's say – Beethoven's symphonies or Allan Petterson's or those of whomever you might choose. Mahler's symphonies are haggis. And it is this kind of Mahlerian formlessness that I dreamed of, or tried to begin imagining. Indeed [I dreamed of] formlessness as form. [...] So from this point of view this book is a failure. In the strict sense, it should have been haggis, but it isn't. It is as carefully composed as is the case with all my books (Magnus Nilsson 2004, 9-10).

The novel is more than a piece of fiction that tells a story. It is as if the novelist has taken on the heuristic exercise of relating to the overwhelming multi-layered ways of life and knowledge, and succeeded, through his powers of condensation and imagination, in creating a many-sided rather than a univocal world. Or, perhaps more precisely: a world of irreconcilable contrasts. Modern man has no option but to reckon with the complexity and multiplicity of the worlds that surround him and fiction is well-suited to exploring and experiencing this complexity. Or as Lindgren puts it: he seeks to write in such a way that the imagined is made flesh (Schueler 1984, 18). The understanding of vision in this case is neither romantic nor functional. Lindgren is not a visionary prophet, but neither is he a post-modern writer playing endlessly on the outskirts and making literature into a tiresome testing ground for illusions and rhetorical power games.

Some might call Lindgren a belated modernist, in so far as he retains a belief in the humanising powers of fiction and a constant concern with form. Imagination is part of the human condition and man's poetic power, his ability to create fiction, is an essential part of his being. From a theological point of view I would not hesitate to call him a religious writer, in so far as fiction is just as necessary a part of religious language and symbols as it is of literature. Literature and religion share certain similarities in terms of reflecting the complex, composite nature of human life. But literature is not a surrogate religion, and in this sense it is irrelevant to define him as a religious writer. What matters is that religion is not taboo in Lindgren's writings; he doesn't harbour any uncritical and bigoted ideas as to what religion is. Moreover, the various books of the Bible, and the ways in which they have been received and transformed in liturgical phrases and everyday language, seem to serve as a kind of equivalent to the "haggis" Lindgren has in mind when composing his novels. However, he is a great novelist, and I often wonder how it is that, whenever I enter one of his imaginary worlds, I feel challenged as a reader to think about the ultimate conditions of human life. I am captivated not by the sense of suspense, but by the depth of subtle irony and humour, the persistent attention to what is unique to man.

In this sense Lindgren may be compared with several other contemporary writers who are equally concerned about the artistic challenge posed by the novel. Milan Kundera, for instance, has specifically referred to the novel as a fabulous heterogeneous universe that gives free rein to the author's imagination (Kundera 1993, 3-6). Jan Kjærstad makes a strong appeal for the hybrid, impure or blurred novel that mixes places, times, different sorts of logic, various religions, dreams, and realities, not for the sake of eclecticism as such but as a reflection of the nature of urban culture (Kjærstad 1999, 17).

One senses a kind of impatient annoyance whenever Lindgren is confronted with questions that suggest that his novels, as non-realist works of fiction, are by that token non-political. For him, such questions imply a careless bias, on the part of materialist critics, against imaginary universes, tall stories, hoaxes as forms of fiction, and a casual rejection of anything that is not empirically concrete. Lindgren brilliantly analyses what happens when the will to power, exercised through self-control, gives rise to a kind of plodding, prosaic anti-humanism, eclipsing the rich variety of potential ways of life and ways of seeing the world. The multiple interpretations to which every piece of art is open, and the great variety of ways in which a novel may explore or embody an idea, are in themselves a token of human value (Nils Gunnar Nilsson 2004, 10-13). Milan Kundera puts forward a similar argument in his defence of the novel as a fabulous heterogeneous universe that gives free rein to the author's imagination. Kundera is blunt: the suspension of moral judgement within this imaginary 'rei(g)n' is itself the very moral of the novel. This is the place where characters, as individuals, are not mere examples of a preconceived truth. Long experience of the European forms of art, particularly the novel, has in Kundera's view taught readers to remain curious about others and trained them in the ability to understand truths that are different from one's own. This exercise is "political" in the sense that it presupposes individuality (Kundera 1993, 8). Lindgren, similarly, points to the importance of the imaginative novel in promoting human understanding; instead of writing univocal literature, he is able to create heterogeneous hybrids and hilarious worlds that are open to endless different interpretations. Just as Kundera puts forward a disjunctive position on the question of morality, Lindgren presents his thinking on the nature of truth and belief. As we saw above, he believes in developing fiction through the process of writing, but at the same time acknowledges that there is no such thing as truth in the novel beyond the investigation. On the other hand, simplifications corrupt language. The novel is not an instrument of plain information, but the bearer of a language through which existential riddles and paradoxes can be presented and examined (Schueler 2004, 14). The transformation and displacement of biblical narratives, phrases and figures of speech throughout Lindgren's work represent part of this endeavour. In his short story about Lot's wife (Lindgren 2001, 75-86), Lindgren playfully dismisses the value of literature. The story is a vigorous, absurdly comic account of how Lot carries his wife along with him on a wagon after she has turned into a pillar of salt. He is hopeful; salt is a substance that can be transformed. He refuses to follow the practical advice of his cook to use her in preparing food. He pities another man whose wife has turned into copper, since copper cannot be transformed into anything else. One day Lot's wife sits up, the blood once more running in her veins. Lot is not surprised. By way of conclusion to this tall story, which never for a moment allows the reader to forget it is fiction, the narrator comments:

Later on rumour had it that Lot, when drunk, had fathered two sons by his own daughters, both the elder and the younger. One was said to be Moab, the other Ammon. For sheer political, not to say geopolitical, reasons malignant forces sought in this way to explain the appearance of the Moabite and Ammonite peoples.
This was literature and nothing more.
Lot's wife knew better, of course (Lindgren 2001, 85).

Faced with this, the reader is left wondering what is going on: if Lot's wife did indeed 'know better', and this story of her life is not fiction, what is it then? The narrator says, more precisely, that it was nothing more than literature. This raises the question as to the extent to which literature makes us 'know better', if it does so at all. Literature demands criticism. It raises thought. By association the laconic phrase 'Lot's wife knew better, of course,' draws a line back to the beginning of Genesis. God said: 'Behold, the man is become as one of us, to know good and evil' (Gen 3:22). So univocal literature is not an option. Lot's wife, like any other human being, knows about good and evil. She 'knew better'. Malignant rumours and one-dimensional accounts of human life and imagination may pass as both meaning and information, but novels and stories cannot be defined as such. Human questions, for better and for worse, may undergo closer investigation in fiction.

Doré's Bible

Lindgren's more recent novel, *Doré's Bible*[3], revolves around Paul Gustave Doré's illustrated Bible or, more precisely, around the unnamed narrator for whom Doré's
version of the holy book has been a lifelong point of reference. The scriptures as such,
their status as the *sola scriptura*, even the institution of the church and its liturgical
reading of the Bible all come second to the illustrated volume itself: this 18th century
version of the Bible that was so popular at the time, becoming a treasured possession
in many people's homes.

The narrator is a cultured man: he is familiar with numerous works of literature
and has a passion for painting, but lacks any formal education and is unable to read.
His father is deeply disappointed in him, regards him as mad and has him confined
to a mental hospital.

As a child the narrator was exposed to Doré's illustrations and, ever since then, the
book has been his main point of reference in interpreting his perceptions and experience of events in his own domestic world. The particular copy of Doré's Bible that he
came to treasure above all else as a child, vanishes in a fire along with his parents and
the family home. But the narrator, who believes that he has a perfect visual memory
of the lost volume, spends years attempting to recreate it with cartouches. He has a
similar capacity to recall stories he has been told or books that have been read aloud
to him. Away from home, and unwillingly parted from the treasured book, he seeks to
make up for his loss by recreating it down to the last detail. Alongside this immense
endeavour, he searches whenever possible in second-hand bookshops to see if he can
find another copy. Miraculously he stumbles on a new copy of Doré's Bible with a red
binding similar to that of the lost volume; the replacement copy had been saved at the
last moment from a fire at a refuse disposal plant. The narrator's success in redressing his
loss is revealed right at the beginning of the novel, but we are not told how this miracle
came about, for the narrator's release from the task of finishing the book in time for a
jubilee celebration of Doré's birth is overshadowed by graver events that have already
reached their dénouement. *Doré's Bible* thus tells, at one level, the simplest of stories:
one of having – losing – regaining. What remains is the hard work of throwing light
on the cause: the task of digging up the evidence that would explain this simple story.
Or, as Lindgren puts it in his definition of the genre of the novel, the work that remains
is that of investigation. In *Doré's Bible*, however, this task becomes the reader's, rather
than the narrator's, because putting the question: What is man? cannot be resolved
simply through the narrator's (re-)possession of a treasured book: it is not just a matter of having. While the narrator is busy trying to replace his lost Bible, the reader is
drawn into other lines of investigation: What are the conditions of becoming a human

---

3   *Doré's Bible* is the last part of a triptycon, the other two novels being *Sweetness* and *Hash*. Each of them can
     be read as separate works. Characters from the two earlier novels appear in this third novel, in an instance of
     Lindgren's endeavour to turn 'formlessness into form'.

being? What does it mean to be humane and assume responsibility? What is the value of a life replete with biblical imagery, but lacking in God?

Formally the novel borrows features from ancient Greek tragedy in the sense that, like Sophocles' *Oedipus*, it consists in an extended recollection. The end of the drama is presented right at the beginning. The course of events, tragic or comic, has already taken place; what is needed now is a more subtle insight into its causes. Oedipus is a drama about collective memory, orchestrated in the theatre by the chorus, which represents the eternal and inescapable laws of fate. In modern times the story of Oedipus has become closely associated with psychoanalytic theory, with its concern for the development of the ego and the independent individual, who becomes rational and realistic by coming to terms with the unrealistic illusions of the immature. In the Freudian remake the drama was shifted to an internal stage. Søren Kierkegaard foresaw and registered the epochal difference between the self of antiquity and the self of modernity; but he managed to relate the psychological and theological categories of the self to each other, rather than dislocating one in favour of the other (Kierkegaard (1843) 1962, 129-151). Lindgren's investigation is of yet another kind: not a psychological displacement of the metaphysical, nor a Bildungsroman in the ordinary sense, in which the main characters are developed and transformed by the course of events. The narrator is remarkably devoid of self-knowledge and self-reflection. He is more like a person grafted onto a large body of language, an imaginary world of images, and indeed sensibly aware of that fact. He is on his knees, a latecomer overwhelmed by tradition. Most of all he is preoccupied with trying to regain his lost property. 'To a certain extent, maybe it was my grandfather's fault, as he stuffed my childhood with words and literature. He never realised that the world cannot be described, but only depicted' (Lindgren 2005, 179). The grandfather represents the inevitable fact that inherited conceptions are transmitted through forms of life, language and imagination.

So what kind of work is *Doré's Bible*? Is it a kind of recollection, a kind of autobiography? In a way it is, but the line of investigation is different. On the periphery one finds information about the narrator's life and doings, fortuitously and casually referred to along the way. All the many incidents that have occurred in the course of the narrator's life seem to vanish into the background. The bits and pieces of his curriculum vitae are either seen in their relation to the narrator's preoccupation with Doré's Bible, or serve to prod our curiosity as readers, as we try to understand what kind of person the narrator is. How are we to understand and evaluate his intimate testimony?

Right from the beginning of the novel the reader is engaged in an asymmetrical relation to the narrator, marked by a difference of ability: the reader is able to read, the narrator is not. We discover that he is a dyslectic who has made a virtue of necessity by naively maintaining the primacy of the spoken word over the written one, and thereby touching upon a well-known theological theme. However, he has a great love and knowledge of literature, derived from his grandfather's retelling of the classics when he was a child.

Here I'll begin to tell my story about Gustave Doré's Bible. I'm telling it into a recorder Sony MZ-N seven hundred and ten. When it becomes a book, it will be embellished with the most wonderful cartouches and illuminations (Lindgren 2005, 7).

The aim is to record a book that will be ready in time for the great Doré Jubilee. Finishing the task will bring him release: indeed, redemption. The voice announces the task and implies its urgency by means of the introductory "Here". At the same time, we are informed of the medium the narrator is using: the story is initially to be recorded, not written. But "here", right at the beginning of the book-making process, the narrator already anticipates the time when the book will be finished, carefully identifying the types of illustration it will contain. He gives no thought, on the other hand, to writing or typography. He notes that the editor who reworks the recording into a manuscript should ignore the clicking noise of the recorder being switched on and off. Thus the universe of the book is framed by the narrator's voice and the imagination; these are what are presented at the beginning, and the reader may wonder how the recorded voice was transformed into a book and whether the volume they hold in their hands is indeed the finished book that the narrator anticipates. It is crucial that the unnamed narrator speaks his text, and significant, too, that the information on the tape-recorder – model 710 – is spelled out: Numerals don't suggest the sound of the numbers in the way that letters do. Moreover, the narrator gives a precise time reference: This particular Sony model was released in 2003. From this we know that the anonymous narrator is our contemporary, though he does not necessarily belong to the same world as ourselves; indeed, this illusion is broken by the fact that he is not an omniscient narrator in the traditional sense. Set on the threshold of the digital revolution – a revolution as decisive as Guttenberg's in the late renaissance, marking the close of one era and the beginning of a new – the novel constructs a world in which the central character is a dyslectic who has been brought up surrounded by narratives, taught by and dependent on the spoken word and images alone. In other words, the novel presents a character who exists in a world of imagination, but without written texts. What kind of person is he? What would it mean to know, and be able to act upon, only what you have been told? And what is the relationship between a reproduction and the original?

On the one hand, the narrator's worldview and self-image are intimately disclosed and mediated by his voice in this first-person novel; on the other hand the narrator's story is reflected not in an introspective relation to the self, but in an exterior object, a book that contains a series of xylographies, that is wood engravings: images that are open and ready for extrospection. The images that fill the narrator's head are not hidden from view; with trustful naiveté, he displays them for everyone to see. This does not mean, however, that the reader is granted access to all the narrator's thoughts. At the psychological level certain painful matters remain known only to the narrator himself. To be sure, in the recording the narrator does share a certain amount of intimate knowledge with the reader. But he adds a further element to the forthcoming work by including within it a letter by his father that he himself has been unable to read.

The playful assumption is made that the reader can be trusted to contribute further knowledge through the very process of reading a letter whose contents have been concealed from the narrator himself. As a result, the reader him/herself comes to play an important role in the investigation. By raising questions as to the nature of high art, the respective value of originals and reproductions, and what is meant by authority, copying and mediocrity, the novel examines the conditions of truth, knowledge, trust, and certainty.

What kind of novel, then, is Doré's Bible? What is its line of investigation? On what stage does it take place? What kind of world does it invent, and what is discovered and uncovered in the making?

In my view, the real subject of the novel is the human imagination, and language itself, as the ultimate creative and powerful ingredients of an inter-subjective world in the making. This theme is playfully materialised and acted out by the dissymmetry established between the narrator and the reader: first through the way in which the novel plays with [the differences between] the spoken word and the written sign, and second through its humour, which creates a confidential alliance between reader and narrator. The extravagant humour recalls that of Kafka, who likewise uses humour as a means to deal with issues of life and death. Third, it is notable that the reader is continuously both repelled and attracted by the use of the engravings and biblical narratives as a counter reference. In this sense the image of Doré's Bible becomes a synecdoche for the way in which, in the 18th century, poetry, myth and biblical narrative were used romantically to explain the religious meaning discerned in the rationality of natural science. A modern solution is available to resolve the distinction between humanism and science, faith and knowledge, a solution that is presented in the novel by the church itself. It is precisely the highest church authority that has commissioned the celebration of the Doré jubilee. The narrator, meanwhile, lives entirely in the world of Doré's images. This is confirmed by his response to his friend Manfred Marklund, when the latter asks: 'Who is Gustave Doré?'

He was the one who made the Bible, I explained. From beginning to end. He made the tablets of law on Mt Sinai and led the people to the Promised Land. He was the one who overthrew the walls of Jericho and drowned the world in a flood. He made sure Jesus was born in Bethlehem and baptised in the River Jordan and held his Sermon on the Mount and was crucified and resurrected on the third day. All of it.

I didn't know, Manfred Marklund said.

Without his Bible I would have been someone else, I said cautiously, not to exaggerate. There isn't one line or figure I haven't studied. The waves of the sea that Jesus walked on. The Samaritan woman's nipples under the linen dress. Herlofernes' head. The robe tied round the waist of the crucified thief. The sword God holds in his hand when he kills the snake. I have devoted my whole life to Gustave Doré. I see everything through his eyes. In everything I notice the contours of Doré. If one doesn't have faith in Doré, one lacks the ability to believe (Lindgren 2005, 46-47).

Metonymically Doré has displaced any reference to God. God is part of the imaginary whole, seen here as he kills the snake, but otherwise the narrator shows no curiosity about Him. Sunday services, the liturgy, prayer or confession in the midst of a congregation are foreign to the universe of the novel. The Swedish church is seen to play a role in commissioning the jubilee volume on Doré, but is otherwise absent. The brief dialogue between the messenger from the church and the narrator suggests the boundaries of the latter's world. The narrator makes it clear that there are no churches in Doré: a few synagogues, but neither churches nor cathedrals. "A regrettable omission", says the man of the church. But the narrator persists: "Doré, I wanted to explain to him, didn't fail to see anything. He didn't even neglect the nonexistent, the straps on Mary Magdalene's sandals, the fact that Jesus has six toes on his left foot when he speaks in the synagogue…'" (Lindgren 2005, 44).

The novel poses the troubling question as to how extensive the narrator's disability really is. We see that he is trapped in Doré's world, yet he appears to be satisfied and content. What is the problem, if there is one? And what are the alternatives? Lindgren has created a world, a point of view, in which the imagery of the Bible plays a crucial role in supplying the narrator with a language in which to come to terms with the surrounding world, as any human being must. The imagery is random, and there is no key to its interpretation, no religious authority, not even a responsible 'I'. Perhaps what the novel offers is precisely a diagnosis of collective imagery in the absence of authority?

Authority and power

It is true of every human being that s/he inherits the world into which s/he is born. The first set of norms and worldviews that s/he acquires are transmitted not through formal education, but through the life forms in which every child participates during his or her upbringing. In *Doré's Bible* the family home was that of a forest superintendent, the narrator's father, who built the house and was in charge of a large area of forest, as well as several state-owned smallholdings. The names given to these small farms were all taken from Christian terminology: The Ends of the Earth, Grace, Salvation, Redemption, Eternity. Thus the rather abstract glosses of Christian spirituality were mapped out in a very concrete form in the boy's immediate surroundings.

His father, the forest superintendent, was the ruler of this small world. His mother was a rather vague figure, with only a subservient role in the traditional patriarchal marriage. Hers was the traditional lot of the housewife: keeping house, playing the piano, doing needlework, looking after the boy and keeping him amused with stories, music, picture books and so on. All this sounds rather innocent, but Lindgren makes clear that it isn't. It was the mother who first introduced the boy to Doré's Bible, showing him the engraving of Nebuchadnezzar slaughtering the infants with Zedekiah as an eyewitness, and soldiers cutting open a child's breast with their swords. Her reason for showing him this picture was simply to test his eyes:

And indeed, I saw! The image burnt itself into me. Like a fire. Exactly like a fire. On the opposite page, which was also turned towards me, Samson was knocking down the columns of the temple. Everyone was trying to escape. But of course they crushed. To crush a human being takes at most a second or two. But it is enough time for the one who will be crushed to think: Now I will be crushed.

I did not understand anything, I said to her now. And nothing parted me from the pictures. I could not defend myself as I lay in the cradle. I was burnt by them (Lindgren 2005, 10).

The child was a victim in the sense that he was captivated by these powerful images, but at the same time these images became his looking glass, providing him with a worldview and a language. Through these well-known pictures the world around him was transformed into something familiar. He loved turning the pages of the Bible and hearing the stories from his mother and grandfather, and he could find a matching story from the Bible for every experience he encountered within his domestic world. Thus from early childhood onwards these pictures, which had made such an impression on him, became the child's key to understanding the world, a counter reference to set against his experience, and a means of access to knowledge not given to him by any other means. From one perspective, then, the novel *Doré's Bible* is a tale about the power of imagination to instruct.

Through the narrator's recorded recollections one gets the picture of a mother who talked and acted as if she observed the opinions of her husband and submitted to his decisions, but in fact did so in a rather low-key manner. In interpreting her role, one might focus on the importance of her domestic duties, and her liking for literature and music, in forging a distinctive worldview, different from her husband's, or one might emphasise her failure to help her son adjust his self-image. Her vague, though loving, attitude may have hindered him in the process of growing up, or, on the contrary, equipped him with the self-confidence to develop his own voice and make an impact on the reader, for his mother, unlike his father, did not judge him by his intellectual abilities.

Another important feature of the boy's upbringing is that he was presented, as a child, with two contrasting versions of paternal authority, his maternal grandfather being part of the household. The dichotomy between father and grandfather functions in the novel as an unmediated allegory for the cultural difference between the arts and sciences. The grandfather was attentive and present to the boy, whereas the father, often absent, demanded mere obedience. The contrast is underlined by the different professions of the two men.

The grandfather was a former professor of literature who suffered from the after-effects of an accident on Twelfth Night shortly after his wife had died, when he lost his way and walked for hours in the cold. By the time he returned, he was completely frozen. It took hours to defrost him, and in the process he lost the ability to read. Or, as it seemed to the boy, perhaps affected by his father's irony: 'Grandfather's brain has been freeze-dried.' He is seen as a victim, yet one who has been rescued from premature death. The father offered this rational explanation:

Because of the freeze-drying, cells and their contents may become fixed in a condition that is as close to the vital as possible, father explained. Other methods of preservation are far from ideal in this respect; the cells undergo innumerable morphological and chemical changes. But in the case of freeze-drying an instant interruption of the processes of life happens, all water-soluble substances are kept exactly where they were at the moment of freezing. Aqueous vapour is liberated, nothing else. If one defrosts the freeze-dried object or preparation and adds fluid, one will observe that by and large it has maintained all its original characteristics. What little has evaporated would mostly be dispensable. One could even claim that freeze-drying removed what was superfluous and dispensable.

In the case of grandfather, it was unfortunately the alphabet that evaporated, father pointed out (Lindgren 2005, 14).

The grandfather, on the other hand, preferred to refer to the incident as the funny episode or his cold stroke of genius.

Luckily the old man knew all the books he really cared about by heart. Over the years he passed on numerous great works of literature to his grandson. They maintained a deep understanding, united by the dyslexia of the old man, who had lost his former ability, and the grandson, who still hadn't reached school age. Together they formed a metaphor of transmittance. The intimate closeness of the two leads the grandson to form childish conclusions, as in the scene when the parents invite the teacher to find out if she thinks it will be possible to teach their only son to read and write. During the conversation the boy sits underneath the table looking at the picture of John baptising Jesus in the river Jordan; his gaze falls upon an old man in a turban sitting on the bank, propping his chin on this hands, and he thinks: 'Maybe Jesus had his grandfather with him.' All the while he continues to gaze at the picture with deep attachment. Similarly, he hears in his head the words to which everyone in the picture is listening: 'This is my son, he is the chosen!' as if they were personally addressed to himself as he hides under the table, listening to his parents and the teacher discussing him.

Confronted with the formal demands of the village school, the narrator recalls that he made the solemn decision not to learn to read. His dyslexia may have been hereditary, but the narrative gives the impression that he felt his disability to be a vocation. When the teacher appealed to him, he felt the desire to read, but this was instantly drowned by a screaming voice in his mind: 'NO, YOU MAY NOT! IT IS FORBIDDEN! YOU CAN'T! YOUR PATH IS NOT THE PATH OF READING!' (Lindgren 2005, 36). His preference was for the world he shared in the close relationship with his grandfather. In his tiny room with a self-playing piano and the mild smell of food from the kitchen, the grandfather let him into the world of literature with freedom, imagination, warmth and genuineness. His grandfather believed that literature was not something to be read, but something one should possess as an inner resource (Lindgren 2005, 33). From his grandfather he heard *The Three Musketeers*, *Death in Venice*, *Comrade Napoleon* and many other works. He remembers how the old man often repeated the phrase from the Corinthians: *for the letter killeth, but the spirit giveth life*. 'Unfortunately Doré hadn't made any picture of that particular passage from the Bible. If he had, the wood engraving could have depicted granddad and me. You know what I mean' (Lindgren 2005, 35). The narrator's attitude is immature, conveying no sense of distance or time; the relationship with the grandfather is both poetic and touching, yet entirely uncritical. At the same time the narrative is ironic, and points to a dilemma: the grandfather is dead. Doré, the engraver, also laid down his creative tools long before the narrator was born. The sympathetic understanding engendered by the grandfather's and grandson's shared dyslexia and the oral transmission of stories appears to have hindered the latter in moving on from his original role model and developing into an adult.

The dichotomy represented by the two contrasting models of parental authority (the narrator's father and grandfather) is deepened by the narrator's different responses to them: whereas he wholeheartedly identifies with his grandfather's worldview, he responds to his father indifferently, obeying him with neither protest nor enthusiasm. His identification with his grandfather reaches its culmination when he is released from the mental hospital to attend the latter's funeral. The mother has taken out the dead man's suit for the grandson to wear at the ceremony: 'And it made me joyful that by wearing the suit I got the opportunity, so to speak, to represent grandfather at his own funeral' (Lindgren 2005, 101). The representation is ironic, implying that the death itself is unimportant and has left everything unchanged. Prior to the funeral, the narrator learns from his parents that the grandfather had regained the ability to read in the last three days of his life. The narrator feels betrayed and insists on knowing what the grandfather had been reading. The mother reads a passage from the last pages of Cervantes' *Don Quixote*, in which Don Quixote confesses his regret at having spent his life reading bad novels of chivalry. The narrator tells us how he continued the passage by heart, unaware of the fact that he was changing the wording significantly. But it would take a reader to check this. In other words he spoke the words in good faith, but was nevertheless untrue to the original. Ignoring the notary's deathbed testimony, in which the latter relates that no knight had ever died in his bed as quietly, and in such a Christian manner, as Don Quixote, the narrator gives a slightly different version: 'Don Quixote died a quiet, conventional, not to say mediocre death in his own bed [...]' (Cervantes (1615) 1993, 475; Lindgren 2005, 99).

It obviously makes no sense to him to characterise Don Quixote's death as Christian. In his interpretation, the present unmistakably intrudes, rendering 'Christian' as 'conventional' and depriving the passage of meaning. The narrator makes rich use of biblical language, yet his narrative is remarkably devoid of any reference to anything religious or metaphysical. This is evident in the culmination of the day of the funeral, when the father invites his son into his study in order to show him Doré's Bible. The father asks the son to kneel down before the cupboard manufactured in the Lindgren workshop. The son is briefly able to touch the binding. The scene is a manifest and ironic demonstration of the disenchanted and secular world. God has been displaced by the imagery of the Bible and the priest by the rational superintendent, who promptly locks the cupboard up again.

The narrator is his grandfather's sole heir, and he has to sign his name in order to acknowledge receipt of his grandfather's legacy, which gives him independent means. The necessary signature is developed to serve the occasion:

Already the same evening I sat on the bed with paper and pencil and invented a signature for myself: It was a short piece of bank down at the Ava stream, three small bushes, two angular stones and finally another two almost creeping bushes. All my life since then I have used that signature (Lindgren 2005, 100).

Fire: fury, destruction and the elementary

Fire represents certain crucial ideas in the novel. The antithesis of the cold that 'freeze-dried' the grandfather's brain, it is a key attribute of the father, ironically contrasting with the cosy kind of warmth and authenticity attached to the narrator's memories of the nursery and his grandfather's presence. By contrast, the father is recalled as a formidable, distant authority: unattainable and unable to serve as a role model. There is nothing cosy about the father; rather, his association with fire makes him God's substitute on earth. At least three semantic levels are brought together by the poetic distribution of fire and utilised to create a grand play of metaphors, connecting themes that are normally treated apart because they belong to different categories or historical epochs. First, there is the psychological level of the relationship between father and son. Second, there is the allegorical level relating to the contrast between science and belief. And third, an anti-metaphysical – metaphysical level that relates to the terms on which the father used to exercise his rational authority, and indirectly raises the question as to how far he still does so. On each of the three levels the nature of truth is questioned.

At the psychological level, we have already seen how the narrator was burnt when his mother exposed him as an infant to the destructive force of Samson. The child's fear on that occasion was transformed into awe of the father, who in his capacity as forest superintendent used fire as a tool, burning down parts of the forest from time to time in order to clear space for the smallholding. This motif is linked directly to the narrator's disability: Prior to his entering the village school and making the decision not to learn to read, a fatal incident had occurred that connected the seemingly dangerous power of reading with the devastating powers of fire. A farmer called Pettersson, who lived on a smallholding called The Solace, often came to visit when the father was away on an official journey. He was pleasant company for the wife and son left behind, taking time to look at the pictures in the book with the boy, and the narrator particularly remembers the time when they looked at the picture of Moses standing before the burning bush. This apparently innocent memory is presented in parallel with the fatal incident that occurred when the superintendent was monitoring the burning of a small piece of land, and equipped Pettersson with a flame-thrower to meet the purpose. The two men, the superintendent and Pettersson, had carefully read the instructions, which the father kept repeating. They had even read the royal protection formula; but instead of placing himself on the edge and making the flame-thrower shoot the flames towards the centre, Pettersson had positioned himself with his back to the middle of the area. Having set the whole edge on fire, he was unable to escape.

The incident is told through the guileless eyes of a young boy, who, perhaps through self-delusion, ends up blaming the accident on the mischievous powers of reading rather than on the father. At the time the authorities and the insurance company wanted every detail investigated and explained. The superintendent was not held responsible for Pettersson's death. As a reader one cannot help but suspect jealousy on the father's part; however, there is absolutely no conclusive evidence. To the boy another of Doré's xylographies provides the conclusion:

I was lying on the floor with my book in the red binding in front of me. Thanks to the picture of Daniel in the burning oven, I realised what had happened. To me it was the most terrible, maybe the only really terrible thing, the persevering and repeated reading that had taken place prior to the incident itself (Lindgren 2005, 26).

Understandably, both parents insist that reading and writing are important skills to learn. The mother even asserts that they are a precondition for knowing the truth. Perhaps neither the boy nor the grown-up narrator ever felt the need to know the truth, and the irony of the story is that the boy could be said to have good reasons not to know. All the way through his narrative, he exhibits veneration and awe towards his father, who constantly claims to be as content and secure as his grandfather. But the misunderstanding between father and son is a chasm of misery. Their relationship is restrained on the surface, but the novel draws a web of lines between various incidents: the very different expectations that the father and the son have of his further education after he completes the village school – the son having considered an academic career, the father having arranged a place for him at a home for the mentally disabled; and the father's letter, of whose contents the son claims to be ignorant. Never having had the letter read to him or read it himself, the narrator records his own preconceived and hopeful version of what it may have said (Lindgren 2005, 200-101).

This letter, composed in wilful, self-protective ignorance of the original, is presented alongside the letter actually written by the father, and this produces a painful contrast. The father reveals an uncompromising contempt for the son, who never managed to fulfil his expectations, and puts forward his own views on truth, God and science (Lindgren 2005, 203-206). Compared with his son the father appears to himself both superior and triumphant, flaunting his rationalistic concept of God, in which he draws on a mathematical-logical notion of eternity associated with the theory that the basic element of all matter is released by fire and becomes the substance phlogiston. The father's adherence to this notion of phlogiston is a token of his intellectual limitations. The reader gets to know him only through the son's awe of him. He appears to have been stiff and unapproachable, and it is difficult not to side with the son and see him as a victim of his father's attitudes.

Oddly enough, however, the mention of phlogiston suggests another possible perspective. The metaphorical reference to fire opens up the allegorical level relating to the distinction between science and belief. In the letter the father's biased view of life is exposed by his putting every aspect of the universe into one rationalistic formula: mathematics, God, any change in the world can all be attributed to a single element: Phlogiston.[4] In his letter, which the narrator encloses but claims never to have read, the father writes:

For example when you asked about eternity, I told you that there are two eternities, one before and one after us, and that they are probably equally long. And you gobbled it up!

Likewise you asked about fire. And I answered that fire consists of phlogiston. And with bleary eyes you were content with that too!

From natural necessity a thinking being, indeed, must ask next: Then what does phlogiston consist of?

But to you, depraved as you are, the word itself was satisfactory!

Actually phlogiston is one of the elements that God made use of when he created the universe; it is quite conceivable that God consists of phlogiston in its purest form. There is phlogiston in all matter.

But now and then it breaks out, blazing and grandiose, in the shape of fire or an explosion or thunder or a devouring glow or melting heat.

The light that will never fall on these pages is also phlogiston and nothing else. When the trees and scrub are burning in the forest, when metals transform into oxides, when metals such as gold and silver are formed, when phosphorus begins to shine, when coal becomes white from heat, then it is phlogiston that is appearing in all its power and authority. Phlogiston is the fatherly element in the world, the essence of fatherliness, at once breeding and breaking, bearing and destroying, unifying and decomposing.

He who has not seen phlogiston has not seen the Father.

As far as eternity is concerned it is naturally one and indivisible. This is what mathematics tells us (Lindgren 2005, 204-205).

Since the theory of phlogiston was proved scientifically invalid and was therefore outdated even before the father was born, his adherence to it raises questions as to the kind of authority and truth value that he represents in the novel.

The two letters, the one demonstrating the narrator's self-delusion on the one hand, and the unread letter from the father on the other, are placed side by side towards the end of the novel. By this point the reliability of the narrator has been called into question in various ways. As a reader one becomes increasingly aware of the stubborn naïveté and immaturity of his self-portrayal. One may even be tempted to adjust one's

---

4   The theory of phlogiston (Robert Boyle: *The sceptical Chemyst*, 1661 and Georg Ernst Stahl, 1703), was put forward in the late 16th century, when the modern science of chemistry began, and maintained through most of the 17th. It was disproved by Antoine-Laurent de Lavoisier's disclosure of oxygen. He reformed the chemical nomenclature, putting forward his anti-phlogistic theory in the 1770s.

impression of the father. The content of the letters transforms the question as to who is the more reliable narrator into the higher question of truth in science and truth in art. The father, who appears to be so knowledgeable, has a one-track mind that rejects the requirements of modern science, while the son is retarded. Both, in their own way, are fundamentalists in the sense that they cannot cope unless everything can be traced back to a principle, an axiom, a dogma.

The third level in this play of metaphor relates to the anti-metaphysical versus the metaphysical. Though all reference to a transcendental sphere is absent in the novel, it is forcefully and ironically re-established through the image of *fire*. Fire, in all its forms, is the medium of God's epiphany in the Pentateuch, the sign of his presence. Yahweh devours the sacrifice by means of fire; he addresses Moses in the burning bush, he leads the Israelites as a pillar of fire through the desert. We have seen how the father's authority is associated with fire. Yet somehow the medium strikes back, both the parents and their home being wiped off the earth by a sudden conflagration. The son, however, is not particularly distressed by the incident, to which he attributes no particular significance.

Condition of life

As the above suggests, heaven and earth, as two incompatible forms of existence, parts of a cosmology that relates God to man, have thoroughly collapsed, leaving, by way of alternative, only Doré's world or phlogiston in its purest form, as God Himself. In this world truth is presented either as a product of man's own imagination, or as an element logically deduced from matter itself. In the novel, education and refined manners are strongly associated with classical literature and art. There are numerous references to these, and the narrator frequently assures us of his contentment. His joy on discovering a copy of Doré's Bible at the disposal plant is the only indication that his spirit is troubled. Significantly, however, the workers at the disposal plant are seen shovelling heaps of books into the fire, destroying all kinds of literature both trivial and sublime, products of the human spirit in a world where such works have no use or meaning.

The novel takes place in a world in which the satisfaction of copying has displaced the questioning mind. The "I" of the novel is retarded; his quest is solely to recover a lost object, not to discover what it means to be human. He is entirely without passion. Any newcomer on the human scene is confronted with the alternatives of abiding by the laws and habits of earlier generations, or of being enlightened by the spirit of the present, and is expected to come to an existential verdict. In the novel these alternatives have been shifted. The doctrine of the letter has been rejected and replaced by the oral transmission of the narrator's cultural heritage; the aim is merely to copy, not to create. The [narrator's] inability to be present in and conscious of his own time is demonstrated in the novel by the sheer fact that it remains unmentioned. As my final comments will show, this perspective is highlighted in at least two ways: by the reference in the novel to two very different purveyors of news: the figure of Jesus on the one hand, and the press on the other.

Throughout the novel we see the narrator spending time with his friend Manfred Marklund, a reporter on a local newspaper. Manfred Marklund, like his father before him, is always on the lookout for stories from daily life. For generations the eldest son in his family has been given the name Manfred and has carried out the same duty. It is through a report in the local paper that the Swedish Church finds out about the narrator and makes the arrangement for the Doré jubilee.

Apart from the information that Jesus, in Doré's engraving, is pictured with six toes when he speaks in the synagogue (Lindgren 2005, 50), there is another ironic reference to him When the narrator's father removes his son to a home for the mentally disabled, the narrator takes with him, among other things, a gift from his mother, a mechanical tinplate replica of Doré's figure of Jesus. On arrival all his personal belongings are put away in the cellar (Lindgren 2005, 70). But much later on in his life, the narrator presents the mechanical Jesus to Manfred Marklund's son, who quickly maltreats the toy with his hammer, removing the winder and other mechanical parts and flattening out the tinplate. In the metaphorical play of the novel the tinplate Jesus is a token of the fatal lack of any kind of qualified presence. Since there is only immanence, the incarnation can be nothing but a toy, a product of human beings' imagination and their skill as copyists.

Bibliography

Aristotle 1927. *The Poetics*. The Loeb Classic Library. London: William Heinemann.

Cervantes Saavedra, Miguel de 1993 (1615). *Don Quixote*. Hertfordshire: Wordsworth Editions Limited.

Eglinger, Hanna & Heitmann, Annegret 2002. *BilddurchSchrift: zum visuelle Diskurs in der skandinavischen Gegenwartsliteratur*. Freiburg: Rombach.

Frye, Northrop 1982. *The Great Code. The Bible and Literature*. New York: A Harvest Book.

Kierkegaard, Søren A. 1843. 'Det Antikke Tragiskes Reflex i det Moderne Tragiske.' In: Søren Kierkegaard 1962. *Enten – Eller*, A. B. Drachmann, J. L. Heiberg, H.O. Lange (eds.). Copenhagen: Gyldendal, 127-152. (*Either – Or*. Ed. & trans. by H. V. Hong & E. H. Hong. Princeton: Princeton University Press 1988).

Kjærstad, Jan 1999 (Norwegian edition 1997). *Menneskets felt*. Copenhagen: Samlerens Forlag.

Kundera, Milan 1993. *Testaments Betrayed*. London: Faber & Faber.

Lindgren, Torgny 1982. *Ormens väg på hälleberget*. Stockholm: Norstedt. (*The Way of the Serpent*. London: Panther Press 1998).

Lindgren, Torgny 1983. *Merabs Skönhet*. Stockholm: Norstedt. (*Merab's Beauty*. London: Harpercollins 1993).

Lindgren, Torgny 1984. *Bat Seba*. Stockholm: Norstedt. (*Bathsheba*. London: Harpercollins 1993).

Lindgren, Torgny 1991. *Til sanningens lov*. Stockholm: Norstedt.

Lindgren, Torgny 1995. *Humlehonning*. Stockholm: Norstedt. (*Sweetness*. London: The Harvill Press 2000).

Lindgren, Torgny 2001 (Swedish edition 1991). *I Brogede Blades Vand*. Copenhagen: Samleren.

Lindgren, Torgny 2002. *Pölsan*. Stockholm: Norstedt. (*Hash*. London: Gerald Duckworth & Co Ltd 2004).

Lindgren, Torgny 2005. *Dorés Bibel*. Stockholm: Norstedt.

Nilsson, Magnus 2004. *Mångtydigheternes klarhet. Om ironier hos Torgny Lindgren från Skolbagateller till Hummelhonung*. Växjö: Växjö University Press.

Nilsson, Nils Gunnar 2004. 'Mahlers pölsa och formlösheten som form.' (Interview with Torgny Lindgren); http://www.panorstedt.se/templates/Norstedts/Page.aspx?id=40317

Persson, Anders 2007. 'Norrlandic Revivalism in the Novels and Short Stories of Torgny Lindgren.' In: Thomsen, Bjarne Thorup (ed.), *Centring on the Peripheries. Studies in Scandinavian, Scottish, Gaelic and Greenlandic Literature*. Norvik Press, 69-77.

Schueler, Kaj 1984. 'Hurudan är Herren? Ett samtal med Torgny Lindgren'. *Ord & Bild*, nr. 3, 12-21.

Tyrbjerg, Anders 2002. *Anrop och ansvar*. Stockholm: Carlssons.

FANTASISING THE FALL

THE RECEPTION AND TRANSFORMATION OF THE BIBLE IN PHILIP PULLMAN'S FANTASY TRILOGY *HIS DARK MATERIALS*

Laura Feldt

Introduction[1]

It is beyond dispute that fantasy fiction currently exerts a strong hold on the global imagination, and no less true that the Bible influences and informs fantasy narratives (Aichele and Pippin 1992, 1997). Studies have shown that fantasy fiction may play a significant role for contemporary worldviews (Partridge 2004, 137) and that it participates in the re-negotiation of religion's place in contemporary society (Harvey 2000; Schofield Clark 2003; Neumann 2006 and Neumann and Nexon 2006; Sky 2006). This article analyses one example of a work of fantasy that participates in this process, the trilogy *His Dark Materials*[2] by Philip Pullman, and focuses in particular on its reception and transformation of the Bible.

I argue in the article that *His Dark Materials* takes its narrative norm from the Old Testament[3] narrative of the Fall (Genesis 3), which also determines its central concern – namely, to give an account of the human condition. Thus I depart from other critics (Manlove 2003, 184; Russell 2003, 68),[4] in arguing that the reason the series lacks a conventional happy ending can be explained by its use of the Fall narrative as a narrative norm. My analysis also shows how the reception of the Fall story in *His Dark Materials,* and the anthropological vision that goes with it, have much in common with the Old Testament view of the human condition as it is currently understood in biblical scholarship. Contrary to the claims often made about it, *His Dark Materials* cannot in this sense be seen as an anti-religious work, either with respect to its use of the Old Testament Fall story or with respect to its anthropological vision.

The article falls into two main parts, the first of which examines the rewriting of the Old Testament Fall narrative in *His Dark Materials* by analysing three specific instances of reception. In the second part, I investigate the reception of the Old Testa-

1   I wish to thank Kirsten Nielsen for valuable feedback on this article.
2   The volumes of the series are abbreviated as follows: GC for *The Golden Compass*, SK for *The Subtle Knife*, and AS for *The Amber Spyglass*.
3   As we can see from the references to the King James version of the Old Testament, to Milton's *Paradise Lost*, to various Christian theological writings, and so on, it is the Old Testament narrative that is used, not that of the Hebrew Bible. *Paradise Lost* in particular is an important inspiration for the work (Squires 2003, 19).
4   Russell 2003 explains the lack of a happy ending in terms of Pullman's post-Christian, post-theistic ethics (Russell 2003, 68), while Manlove argues that Pullman fails to prepare us for the unhappy ending, a sign that he was over-hasty in drawing the narrative threads together at the end (Manlove 2003, 184).

ment Fall story in *His Dark Materials* in terms of its implicit anthropological vision, and show how, in its transformation of the biblical material, the trilogy both testifies to a contemporary religious imagination, yet remains tied to the anthropology implicit in the biblical narrative of the Fall.

Summary of and introduction to His Dark Materials

The complex structure of the trilogy resists simple summary, but some words of introduction are of course needed. The books revolve around two youngsters, *Lyra* and *Will*, who come from different worlds. Will's world resembles our contemporary world, while Lyra's differs from ours in many respects, bearing traces of mediaeval or pre-Reformation times. An important feature of Lyra's world is that everyone in it has a visible dæmon in the form of an animal. The dæmon has a separate identity from the person to whom it belongs, yet is also an integral part of that person. In some of the other worlds described in the trilogy, notably Will's, dæmons are invisible and non-physical. Until a person enters adulthood, the dæmon changes shape according to circumstances, but in adulthood it settles into its final form.[5] Moreover, both Lyra and Will possess a unique object that gives them access to knowledge: Lyra has the Golden Compass (the title of the first book), also known as the alethiometer, which communicates the truth about any given situation to anyone who can read its symbols. Will has the Subtle Knife (the title of the second volume), which can cut open windows to the multiple other worlds in the trilogy's universe.

In the first volume Lyra undergoes various separate adventures involving a search for some missing children and for the meaning and significance of something called *dust* or *original sin* (established as the primary theme of the trilogy), but once Lyra and Will meet it becomes clear that they are to be the protagonists in a re-enactment of the Fall narrative. They find themselves in the middle of a war between God, *the Authority*, and *Lord Asriel* (Lyra's father, a rewritten Satan-figure), who wants to replace the old, authoritarian Kingdom of Heaven with the Republic of Heaven. The Church in Lyra's world is staged as a combination of the worst of Inquisitorial Catholicism with that of Calvinism. In its attempt to control free thought it resorts at times to torture and murder, as we see in the character of *Father Gomez*, who has done pre-emptive penance for most of his life and is given absolution in advance so that he is free to murder Lyra. He fails, however, and towards the trilogy's end the ex-nun turned physicist, *Dr. Mary Malone*, succeeds in playing the part of the tempting serpent in the final re-enactment of the Fall narrative, with Lyra and Will as Eve and Adam. After a loving union in a 'garden' (the scene of the Fall), their respective dæmons settle into their final forms, and the trilogy ends with Lyra and Will having to separate and live apart in their original

---

5   This final form reflects the individual's personality: A dog dæmon may indicate a tendency to follow authority; a cat dæmon may indicate independence.

worlds, unable to communicate with one another, in order to halt the drift of dust from the universe and thereby save it from disintegration.

Reception and transformation

Before we proceed to the analysis, it is appropriate to reflect briefly on the various ways in which the Bible has been received and transformed in literature. As Robert Alter suggests, the encounter between biblical literary tradition and new works of literature involves both continuity and change, both iconoclasm and traditionalism (Alter 2000, 1-20). Although modern literature may put biblical motifs and themes in new contexts, thereby redefining and challenging them, the authors' stance towards the Bible may nevertheless be positive – even if combative (Alter 2000, 8-9). Any reception and transformation of an earlier work in a work of contemporary literature may be said to participate in the perpetuation of the earlier work in cultural memory,[6] even when the author questions or challenges central ideas in the earlier work (Alter 2000, 19). Thus reception and transformation are always, at the same time, a reaffirmation of the continuing authority of the earlier work, in this case the Bible, in cultural memory (Alter 2000, 20).

As Alter further points out, the Bible also plays an especially powerful role in secular literature because of its canonical status as a body of founding texts. The Bible thus marks out 'one of the primary possibilities of representing the human condition [...]' (Alter 2000, 17-18). My argument is that *His Dark Materials* uses the Fall narrative precisely in the sense of a primary, powerful, and normative possibility for representing the human condition still relevant today.

However, in a radical, and perhaps trivial, sense, every reception of a text involves a transformation of some kind. In this article, 'reception' is therefore used of an inter-textual[7] referencing of an earlier work, whether in the form of direct quotation or as a reference to characters, metaphors, motifs, names, structures, or other elements. Such referencing may be very explicit or implicit and graspable only by specialised readers. Here, I analyse only examples of explicit forms of reception of the Old Testament Fall narrative, since there is no lack of such in His Dark Materials and since these have not previously been analysed. I use the term 'transformation' to denote the overall view of the Old Testament narrative that *His Dark Materials* presents through its various instances of reception, in so far as this view not only re-actualises the received text, but clearly transgresses its framework.

---

6   I follow Lachmann 2004 in using the term 'cultural memory' in relation to literature.
7   For this term, I refer to Kirsten Nielsen's article in this volume.

1 Rewritings of the biblical Fall narrative in His Dark Materials

Although Milton's *Paradise Lost* is the principal source of inspiration for *His Dark Materials*[8] (Squires 2003, 19), I argue in this section that the narrative norm for the trilogy is in fact provided by the Old Testament narrative in Genesis 3. The trilogy's relationship to *Paradise Lost* is different, since both works can be seen on a par as alternative receptions of Genesis 3.

Three versions of the Old Testament Fall narrative are embedded in *His Dark Materials*. The first (henceforth version A) is the one that Lord Asriel reads to Lyra from the Bible, a version adapted from the real-world Old Testament text in the King James Version. The second (version B) is narrated to Mary Malone by the mulefa people[9] and constitutes an alternative Fall story. The third (version C) is an interpretative re-enactment of the Old Testament story in which Lyra is Eve and Will, Adam. In this section, I analyse the reception and transformation of the biblical Fall narrative in these three parts of the text, and argue that all three instances of reception show that the Old Testament story of the Fall plays a normative function[10] in *His Dark Materials*.

In version A, Genesis 3 is quoted from directly, but its text is subtly altered, as the following extract shows:

> But of the fruit of the tree which is in the midst of the garden, God hath said, Ye shall not eat of it, neither shall ye touch it, lest ye die. And the serpent said unto the woman, Ye shall not surely die: For God doth know that in the day ye eat thereof, then your eyes shall be opened, and your dæmons shall assume their true forms, and ye shall be as gods, knowing good and evil (GC, 371-372).

As we see here, the Old Testament story of the Fall in the King James version is used as the matrix for the new text. This first instance of reception occurs towards the end of GC, when Lord Asriel explains to Lyra about the nature of dust. Asriel reads to Lyra from this altered King James version of Genesis 3 and explains his interpretation of the text. He insists on the relevance of the story to Lyra (GC, 372-373) while at the same time questioning the Church's understanding of it (GC, 374-375). He tells her about the Church's experiments in attempting to separate the dæmon from the body without killing the person. If the dæmon is severed from a person, the person will turn into a '*zombi*': 'It has no will of its own; it will work day and night without ever running away or complaining. It looks like a corpse…', explains Asriel. The procedure of cutting the dæmon from the person, unequivocally staged as evil

---

8   The title of the trilogy is taken from *Paradise Lost* Book II (cf. the epigraph to GC).

9   The mulefa are an alien species of friendly, sentient, intelligent beings, antelope-like in form, who move about on wheels and live in an idyllic society. Mary Malone enters the mulefa world through one of the windows cut by the subtle knife and quickly makes friends with them.

10   The way the Bible is generally handled in His Dark Materials suggests that it is girded with authority and sacredness, as in traditional Christian communities today. For an analysis of how the Bible functions in a traditional Christian community, see Malley 2004. Malley aims to show that what people expect from the Bible are seriousness, authority, and relevance to individual life. Similar expectations seem to be at work in *His Dark Materials*.

in His Dark Materials (cf., e.g., Lyra's reactions, GC, 374), is a result of the Church's obsession with original sin.

In Asriel's understanding, the Fall narrative discloses the secret of what happens when innocence changes to experience, and also reveals the nature of the tie between dæmon and person. Asriel wishes to undo the consequences of the Fall by ridding the world of sin, shame, and death (GC, 372, 377). He is interested in the Fall story as a source of knowledge about humankind and the nature of dust, and in the immense power and energy that link body and dæmon. In particular, he would like to harness this power scientifically to put an end to original sin as he understands it: 'Human beings can't see anything without wanting to destroy it, Lyra. *That's* original sin. And I'm going to destroy it. Death is going to die' (GC, 377). We note however that Asriel's interpretation of the story is not accepted in *His Dark Materials*. In order to access the other world in which he believes the source of dust and original sin to be located, Asriel later kills Lyra's friend Roger, a sacrifice that is wholly condemned in the trilogy, as is any sacrifice of human life for a 'higher' cause, such as the experiments to cut the dæmon from the body. The following representation of Lyra's thoughts is an example of such condemnation:

They [the members of The General Oblation Board] were too cruel. No matter how important it was to find out about original sin, it was too cruel to do what they'd done to Tony Makarios and all the others. Nothing justified that (GC, 376).

Version A testifies that *His Dark Materials* stages a far-reaching interest in the correct interpretation of the Old Testament Fall story, both on the societal level in all the worlds of His Dark Materials, as well as on an the individual level. The Church in *His Dark Materials* has a crucial interest in the interpretation of the story and will go to great lengths to suppress alternative interpretations that question the sanctioned theological interpretation. Further, as Asriel tells Lyra here, various scientists are offering their own interpretations, while individuals such as Mrs. Coulter (Lyra's mother) and Asriel himself are on personal quests for the meaning of the story. The two protagonists, Lyra and Will, are intrigued by the Fall narrative and by the quest to understand the significance of original sin/dust. In these ways, *His Dark Materials* presents the Fall story as being of decisive importance for an understanding of human life. The importance for the trilogy as a whole of this discussion of the correct interpretation of the Fall can hardly be overstated.

For the Church in *His Dark Materials*, the Fall narrated here is the source of original sin (GC, 371), of the transition from innocence to experience, and of fixing the dæmon in its true form. When they eat the fruit, Adam and Eve's eyes are opened, they see the true form of their dæmons and are able to speak with them. They come to understand the difference between themselves and the other animals, they discover good and evil, and in their shame they sew fig leaves together to cover their nakedness (GC, 372). This version of the Fall narrative is staged as the 'original' version in *His Dark Materials*. The Church's interpretation of it bears some similarities to the traditional Christian interpretation of the Fall, in the sense that there is a transition from good (innocence) to bad (experience), as well as from a pre-sexual or non-sexual state (good) to a state of sexual awareness (bad, shameful), and also from self-ignorance (not knowing the true form of one's dæmon) to self-knowledge (realising one's dæmon's true form).

Asriel explains to Lyra that the Church's disapproval of the onset of sexual maturity goes back to this founding story of Adam and Eve. However, the meaning of the story is by no means presented as settled, but is, rather, the object of an interpretative quest, for, as we have seen, *His Dark Materials* offers several alternative interpretations simultaneously.[11] The theme of solving the mystery of dust, introduced already in the first two chapters of the trilogy (GC, 5-32) as the central quest of *His Dark Materials*, is further maintained and unfolded in version A. This quest is inextricably tied to the Fall story of the Bible. In spite of the many possible interpretations, version A clearly presents the post-Fall condition as the natural mode of human existence, for when severed from their dæmons, i.e., when forced back to a pre-lapsarian state, humans become less-than-human: they become, 'zombi's', losing consciousness, personality, will, and the joy of life. So while the quotation from the Fall story in this version becomes a platform for multiple discussions of its interpretation, we are clearly shown that the Fall story is of decisive importance for an understanding of human life – even though the Church's interpretation is incorrect.

Version B is an alternative account of the Fall that nevertheless makes overt reference to the Old Testament narrative. The reader is informed in advance that the Old Testament story is the lens through which we are meant to see the subsequent narrative (AS, 223). It is further stated that version B is to be understood metaphorically (AS, 224).[12] However, this version is not, as version A was, a platform for interpretative discussions of the story's meaning, but an alternative version of the Fall story itself that bears some similarity to an indigenous myth. Yet by implication it is, of course, a re-interpretation of the received Fall story, and as such contributes to the discussion of its meaning, or, in other words, to the interpretative quest of *His Dark Materials*.

The context of this alternative Fall story, the mulefa version, is that Mary Malone is talking to the female mulefa Atal about dust (*sraf* in the mulefa language). The mulefa are able to see the dust surrounding all sentient conscious beings (both themselves and humans – for example Mary), whereas Mary and other humans are not. To Mary's question of how this came about, Atal replies by retelling the mulefa Fall story. Long ago, a female mulefa discovered a seedpod and started playing with it. A snake that

---

11   In Lyra's world, scientific discovery provides 'a physical proof that something happened when innocence changed into experience' (GC, 373). The scientist Rusakov discovered a new elementary particle clustering around human adults (GC, 370). Through reference to the Bible (Genesis in the King James version: 'in the sweat of thy face… unto dust shalt thou return'), this particle came to be named Dust. Dust is the physical proof of a child's transition to adulthood and is connected to sexuality. The Church's name for it is therefore original sin.

12   The mulefa Atal explains that the story is 'a make-like', the mulefa word for metaphor (AS, 222).

had coiled itself into the pod asked her what she knew and what she remembered. When she answered that she knew and remembered nothing, the snake told her that if she put her foot through the hole in the seedpod, she would become wise. She did as the snake suggested, and the seedpod oil entered her blood, enabling her to see *sraf*. She then shared this experience with her fellow mulefa. She and her mate then took the seedpods, thus becoming self-aware, conscious, and wise. They started to name each other, as well as the trees, their fellow creatures, and the plants. Subsequently, the mulefa realised that they had to plant more seedpod trees in order to maintain their supply of the precious oil. Unfortunately, the pods were so hard that they only very rarely germinated, and this threatened the trees' survival. At this point, the mulefa and the seedpod trees entered into a happy symbiosis: the mulefa started riding the seedpods as wheels, which would, eventually, crack them and make them germinate. This generated new trees to the benefit of both parties. Since then, the trees and the mulefa have lived together in happy mutuality (AS, 128-129, 224-225).

One of the most striking differences between this narrative of the Fall and the Old Testament version in its traditional Christian interpretation is the lack, in the mulefa version, both of a creator authority (God) and of any sense of prohibition – here there is no temptation and no transgression. Moreover, the snake is not evil, and there are no allusions to sex or to food, no negative moral connotations are indicated, and the transformation that the mulefa undergo as a result of *sraf* (dust, original sin), from a pre-conscious state to a state of self-knowledge and world-recognition, to 'memory and wakefulness' (AS, 224), is depicted as entirely positive (joyful, good, beautiful, AS, 234), as is their new relationship with their environment, which is seen as healthy and beneficial to both mulefa and trees. The continuities between the Fall story and this rewriting are made especially obvious by the overt referencing of the Old Testament story of the Fall prior to Atal's retelling of it; shared motifs include the idea of a female instigator of change, the role of the snake, and the fact that the resulting change is coded as a transformation from a state of none-awareness of the self to one of self-awareness.

The mulefa version of the Fall story is not presented as *the* true version, but rather as an alternative, beautiful version that points to one possible way for conscious beings to live in harmony with themselves and the environment[13] – and to a possible way of understanding the Fall and dust/original sin in a positive light. As I mentioned above, it is explicitly stated in *His Dark Materials* that the story is to be understood metaphorically. Squires sees the trilogy as a tale of evolution (Squires 2003, 54) rather than of the Fall, but its narrative form, its overt references to the Old Testament narrative of the Fall, and its attention to the mysterious beauty of *sraf* (dust) suggest that it is more than that. Several indications are given as to what we are to understand by dust.

---

13   However, this relationship is threatened by the drift of dust out of the universe – a problem created by the many windows cut by the Subtle Knife, invented only recently (about 300 years before the present time of the novels). The threat is averted by Lyra and Will's re-enactment of the Fall.

Indeed, Mary Malone's stay with the mulefa (AS, 120-133, 221-235, 270-276, 365-370) prior to the arrival of Lyra and Will centres on the quest for the meaning of dust, which comes across as ever more mysterious and interesting. Dust in the mulefa version is connected to memory, consciousness, beauty, life, hope, and joy. It is almost mystically present in everything that co-exists (Bird 2005, 190) and its presence apparently serves both to identify each individual as a sentient being and to connect all sentient beings to one another. Version B shows us dust as the *possibility* of happy coexistence between sentient beings and the environment. In version B, what comes into the world as a result of the Fall is not dust in the negative sense expounded by the Church in *His Dark Materials*, but dust in a positive sense that is linked to consciousness, hope, and imagination.

Taken together, versions A and B thus reveal the dual nature of dust as being at once material/physical *and* spiritual, potentially good *and* potentially destructive, dark matter *and* consciousness, imagination, hope (see also Bird 2005, 191). Version B stresses that dust and matter are interdependent, since the existence of dust is contingent on mutuality and love between sentient beings (AS, 451-452, 443[14]). Version B is framed by Mary's stay with the mulefa and her quest for the meaning of dust, which gives her back the sense of meaning and purpose in life that she had lost when she stopped believing in God (AS, 448-454). I therefore suggest that in version B dust is to be understood as a possible new focus of spirituality, a source of wonder and mystery that may return the sense of purpose and meaning to humans after the death of God the Authority (cf. AS, 411-413). The many diverging descriptions of dust throughout the trilogy, its amorphousness and great adaptability (Bird 2005, 196-197) affirm that this new focus of spirituality cannot be identified as a single object or entity, or captured in one metaphor, but must forever remain the object of an interpretative quest: divine[15] but ineffable, and essential to conscious human existence.

Version C, the third reception of Genesis 3, occurs in AS (AS, 463-470). For Lyra and Will this version of the Fall involves the joyful union of bodily and spiritual love.[16] Contrary to the view of original sin put forward by the Church in *His Dark Materials*, their love is depicted as liberating and positive (AS, 470; Squires 2003, 49). In this account of the Fall, Lyra and Will are filled with dust, understood as consciousness, experience, knowledge, joy, and love, but the Fall does not obliterate the physical,

---

14   Here Mary argues that no human being can be fulfilled and happy on his/her own without the love of another.

15   Note that dust, a.k.a. sraf, is also sometimes referred to as 'shadows'. These shadows have told Mary that they are angels (AS, 440-441).

16   It is not made clear whether this Fall involves intercourse, but a loving union is surely meant. A parallel to the loving relationship between Lyra and Will emerges in this chapter when the angel Balthamos, who rescues Will and Lyra from Gomez, refers to his homosexual relationship to the angel Baruch (AS, 469). Cf. also AS, 498, when Lyra and Will stroke one another's dæmons: an instance perhaps of a more concrete bodily union between the two.

potentially dark and destructive side of dust;[17] it simply shows that, for better or worse, the world and human beings as we know them were saved by the Fall.

Mary's narration of her sexual experience spurs Lyra on to fulfil her destiny as Eve (AS, 441-447). Will and Lyra enter a little wood (the garden) as 'the only people in the world' (AS, 458). The Church's interpretation plays a significant role in this reception of the Fall story since it is embodied in Gomez, the assassin sent by the Church. In the view of the Church, Lyra's and Will's love for one another and their adolescent sexuality constitute a mortal sin, and Gomez is sent to kill Lyra to stop the Fall taking place. He is prevented from doing so by the angel Balthamos, who vehemently declares that he and Gomez are not on the same side, and eventually kills the latter (AS, 464, 468). In seeking to understand the role of the Bible and religion in *His Dark Materials* it is highly significant that an angel, by definition a divine emissary, is on the side of Lyra and Will rather than the Church. This strongly suggests that in *His Dark Materials* the source of true spirituality, true religion – of dust itself – is not the caricatured Church, but rather the mysterious, ineffable, mystical interconnectedness of everything (AS, 478). Further, the context of this reception of the Fall story involves a discussion among the principal characters about the many striking coincidences that make up their life stories, in which an elapse of seconds would often have made a crucial difference – preventing Will from meeting Lyra, for instance (AS, 437-438). Chance or coincidence often plays an important role in fantasy literature, leading the reader to suspect the existence of a plan behind events and to ponder the possibility of supernatural causes (Lachmann 2002, 117-150; 2004).

In the pages immediately following version C of the Fall, we learn more about human life through descriptions of dust. Human life is described as a journey towards wisdom (AS, 473). The pursuit of wisdom produces dust, and the passing on of wisdom renews it (AS, 491-492). The benevolent angels of the universe, those led by Xaphania, a divine female angel who is very favourably portrayed, work towards the goal of multiplying wisdom and preventing the proliferation of stupidity. We learn, too, that dust and dæmons are related (AS, 486). On the one hand dæmons/dust are an inescapable part of human nature; they are what allow us to be fully human. At the same time the various discussions of dust in *His Dark Materials* suggest that it is a mysterious substance that transcends the human and perhaps has a divine source.

Just as the Old Testament story of the Fall ends badly, so there is no happy ending to this account of the Fall. Once they have come into their inheritance as adult humans, Lyra and Will are obliged to separate. The difference between the pre- and the post-lapsarian states is portrayed in terms of a move from intuitive knowledge, grace, joy, and love, to hard work,[18] conscious understanding, education, the sense of being alone and lost, the search for wisdom and a longing for love and community (AS,

---

17   As Bird shows, dust in *His Dark Materials* is not *either* matter *or* spirit, but both-and (Bird 2005, 190): matter and spirit are one (SK, 260). Both the physical and the metaphysical belong positively in a vision of the human. Dust is both dark material (NL, 370, 371, 390) *and* consciousness, imagination, hope (SK, 90-92, 260).

18   The references to work (AS, 518) in particular express a continuity with the Old Testament story.

491-493, 513-514, 517). It is made starkly clear, moreover, that it is impossible to change the fundamental shape of the world and that there is no going back, no re-opening of the windows between the worlds (AS, 493). This world is always the most important place, and humans can only do good and build something positive if they cooperate and do not put themselves first. However, a little indication is offered that the human feeling of loss and longing may one day be assuaged. Towards the very end of the trilogy we are told that, while the angel Xaphania shares Lyra's and Will's immense sorrow and their longing for love and community, she 'could see farther than they could, and there was a calm hope in her expression' (AS, 493). For now, however, the only way for humans to travel to other worlds and to appease their sorrow and longing is by means of imagination (AS, 494-495). This, in sum, is the vision of life, the state of the world and the human condition presented in *His Dark Materials*: a vision that embraces the whole of human nature, including the body (AS, 439), and accepts the world as it is (AS, 450-451).[19]

My analysis has shown that *His Dark Materials* is committed to an interpretative quest for the meaning of the Fall story (version A), that it plays with the central themes of the Fall narrative, providing alternative images of the narrative's meaning (version B), and that it stages a re-enactment of the Fall narrative as a normative vision of human life (in version C). It is thus plausible to suggest that the Old Testament story of the Fall functions as the guiding norm for the trilogy as a whole. As such it explains the lack of a happy ending (the separation of Lyra and Will, the lack of communication between worlds), and ultimately determines the view expressed in the trilogy as to the fundamental characteristics of human existence. The trilogy as a whole can be seen as a transformation of the Old Testament narrative of the Fall, one that is marked by both continuity and change, in its attempt to reconstruct the true meaning of the Fall narrative under the palimpsest of the earlier interpretations (especially those of the Church). Rather than rejecting religion, *His Dark Materials* affirms a religious viewpoint by presenting the Fall narrative as central to an understanding of human life and by seeing the divine as a mystery.[20] In its transformation of traditional Fall theology the trilogy upholds the value of choice, individualism, the empowering of women, mystery, and the importance of questioning and seeking (GC, 398). These values accord more with contemporary spirituality than with 'traditional' theology (Partridge 2004, 2006, Lyon 2000). In the next section I will discuss in more detail how the anthropological vision expressed in *His Dark Materials* through its reception and transformation of

---

19   The windows between the worlds cut by the Subtle Knife are seen as unnatural, damaging. The current state of the world is portrayed as the proper and natural way for the world to be.

20   The work affirms the centrality of the Old Testament narrative in understanding human life, even though the moral value the Church has traditionally put on the Fall is reversed from negative to positive. Although the deity known as The Authority is killed in the trilogy, the angel Balthamos makes it clear that this Authority is *not* God (AS, 31-32).

the Bible is indebted to the Old Testament narrative of the Fall in a way that is neither anti-theological nor anti-religious.[21]

2 The anthropological vision in His Dark Materials

Critics and readers frequently make the claim[22] that *His Dark Materials* is atheistic and anti-religious.[23] I will argue that this view is misguided and that this is particularly evident in the anthropological vision that the trilogy presents. Critics who perceive the work as anti-religious often base their view on isolated statements such as 'the Christian religion is a very powerful and very convincing mistake' (AS, 441),[24] and in doing so overlook the pervasive religious themes in the trilogy (Leet 2005, 182). Although it challenges and transforms traditional views on the afterlife, original sin, the soul, and so on the trilogy transforms such traditional views while remaining faithful to the basic theo-anthropological concerns of the Christian tradition, as we see in the various receptions of the Old Testament narrative analysed here. Thus the work makes clear that a utopian vision of the world without sin would be unnatural. There is no going back beyond the cherubim, just as there is no re-opening of the windows between worlds. In *His Dark Materials*, as in the Old Testament, the Fall is the distinctive mark of human existence, and, as I have tried to show, the trilogy's adherence to the Old Testament account of the Fall leads naturally to its 'unhappy' ending. Through its various receptions of the Fall story and its interpretative quest for the meaning of the Fall, *His Dark Materials* seeks to recover a vision of the human condition that is freed from centuries of negative theological interpretation. And in fact this vision corresponds well to the interpretation of Genesis 3 put forward by contemporary scholars of the Bible.

Old Testament scholar Claus Westermann has pointed out that the terms 'original sin' and 'the Fall' played no part in the original/ancient understanding of Genesis 3 or the larger primeval history in which it is embedded (Westermann 1984, 275). Westermann also stresses that there are important differences between the Old Testament

---

21   Personal statements by the author Philip Pullman are not regarded as relevant here, since the focus of this investigation is on the text itself.

22   E.g., Marr, Johnson, Dirda (references in Squires 2003, 72-73), Squires (2003, 51-54), Tucker (2003, 124-130). Examples: 'Pullman does for atheism what CS Lewis did for God' (Marr); 'the most savage attack on organised religion I have ever seen' (Johnson).

23   While *His Dark Materials* can certainly be enjoyed by secular readers, a certain interest in Christianity would seem to be a prerequisite for understanding the work more fully. The reception of the Bible seen in the trilogy differs from that in classical works of fantasy such as those of J.R.R. Tolkien, which make only oblique use of the Bible (Manlove 1992, 262-263). By contrast, *His Dark Materials* uses the Bible and the theological tradition directly and is thus less open to appropriation by other religious communities, since the Christian religion is used so explicitly as its frame of reference. For this reason, the debates have centred on whether *His Dark Materials* is atheistic or Christian in its view of the world.

24   This sentence is uttered by the former nun Mary Malone, and, read in context, it clearly relates to this prehistory. Further, in her description of her life as a nun Mary says that she tried to be too holy, that she was too proud (AS, 441) – in other words, that her approach to religion was wrong, not that religion or spirituality *per se* are wrong. In AS, 470-476 it is argued that the absence of God is not necessarily a positive liberation, but may be another form of slavery – and that it leaves a spiritual void (AS, 447, 449; Bird 2005, 195).

text itself and the Church's traditional interpretation of it. The text of Genesis 3 by itself provides no basis for the notion of original sin or for the Church's unequivocally negative interpretation of the Fall (Westermann 1984, 81).[25] Instead, what is important in Genesis 3, Westermann argues, is that it establishes the fundamental conditions of human life in this world. In the vision put forward in Genesis 3, perfection or infallibility is inhuman;[26] human life is characterised, instead, by hard work and the search for wisdom, and as such can be seen to be founded on God's creative act (Westermann 1984, 83-85). Both the Old Testament narrative and His Dark Materials tell us, in short, that without the Fall we would not be human. In transforming the traditional Church reading of the Fall by assigning a positive rather than a negative value to experience, the body, matter, knowledge, and sex, and presenting them as thoroughly natural (SK, 50), the trilogy in fact presents a view of human life that does not differ radically from that of the Old Testament.

John Milbank argues that *His Dark Materials* puts forward an ethical prescription that is materialist Gnostic rather than orthodox Christian (Milbank 2005), but in the light of my analysis this view seems ill-founded. The created world in *His Dark Materials* is by no means evil, even though the deity who *claims* to be God the creator turns out to be evil himself. But it is made clear in the trilogy that this Authority is not the real creator but an impostor (cf. AS 439). In this sense *His Dark Materials* has closer affinities with Old Testament anthropology than with the traditional teachings of the Church in its positive affirmation of the created world and the pursuit of wisdom. In both narratives, human existence is understood as a combination of the material and the spiritual, neither of these being essentially evil or essentially good.[27] Thus both *His Dark Materials* and the Old Testament affirm a loyalty to this world and the human condition. This is not Gnosticism, at least not as it is traditionally understood. The price of the Fall is the same in Genesis 3 and in *His Dark Materials*: separation. Dust – meaning consciousness, wisdom and understanding – is the goal of the quest in *His Dark Materials*, but – as the trilogy amply demonstrates – these values come at a price and may be used for evil purposes. The price of the Fall is separation, ambiguity, and distance, for to stop the drift of dust and the consequent disintegration of the universe, Lyra and Will must close all passages between the worlds and thus end up without passage to one another, facing everyday life as adults in their normal, separate worlds.

Other continuities between *His Dark Materials* and the Old Testament Fall narrative's anthropological visions can be found in the description of the passage from community and blessedness to hard work, pain, and separation. In defining the human

---

25 Instead, he suggests that these ideas probably stem from the Jewish tradition, specifically IV Ezra (7,118), which was then further elaborated by Augustine (Westermann 1984, 81). One could therefore plausibly argue that *His Dark Materials* seeks to recover a pre-Augustinian interpretation of the Fall. *De civitate Dei* 14,13 is said to have given the symbol of the Fall its full Christian-theological import in terms of original sin.

26 Similarly, all the various worlds in *His Dark Materials* are portrayed as a mixture of civilisation and barbarism (Manlove 2003: 181).

27 The trilogy rejects the metaphysical dualism in which matter/the body is seen as evil and the spirit as good (Hatlen 2005, 79).

condition in terms of toil, pain, separation, sex, and the search for love and wisdom *His Dark Materials* also echoes Old Testament anthropology. Moreover, in both stories the work is not done when the story concludes; indeed, the real work begins once the story is over. In this sense *His Dark Materials* is closer to the Old Testament than to Gnosticism, and this is confirmed by the fact that, in the trilogy, human love is seen to halt the disintegration of the universe (Squires 2003, 99). Thus the anthropological vision put forward in *His Dark Materials* seems to correspond more closely to the Old Testament story of the Fall, as we understand it today, than to Church's version of the story as presented in the trilogy.

The anthropological vision put forward in *His Dark Materials* certainly transforms the traditional theological interpretation of the Fall, but it is not opposed to all forms of Christian theology. In fact, the values implied in this transformation are congruent with many strands of contemporary Protestant theology: gender equality (cf. the predominance of female heroes – the prophetess Lyra, the powerful and dignified witch Serafina Pekkala, the scientist Mary Malone, the sacred supernatural figure Xaphania), tolerance of sexual orientation (homosexual angels), sexual intercourse as a positive and life-affirming act (Lyra and Will), individual will and imagination as positive entities (dæmons as vitality, life force), tolerance towards other ethnicities (multiple races, multiple worlds), anti-imperialism (the mulefa case), anti-authorianism (passim), the focus on mystery and the search for spiritual meaning.

What is certain – despite some critics' claims to the contrary – is that the worldview expressed in *His Dark Materials* is neither scientist nor atheist. The trilogy does not condone Lord Asriel's war against The Authority, for Asriel's and Mrs. Coulter's willingness to sacrifice human life (that of Lyra's friend Roger and the children at Bolvangar) in the cause of war is clearly condemned (Manlove 2003, 181). Rather than opposing religion as such, *His Dark Materials* attacks authority-bound religions and ideologies and argues instead – in accordance with contemporary transformations of the religious landscape – in favour of self- or individually-based religions (Lyon 2000). In the prominence it gives to receptions of the Fall narrative and its quest for the meaning of the story, *His Dark Materials* contributes positively to perpetuating the Fall narrative as a vital option for, or means of, representing the human condition today, while at the same time transgressing the traditional framework in which it is couched. But to really break with a predecessor, especially so great an authority as the Bible, one would need not to defy its commands, to question or rebel against it, but to enter into a quite different logic, a different genre (Žižek 2001, 118-121). This, certainly, is not Pullman's project in *His Dark Materials*.

Conclusion

Biblical texts continue to shape, and be re-interpreted by, not only high culture but popular cultural products such as fantasy fiction. Indeed, it appears that fantasy literature is able to re-enact central biblical stories in a modern context in a way that reaches out to a greater public than the Bible itself.

In its time, *Paradise Lost* recast the biblical story of the Fall in epic poetry, and Milton developed the narrative beyond the framework of Genesis. The fallen angels and Satan as Eve's tempter were set against the autocratic power of God. But did *Paradise Lost* depict God and Christianity as cruel, free will as a trap for mankind, and the desire for knowledge as wrong? This is a central dispute in *Paradise Lost* scholarship (Squires 2003, 19; Hatlen 2005, 84-85), and it also demarcates the central theme of *His Dark Materials*. In the trilogy the Fall is clearly represented in positive terms as essential to human life, and the same goes for free will and the human desire for knowledge. But does that make Pullman's trilogy anti-religious and atheistic? I have argued that it does not.

The trilogy's dependence on the Bible and its reception and transformation of the Old Testament narrative of the Fall produce a vision of human life that corresponds closely to that of Genesis 3 as it is understood in contemporary exegesis, and thereby affirms the value of the Old Testament as a resource for understanding human life. Although His Dark Materials questions the values traditionally associated with Christianity and criticises organised religion, its transformation of the Christian vision of humankind is premised on the acceptance of theism and affirmatively indebted to the anthropology of Genesis 3. Many theologians and philosophers have also seen the Fall as a necessary Fall into existence, just as there is a long Christian tradition of *felix culpa* (Gestrich 1997, 82-129, 225-248).[28] *His Dark Materials* should thus sooner be seen as an attempt to turn (what is staged as) traditional Christianity into a more genuine religion. Traditional theology and the Church are presented in such a hyperbolic manner in the trilogy that its attack upon them must be seen not so much as an attack on any actual church, but rather on any form of authoritarianism. The reception and transformation of the Bible that *His Dark Materials* attests to is thus congruent with a shift away from 'traditional theology' to another form of spirituality documented by sociologists of religion: one that places value on multiple interpretations, the proliferation of theological meanings, doubt,[29] the mystical experience and an unlimited space for individual reflection and spiritual search, and which sees God as interdependent with humans (Partridge 2004, 2006; Lyon 2000).[30]

The interest expressed in *His Dark Materials* in the meaning of the Fall and in fantastic and supernatural creatures, and the anthropological vision that it puts forward

---

28 I am grateful to Marie Vejrup Nielsen for this reference.

29 Cf. Mary Malone who starts to doubt but who does not lose her morality or stop searching for meaning (Squires 2003, 49).

30 Many scholars of religion have suggested that popular culture plays an important role in the current re-enchantment. This article has indicated how fantasy fiction may participate in this process, because although church attendance, for instance, is in decline, it seems that other forms of Christian influence permeate contemporary culture (Partridge 2004, 208).

show that the trilogy is, in effect, a theological work of literature.[31] It bears witness to a love of theological speculation and re-interpretation that serve to render Christianity and the theological tradition still fascinating, and which are not, in the end, unbiblical.[32] There are too many echoes of God in the trilogy, too evident an interest in and love for theology and the Bible, for the work to be called anti-religious. While *His Dark Materials* may not clearly espouse any one theological view, it engenders a love of theological reflection[33] and attests to the value of the spiritual search as a central aspect of what it means to be human. Indeed, theological reflection on the biblical narratives might even be seen in the trilogy as indispensable for thinking human existence:

But think of Adam and Eve like an imaginary number, like the square root of minus one: you can never see any concrete proof that it exists, but if you include it in your equation, you can calculate all manner of things that couldn't be imagined without it (GC, 372-373).

Bibliography

Primary sources

Pullman, Philip 1995. *The Golden Compass* (GC). New York: Dell Yearling / Random House Children's Books.

Pullman, Philip 1997. *The Subtle Knife* (SK). New York: Dell Yearling / Random House Children's Books.

Pullman, Philip 2000. *The Amber Spyglass* (AS). New York: Dell Yearling / Random House Children's Books.

Secondary sources

Aichele, George and Pippin, Tina (eds.) 1992: *Fantasy and the Bible*. Special issue of *Semeia*. No. 60.

·Aichele, George and Pippin, Tina (eds.) 1997. *The Monstrous and the Unspeakable. The Bible as Fantastic Literature*. Sheffield: Sheffield Academic Press.

Alter, Robert 2000. *Canon and Creativity. Modern writing and the authority of scripture*. New Haven and London: Yale University Press.

Bird, Anne-Marie 2005. 'Circumventing the Grand Narrative: Dust as an Alternative Theological Vision in Pullman's His Dark Materials'. In: Lenz and Scott (eds.), *His Dark Materials Illuminated. Critical Essays on Philip Pullman's Trilogy*. Detroit: Wayne State University Press, 188-198.

---

31   I thus disagree with Manlove (2003, 184), who finds that although Pullman allows for angels, a land of the dead and similar features, he ends up in materialism. Such a view is reductive to the complexity of the trilogy, to the variety of interpretations of the supernatural phenomena used in His Dark Materials, the use of the Fall narrative.

32   In Nielsen's contribution to this volume it is suggested that continual re-interpretation inheres in the biblical tradition itself (Nielsen, 185-186).

33   Squires' comments on the not clearly resolved questions of His Dark Materials point in a similar direction (Squires 2003, 63-65).

Gestrich, Christof 1997. *The Return of Splendor in the World. The Christian Doctrine of Sin and Forgiveness*. Grand Rapids: William B. Eerdmans.

Harvey, Graham 2000. 'Fantasy in the Study of Religion. Paganism as Observed and Enhanced by Terry Pratchett'. *DISKUS* 6 [e-journal]. Bath: Study of Religions Department. Lampeter: Theology and Religious Studies Department.http://web.uni-marburg.de/religionswissenschaft/journal/diskus/harvey_2.html accessed on October 26th 2007 11.48 a.m.

Hatlen, Burton 2005. 'Pullman's *His Dark Materials*, a Challenge to the Fantasies of J.R.R. Tolkien and C.S. Lewis, with an epilogue on Pullman's Neo-Romantic Reading of *Paradise Lost*'. In: Lenz and Scott (eds.), *His Dark Materials Illuminated. Critical Essays on Philip Pullman's Trilogy*. Detroit: Wayne State University Press, 75-94.

Lachmann, Renate 2002. *Erzählte Phantastik. Zu Phantasiegeschichte und Semantik phantastischer Texte*. Frankfurt am Main: Suhrkamp.

Lachmann, Renate 2004. 'Cultural Memory and the Role of Literature'. *European Review* 12,2, 165-178.

Leet, Andrew 2005. 'Rediscovering Faith Through Science-Fiction'. In: Lenz and Scott (eds.), *His Dark Materials Illuminated. Critical Essays on Philip Pullman's Trilogy*. Detroit: Wayne State University Press, 174-187.

Lenz, Millicent and Scott, Carole (eds.) 2005. *His Dark Materials Illuminated. Critical Essays on Philip Pullman's Trilogy*. Detroit: Wayne State University Press.

Lyon, David 2000. *Jesus in Disneyland. Religion in Postmodern Times*. Cambridge: Polity Press.

Malley, Brian 2004. *How the Bible Works. An Anthropological Study of Evangelical Biblicism*. Walnut Creek, CA: Altamira Press.

Manlove, Colin 1992. *Christian Fantasy from 1200 to the Present*. London: MacMillan.

Manlove, Colin 2003. *From Alice to Harry Potter. Children's Fantasy in England*. Christchurch: Cybereditions.

Mikaelsson, Lisbeth 1999. 'Magi, fantasi og fiksjon'. In: Alver, B.G., Gilhus, I.S., Mikaelsson, L., Selberg, T. (eds.), *Myte, magi og mirakel i møte med det moderne*. Oslo: Pax.

Milbank, John 2005. 'Fictioning Things: Gift and Narratives'. *Religion and Literature* 37.3, 1-35.

Neumann, Iver 2006. 'Pop Goes Religion. Harry Potter Meets Clifford Geertz'. *European Journal of Cultural Studies* 9.1, 81-101.

Neumann, Iver and Nexon, D. 2006. *Harry Potter and International Relations*. Lanham: Rowman and Littlefield.

Partridge, Christopher 2004 (vol.1) / 2006 (vol.2). *The Re-Enchantment of the West. Alternative Spiritualities, Sacralization, Popular Culture and Occulture*. London: T&T Clark.

Possamai, Adam 2005. *Religion and Popular Culture. A Hyper-Real Testament*. Bruxelles: Peter Lang.

Russell, M.H. 2003. 'Ethical Plots, Ethical Endings in Philip Pullman's *His Dark Materials*'. *Foundation. The International Review of Science Fiction* vol. 32, no. 88, 68-75.

Schofield Clark, Lynn 2003. *From Angels to Aliens. Teenagers, the Media and the Supernatural*. Oxford: Oxford University Press.

Scott, Carole 2005. 'Pullman's Enigmatic Ontology: Revamping Old Traditions in His Dark Materials'. In: Lenz and Scott (eds.), *His Dark Materials Illuminated. Critical Essays on Philip Pullman's Trilogy*. Detroit: Wayne State University Press, 95-105.

Sky, Jeannette 2006: 'Harry Potter and Religious Mediatization'. In: Sumiala-Seppänen, J.; Lundby, K. and Salokangas, R. (eds.), *Implications of the Sacred in (Post)Modern Media*. Nordicom, 235-253.

Squires, Claire 2003. *Philip Pullman's His Dark Materials Trilogy*. New York: Continuum.

Tucker, Nicholas 2003. *Darkness Visible. Inside the World of Philip Pullman*. Cambridge: Wizard Books.

Westermann, Claus 1984. *Genesis. A Commentary*. Vol. 1: Genesis 1-11. Minneapolis, Augsburg, London: SPCK.

Žižek, Slavoj 2001. *On Belief*. London: Routledge.

THE IMAGINARY PARADISE OF THE NOVEL

THE RECEPTION AND TRANSFORMATION OF A BIBLICAL THEME IN MILAN KUNDERA[1]

David Bugge

When dealing with *the Bible and literature*, we usually focus on the narrative or stylistic similarities of the texts in question. We investigate how a biblical story and its characters live on in later fictional writings, if only as a counter story, or we examine the figurative language of the Bible and its revitalisation in modern literature. In both cases, our attention is concentrated on the reception and transformation taking place *within* the literary works.

There is, however, another way of approaching the Bible and literature. Instead of dwelling on the specific literary texts, we can take a step back and look at imaginative literature as such. This gives rise to the interesting question as to how literature and its particular way of exploring human existence relate to the Gospel. Is there any link whatsoever? As the Bible contains not one but several distinct and mutually conflicting theologies, the answer naturally depends on one's interpretation of the Christian Gospel. What may seem truly Evangelical to one interpreter may seem, to another, to miss the very core of the Gospel – a hermeneutical difficulty that applies, however, to any theological statement.

So when I argue below that there is a striking parallel between the Christian Gospel and Milan Kundera's meta-literary reflections on the art of the novel, my main emphasis is on two components of the former, both representing a certain tradition within the history of Christian theology, namely the criticism of ethics (the unmasking of carping Pharisaism) and the idea of a divine, unconditional and *all*-embracing mercy. Now, when Kundera states that the novel is 'the imaginary paradise of individuals', one might ask if this 'paradise' is so different after all from that of Christianity, otherwise known as the Kingdom of God.

Kundera is no Christian novelist. On the contrary, he frames his theory of the novel in explicit opposition to any sort of religion. So the aim of the present article is certainly not to turn him into a 'closet Christian'. Rather, my intention is to demonstrate that Kundera's criticism of religion and his alternative concept of 'the imaginary paradise' of the novel can be considered a reception and transformation, within a thoroughly *literary* realm, of the essence of the Christian Gospel. In this sense the criticism of religion may remain one of the most valuable theological resources for profiling the

---

1   This article is a revised version of a previous publication in Danish, 'Romanens moral – et tema i Milan Kunderas poetik'. In: David Bugge & Ole Morsing (eds.) 2006, *Milan Kundera i syv sind*. København: Anis, 83-100.

Evangelic core and defending it against the forms of decay so often laid bare by critics of religion.

The article falls into four parts: (1) a short introductory section describing the importance Kundera attributes to the particular features of the novel as a genre; (2) a study of the way in which Kundera works out his novelistic theories by contrasting the novel with lyrics; (3) an inquiry into two of the main characteristics of the novel, which, according to Kundera, constitute 'the imaginary paradise': the suspension of moral judgment and a fundamental tolerance; and finally, (4) a demonstration that this 'imaginary paradise' of the novel and the Christian Gospel meet, after all, in the motif and vocabulary of one of Kundera's own novels.

1. The morality of the novel

In 1935 Husserl gave his famous lectures in Vienna and Prague on the crisis of European humanity. He located the roots of the crisis in the beginning of the Modern Era as personified by Descartes. Gradually, he said, the Modern Era has reduced the world to a mere object of technical investigation, disregarding the concrete 'lifeworld'. Later Heidegger cemented this diagnosis in his assertion that man has lost the sight of his own self and in his phrase 'the forgetting of being'.

With these reflections Kundera opens 'The Depreciated Legacy of Cervantes', a chapter of his essay *The Art of the Novel* (Kundera 2005, 3-4). It is true, he argues, that in their diagnosis the two phenomenologists had indeed exposed an important aspect of modernity, especially in the case of philosophy and science. But in their judgment of the epoch, Kundera says, they forgot (!) that Cervantes was just as much a founder of the Modern Era as Descartes. As he puts it in his essay *Testaments Betrayed*: 'Heidegger, a poetry lover, was wrong to disregard the history of the novel, for it contains the greatest treasury of existential wisdom' (Kundera 1996, 165).[2]

With Cervantes, Kundera goes on, a new form of European art arose, the purpose of which is to explore precisely what philosophy and science have neglected, in other words man's being. For the 'provision' of the novel, in Henry Fielding's words, is 'no other than *Human Nature*' (*The Curtain*, Kundera 2007, 11-12). And indeed, over the four centuries of its existence the European novel has explored all the great existential subjects that Husserl and Heidegger accused the European philosophers of neglecting. Like Hermann Broch, Kundera regards the novel's exploration of human nature as the sole proper *raison d'être* of the novel: 'A novel that does not discover a hitherto

---

2   In a way, Heidegger and Kundera have the same axe to grind and a common enemy, i.e. the tradition of Western metaphysics. But as Richard Rorty points out in his essay on 'Heidegger, Kundera, and Dickens', their alternatives differ widely: 'For Heidegger the opposite of metaphysics is Openness to Being, something most easily achieved in a pretechnological peasant community with unchanging customs. (…) Kundera's utopia is carnivalesque, Dickensian, a crowd of eccentrics rejoicing in each other's idiosyncrasies, curious for novelty rather than nostalgic for primordiality' (Rorty 1991, 75).

unknown segment of existence is immoral. Knowledge is the novel's only morality' (*The Art of the Novel*, Kundera 2005, 6-7; cf. *The Curtain*, Kundera 2007, 61).

This double definition indicates the relation between the novel and morality: *negatively*, by rejecting as immoral all novels that do not contribute to our knowledge (Fr. *connaissance*) of existence; *positively*, by defining the morality of the novel as consisting in nothing but knowledge. In both cases the definition of the relation is exclusive ('does not', 'only'), and in both cases the concept of morality, in contrast to current usage, is confined to a question of cognition.

Indeed, Kundera's definition proves to be polemically aimed at any attempt to subordinate the novel to morality in the traditional sense of the word. Thus in *Testaments Betrayed* he characterises the business of the novelist as one that rules out 'identification with any politics, any religion, any ideology, any moral doctrine, any group; a considered, stubborn, furious *nonidentification*' (Kundera 1996, 158). Painting and music, which for centuries remained in service to the Church, did not thereby lose their beauty: 'But putting a novel to the service of any authority, however noble, would be impossible for a true novelist' (*The Curtain*, Kundera 2007, 60). In the context of the present article this statement is of great importance, since Kundera's rejection of any obligation to a *religious* doctrine is decisive to his *literary* trans-formation of the paradise theme.

2. Make-up on desolation

Kundera often highlights the distinctive characteristics of the novel by contrasting it with lyrics (or lyricism, as he derogatorily calls it), but time and again the two concepts expand from mere genre indications to two fundamentally different attitudes to life: 'For me, the lyrical and the epical extend beyond aesthetics; they represent two possible attitudes that man might take toward himself, the world, other people' (*The Art of the Novel*, Kundera 2005, 138). In this connection, Kundera distinguishes between *lyrical* and *poetic*, arguing that the novel may well be poetic without being lyricised: 'Novel: antilyrical poetry' (p. 144).[3]

The lyrical attitude to life is marked by an embellishment and veiling of reality in which you are carried away and amalgamated with the world. It is to be found above all in the juvenile longing for totality and in the revolutionary reign of terror:

That's why young people are such passionate monists, emissaries of the absolute; that's why the poet weaves his private world of verse; that's why the young revolutionary (in whom anger is stronger than anxiety) insists on an absolutely new world forged from a single idea; that's why

---

3   As Robert Porter points out, Kundera began his writing career as a poet, so his criticism of lyrics may also be considered a self-criticism: 'the author had himself served a successful apprenticeship in poetry and so his polemic against lyricism must imply a certain uneasiness with his own early writings' (Porter 1981, 54).

such a person can't bear compromise, either in love or politics, the rebellious student hurls his *all or nothing* in the face of history (*Life is Elsewhere*, Kundera 1991, 206).

As we will see, it is this overburdened 'all or nothing' that the novel seeks to relieve by its particular humour.[4]

In his portrait of the young poet Jaromil in the novel *Life is Elsewhere* Kundera has displayed the self-staging escapism of lyricism: 'The independence of the poem provided Jaromil with a marvellous world of concealment, the possibility of a *second existence*' (Kundera 1991, 57). As the fictional biography of a poet, the novel describes a pseudo-life, a 'substitute world' in which everything is reduced to a 'tragedy', a 'theatrical performance', a 'scene' (pp. 205, 249, 50, 110):

In rhyme and rhythm resides a certain magic power. An amorphous world becomes at once orderly, lucid, clear, and beautiful when squeezed into regular meters. Death is chaotic. But if a woman *weary of breath* has *gone to her death*, dying becomes harmoniously integrated into the cosmic order. Even if such a poem were intended as a bitter protest against mortality, death, adorned by rhymed couplets, would turn protest into celebration. Bones, funeral wreaths, gravestones, coffins, everything in a poem becomes transmuted into a ballet in which both the reader and the poet perform their dance. Through poetry, both the poet and the reader signify their agreement with existence, and rhyme and rhythm are the bluntest ways of eliciting consent (*Life is Elsewhere*, Kundera 1991, 179).

So poetry transforms the chaos of life into a cosmos, but Kundera, departing from conventional wisdom, takes a negative view of this, for the transformation is due to a misrepresentation of the harsh realities of the world. It may afford momentary happiness in the lyrical ecstasy it produces, but in the long run its seductive embellishments engender a fatal acceptance of destiny that hampers us in our struggle against misery. The beautiful form of poetry endows it with such powers of conviction that the poem loses its anchorage in real life, so that now one statement is true, now its diametrical opposite:

Lyrical poetry is a realm in which any statement is immediately accorded veracity. Yesterday, the poet said, *life is a vale of tears*; today, he said, *life is a land of smiles*; and he was right both times. There is no inconsistency. The lyrical poet does not have to prove anything. His proof is the pathos of his own experience (*Life is Elsewhere*, Kundera 1991, 198).

---

4   In many respects, Kundera's defence of the novel at the expense of lyrics corresponds to Iris Murdoch's position. In her philosophical writings we find an almost identical definition of the genre: 'Prose literature can *reveal* an aspect of the world which no other art can reveal, and the discipline required for this revelation is *par excellence* the discipline of this art' (Murdoch 1959, 267). She, too, sees a constant temptation in the veiling *consolation* that the form of poetry and the *dry symbol* offer, arguing that: 'The proper home of the symbol (…) is poetry' (Murdoch 1961, 19-20). In this sense she dissociates herself from T.S. Eliot's Romantic use of symbol and his disparagement of prose: 'So it is not surprising that he makes no place for imaginative prose literature which is *par excellence* the form of art most concerned with the existence of other persons' (Murdoch 1959, 264).

A key concept in this connection is that of *kitsch*, 'the *supreme aesthetic evil*' (*The Curtain*, Kundera 2007, 51). Kundera follows Herman Broch in seeing the modern novel as an (apparently vain) endeavour to struggle against the 'tide of kitsch', the latter arising from the desire to please everyone at once and confirm them in their received ideas: 'Kitsch is the translation of the stupidity of received ideas into the language of beauty and feeling' (*The Art of the Novel*, Kundera 2005, 163). By way of this, the unconditional acceptance of reality that is characteristic of lyrics recurs in the aesthetic ideal of kitsch.[5]

Kundera also defines kitsch as 'the absolute denial of shit', and insists that this denial is essential to religion and its '*categorical agreement with being*' (*The Unbearable Lightness of Being*, Kundera 1984, 248). The most 'onerous theological problem', he asserts, is not that of evil; man's crimes may be due to his freedom: 'The responsibility for shit, however, rests entirely with Him, the Creator of man' (p. 246).[6]

Because of his truth-loving zeal for knowledge, Kundera pays little heed to the positive role that lyricism may play in veiling and embellishing reality – given that mankind is fragile and in need of consolation. Kundera doesn't seem to recognise that, by veiling the world, lying may be a positive act, though this is advocated by a few of his characters, among them Chantal's advertising manager in the novel *Identity* of whom she relates:

He likes to tell about how in the nineteen twenties, in Germany or somewhere, there was a movement for a poetry of the everyday. Advertising, he claims, is realizing that poetic project after the fact. It transforms the simple objects of life into poetry. Thanks to advertising, everydayness has started singing (Kundera 1999a, 25).

5   In other words, kitsch is an affirmation of 'banality', and in this sense kitsch as 'our everyday aesthetic and moral code' (*The Art of the Novel*, Kundera 2005, 163-164) comes close to Knud Ejler Løgstrup's concept of 'triviality' as an aesthetic *and* ethical category. Unlike Kundera, however, Løgstrup does not regard poetry as an affirmation of, but rather as a corrective to triviality: 'The antithesis of poetry is triviality. However, triviality is not only an aesthetic category. It is also an ethical category. Triviality is to be complacently arrogant. To make oneself comfortable with triviality is to cultivate one another's self-righteousness, possibly so continuously that it is actually reflected in the voice, so that regardless of what is being related – accidents, crimes, illnesses, or deaths – it is recounted in the most self-satisfied tone of voice intended to make the other person comfortable' (Løgstrup 1997, 196).

6   Frank Brown raises two interesting objections against Kundera: For one thing, Kundera makes it sound as if religious art is kitsch *by definition*, which would 'mean that even the epics of Milton and Dante should be regarded as kitsch'. For another, the writer's 'need to shock or disgust' may become 'a perverse sort of kitsch' itself, as, following Karsten Harries, some 'modern kitsch becomes downright sour, by taking itself too seriously in an effort to compensate for having lost religious weight'. According to Brown, Kundera's novels may sometimes suffer from this flaw, their cynicism seeming 'mannered and pretentious – marred by pseudo-profundities' (Brown 2000, 130-131). To Brown's second objection one might add that the cynic's mannered, pessimistic kitsch, like the traditional, embellishing form of kitsch, may serve as a flight from the very ambiguity of life that Kundera otherwise advocates so eagerly.

Hence his (but hardly Kundera's) enthusiastic applause for the (poetic) strategy of advertising: 'We put make-up on desolation!' (p. 133; Fr. *Nous sommes les maquilleurs de la misère!*).[7]

Kundera's uncompromising search for an unvarnished picture of human existence, which he sees as the sole mission of the novel, leads us to the subject of the next part of this article.

3. The imaginary paradise of the novel

'Knowledge is the novel's only morality': knowledge, that is, of human life in all its ambiguity, the very cognition of existence and identity that philosophy has missed. Because the novel must present a *concrete* gallery of characters, it is particularly well suited to exploring these fields: 'Over what period of time can we consider a man identical to himself? Only the novel can, in concrete terms, explore this mystery, one of the greatest known to man' (*Testaments Betrayed*, Kundera 1996, 215).

So, in our atomised age, the novel is 'the last observatory from which we can embrace human life as a whole' (*The Curtain*, Kundera 2007, 83). And while, traditionally, philosophy sets forth its thinking within an abstract space, the forte of the novel consists in the fact that its ideas are incarnated in fictional characters: 'Like Penelope it undoes each night the tapestry that theologians, philosophers, and learned men have woven the day before' (*The Art of the Novel*, Kundera 2005, 160).[8]

Thus: 'The novel is a meditation on existence as seen through the medium of imaginary characters' (*The Art of the Novel*, Kundera 2005, 83), it is 'a kind of optical instrument he [the novelist] provides the reader so he can discern what he might never have seen in himself without this book' (*The Curtain*, Kundera 2007, 96). The novel un-veils in the precise sense of the word: 'it is by tearing through the curtain of pre-interpretation that Cervantes set the new art going' (Kundera 2007, 92).

---

7   In the novel *The Farewell Party* we are presented with a (loyally described) pragmatic attitude towards truth. At one point Jakub has asked Dr. Skreta to manufacture for him a pale blue tablet so that he can die easily at any time. But when Jakub (erroneously, by the way) realises that the tablet is just a harmless placebo, everything suddenly seems absolutely clear to him: 'the pale blue pill which he had been carrying in his pocket as a guarantee of his freedom was a fake. His friend had merely given him an illusion of death' (Kundera 1998, 170). Gradually he comes to realise the faking doctor's wisdom: 'Skreta had acted wisely, much more wisely than others, who had turned down Jakub's plea. Skreta had simply given him a harmless illusion of peace and certainty' (p. 171). And immediately afterwards this illusion is compared with religious belief: 'Although he was sceptical about everything in this world, his faith in the pill was like faith in the Gospel' (p. 170). – Cf. also the characterisation of Madame de T. in the novel *Slowness*: '(…) she lied to her husband, she lied to her lover the Marquis, she lied to the young Chevalier. It is she who is the true disciple of Epicurus. Lovable lover of pleasure. Gentle protective liar. Guardian of happiness' (Kundera 1997, 141).

8   In his rejection of (philosophical) systems, Kundera is indebted to Nietzsche's ideal of the philosopher as an *experimenter* (*Testaments Betrayed*, Kundera 1996, 174-75). And as Andrew Hass points out, Kundera is influenced by this ideal even in his own novelistic writings: 'His writing style is neither rigid nor imposed upon by a system; his novels experiment, are broad in theme, go in various directions. And yet they philosophize.' Kundera's philosophy, however, never appears in the guise of an inner monologue by one of the characters; the author simply breaks off to display his thinking, though this is never 'outside the *context* of his story' but arises from it (Hass 2003, 125-26).

As an émigré Kundera naturally chooses the travelling metaphor to express the project of the novelist. He is neither historian nor prophet, but an 'explorer of existence' who 'draws up *the map of existence* by discovering this or that human possibility' (*The Art of the Novel*, Kundera 2005, 43-44).

But what does his explorer's map look like? What characterises the lifeworld that the novelist creates in his narrative universe? Once again, the answer is connected with the genre's background in modernity – or rather with the joint project of the novel and modernity:

As God slowly departed from the seat whence he had directed the universe and its order of values, distinguished good from evil, and endowed each thing with meaning, Don Quixote set forth from his house into a world he could no longer recognize. In the absence of the Supreme Judge, the world suddenly appeared in its fearsome ambiguity; the single divine Truth decomposed into myriad relative truths parcelled by men (*The Art of the Novel*, Kundera 2005, 6).

In other words, the '*spirit of the novel*' (Kundera 2005, 14) is a spirit of relativity in which everything is much more complicated than we usually realise.[9]

Here the keyword is *humour*. Kundera concurs with the Mexican writer Octavio Paz in connecting the appearance of humour with modernity and the novel: 'Thus humor is not laughter, not mockery, not satire, but a particular species of the comic, which, Paz says (and this is the key to understanding humor's essence), "renders ambiguous everything it touches"' (*Testaments Betrayed*, Kundera 1996, 5-6). And this ambiguity, this 'carnival of relativity' (p. 27) arises from the many-stringed composition where nothing can be taken in isolation, every claim, every situation, or idea being complicatedly confronted with other claims, situations, and ideas.[10]

In *The Art of the Novel*, as I mentioned above, Kundera defined the morality of the novel exclusively in terms of its endeavour to uncover fresh knowledge of human life, to fill in another blank spot on the map of existence, and denounced as immoral any other view of the novel's mission. However, in his later book *Testaments Betrayed*, Kundera supplements this definition as follows: 'a novel: that is, a *realm where moral judgment is suspended*'. And immediately afterwards he formulates this explicitly: 'Suspending moral judgment is not the immorality of the novel; it is its *morality*' (Kundera 1996, 7). Whereas, in *The Art of the Novel*, his definition of the genre was framed in

---

9   This announcement of the 'fearsome' new world was certainly by no means entirely positive. As Scott Robertson mentions in his comment on the passage quoted above, the novel 'holds a dual faceted function'. By telling stories, the novel points to tradition and the familiar, and in so doing offers some security in the strange ambiguous world. By creating worlds of its own, however, it points to the (fearsome) openness of the world. Stories 'are our memories writ large. The novel form progresses this tradition in a new and potentially threatening context. This threat is found within the created worlds of the novel' (Robertson 2007, 432).

10   As to the personal background to Kundera's appraisal of humour, cf. his statement in an interview by Philip Roth: 'I learned the value of humor during the time of Stalinist terror. I was twenty then. I could always recognize a person who was not a Stalinist, a person whom I needn't fear, by the way he smiled. A sense of humor was a trustworthy sign of recognition. Ever since, I have been terrified by a world that is losing its sense of humor' (Roth 2001, 94).

cognitive terms, in *Testaments Betrayed* Kundera defines the morality of the novel in terms of the interpersonal space of love.

In 'the unillusioned territory of the novel' (*Testaments Betrayed*, Kundera 1996, 159) humour, like a divine flash of lightning, serves to expose the world in all its moral ambiguity. In the process, as we saw in *The Art of the Novel*, our propensity for judging before understanding becomes itself the object of judgement, as does our inability to tolerate 'the essential relativity of things human' and to accept 'the absence of the Supreme Judge' (Kundera 2005, 7). For this reason the wisdom of the novel, i.e. 'the wisdom of uncertainty', is constantly at odds with our native desire for 'a world where good and evil can be clearly distinguished'. And it is on that desire, according to Kundera, that religions and ideologies are founded (p. 7).

The novel creates its own, relative universe in opposition to our habitual either-or thinking in which, as Kundera puts it, either Anna Karenina is the victim of a tyrant or Karenin is the victim of an immoral woman (p. 7). It is not that the novelist is supposed to be morally superior to ordinary mortals or free from the vice of moral carping; nor does the novelist deny the legitimacy of moral judgment in general. But in the very process of creating he forgets, so to speak, his personal moral convictions and listens instead to the 'suprapersonal wisdom' of the novel. As a result, an imaginary realm arises in which no one has a monopoly on the truth but 'everyone has the right to be understood' (p. 157-65). The novel thus encourages a fundamental respect for the individual, as the reader learns to be curious about the other person and to try to understand him (*Testaments Betrayed*, Kundera 1996, 8).[11]

There is no room for hatred in the universe of the novel, in which relativity prevails. Even in Salman Rushdie's imaginary portrait of Khomeini in *The Satanic Verses*, there is 'an almost respectful understanding' (Kundera 1996, 27).[12] Incidentally, this attitude on the part of the novelist is sometimes evinced by the characters themselves in Kundera's fictional writing, e.g. by the lawyer Paul in the novel *Immortality*, who becomes fond of his defendants and tries to understand their crimes, his half-joking *bon mot* being: 'I am not a lawyer, I am the poet of the defence!' (Kundera 1999b, 124).

The novelist's 'all-loving' attitude arises not only from the inherent relativism of the genre and the suspension of moral judgment that it entails; it may also derive from the almost fatherly care that the creation of fictional characters involves. Many novelists have remarked on this relationship between author and characters, and Kundera comments on it himself in *The Unbearable Lightness of Being*: 'The characters in my

---

11   Kundera goes so far as to consider the genre of the novel one of the important conditions for the emergence of Human Rights in Western society: 'before a man could have rights, he had to constitute himself as an individual, to consider himself such and to be considered such; that could not happen without the long experience of the European arts and particularly of the art of the novel, which teaches the reader to be curious about others and to try to comprehend truths that differ from his own' (*Testaments Betrayed*, Kundera 1996, 8).

12   In Kundera's view, the saddest thing about the whole story of *The Satanic Verses* is not Khomeini's fatwa itself but Europe's incapacity to defend the most European of all arts, i.e. the novel (*Testaments Betrayed*, Kundera 1996, 27).

novels are my own unrealized possibilities. That is why I am equally fond of them all and equally horrified by them' (Kundera 1984, 221).

Of course, you might call the novelist's fondness for his *own* fictional characters a hidden preferential love. Nevertheless, it is worth noting that Kundera is talking here about *all* the characters in his novels; he is equally fond of and equally frightened by each of them: the fear, in other words, does not eliminate the fondness. Here, then, we can observe a certain similarity between Kundera's love as a novelist for his characters and the Gospel's all-embracing divine love of mankind, though the latter is entirely free of partiality.

In this light one may wonder why Kundera sees such an implacable opposition between the spirit of the novel and all forms of religion.[13] His repeated emphasis on Europe as the cradle of the novel, and the novel itself as the cradle of modernity, leads one naturally to ask whether modern Europe itself, and the novel as one of the hallmarks of European culture, are conceivable at all outside a Christian context, since the boundless value given to each individual in the novel may originate in the Gospel's notion of radical love and forgiveness. Indeed, Kundera sometimes resorts to a religious vocabulary when expressing his views on the exceptionality of the universe of the novel, e.g. in his reference to the *agélaste*, one of Rabelais' forgotten neologisms, meaning a man who has no sense of humour:

No peace is possible between the novelist and the *agélaste*. Never having heard God's laughter, the *agélastes* are convinced that the truth is obvious, that all men necessarily think the same thing, and that they themselves are exactly what they think they are. But it is precisely in losing the certainty of truth and the unanimous agreement of others that man becomes an individual. The novel is the imaginary paradise of individuals (Fr. *Le roman, c'est le paradis imaginaire des individus*) (*The Art of the Novel*, Kundera 2005, 159).

And if Kundera is not to contradict his own point, there must be room for the *agélaste* as well in the imaginary paradise of the novel.

4. A modern version of the Gospel

Thus despite his scepticism towards religion, Kundera seems to have been influenced, more or less consciously, by the spirit of the Christian Gospel in his *theory* of the novel. But most surprisingly, the Gospel has clearly had an impact on his novelistic *practice* as

---

13   On the notion of hell as contained in the dream of creating paradise on earth, Kundera remarks in the interview by Philip Roth: 'If totalitarianism did not exploit these archetypes, which are deep inside us all and rooted deep in all religions, it could never attract so many people, especially during the early phases of its existence' (Roth 2001, 95-96). In other connections, however, Kundera's views on religion seem more ambiguous. In another interview, by Francine de Plessix Gray, he says: 'Ideologically I'm an agnostic, a skeptic', but adds shortly afterwards: '(...) I've always felt a considerable interest in religion and theology, and even a great fondness for it, without myself being able to believe. You might almost call it the love of a non-believer for religion' (Gray 1999, 49).

well: specifically on the plot of the novel *The Farewell Party*, which involves a straight reception and transformation of the Gospel's 'paradise' theme.[14]

In various respects *The Farewell Party* differs from Kundera's other works. Unlike his usual polyphonic compositions, which unite heterogeneous elements within an architecture based on the number seven, this novel is absolutely homogeneous, narrated at an even tempo and with no digressions, almost like a stage play (*The Art of the Novel*, Kundera 2005, 86, 89).

With regard to its contents, moreover, *The Farewell Party* is exceptional among Kundera's novels in being so imbued with the Christian narrative that it might be read as the novelist's 'modern version of the Gospel'. Indeed, this expression is applied to the main character of the novel: 'It seemed to Klima that everything Bartleff said could serve as homily, a parable, an example, a chapter out of some modern version of the Gospel' (Kundera 1998, 27). Here, there are none of the usual authorial remarks or metaliterary reflections that one finds in most of Kundera's novels. Rather, it seems here as if the Gospel keeps up the imaginary paradise that is usually ensured by the novel as a genre. Most interestingly, Kundera has called *The Farewell Party* 'the novel dearest to me, in a certain sense' (*The Art of the Novel*, Kundera 2005, 92).

The novel is set in a small Czech health resort where Dr. Skreta treats seemingly sterile women by inseminating them – unbeknownst to the women themselves – with his own semen. The plot consists in a number of ramifying mistakes and delicate intrigues, all revolving around one character, a rich and generous American man-about-town named Bartleff. He is at once a hedonist and a Christian mystic, an adventurer and an ardent believer, and an enthusiastic painter, though convinced that the aesthetic criterion does not originate from God but from the Devil. An aura of mystery surrounds him, making him the very pivot of the novel.[15]

While the other guests at the health resort are losing their footing in a more and more despairing and hopeless world, only Bartleff never falters. He has been seen as an ironic representation of a Nietzschean superhuman in the shape of a hedonistic saint capable of saying a life-embracing 'yes' even from the deepest despair (Boisen 2001, 104-105). In fact, however, Bartleff represents a transformed version of an even more fundamental figure in our culture, as the following episode in the novel shows.[16]

The episode takes place when the despair has grown to its height. By chance, two female rivals are seated at the same table in a filthy café with a bunch of noisy, lecherous men when Bartleff enters unexpectedly: 'Nobody had seen him coming, and sud-

---

14   'I wrote this novel counter to myself', Kundera says in an interview by Alain Finkielkraut, and continues: 'Moreover, I believe that this is how one writes novels. If the novel is successful, it must necessarily be wiser than its author' (Finkielkraut 1999, 42).

15   In her profound analysis of *The Farewell Party*, Maria Nemcova Banerjee calls Bartleff 'one of the most puzzling of Kundera's creations', and says of the novel that it 'may be the most metaphysical piece Kundera has written' (Banerjee 1991, 115). Among other things, Banerjee makes a convincing comparison between Bartleff and Dostoevsky's holy fool, Myshkin, pointing out the differences, e.g. that Bartleff is 'a sensually complete human being' (Banerjee 1991, 117).

16   Thus Robert Porter seems to miss a point, saying: 'In the figure of Bertlef, Christian virtue is founded on nothing but conceit and material wealth' (Porter 1981, 75).

denly there he was'. They are all astonished, so Bartleff has to explain: "'Forgive me,'" he continued. "I have the peculiar habit of appearing rather than arriving'" (Kundera 1998, 140).

The obvious Christological undertone continues. In the dirty café the party are reduced to drinking a miserable wine. Bartleff, however, knows the innkeeper, and soon he has conjured up a *remarkable and excellent wine* and a platter of delicious cheese. None of the men present, among them the 'anthropomorphized vat of vinegar' (p. 142), are keen on the intruder's appearance; but both of the *women* enjoy his company. However, as the miracle of the wine takes effect, the tension dissolves in a cheerful conversation. And they all 'wondered' how on earth this meal could have been provided (p. 144).

This almost sacral meal throws light on Bartleff's role throughout the novel. It anticipates his later attempt to *take the blame for a murder, though innocent himself.* Even more essentially, however, it qualifies the theology that the reader has heard him utter from the very beginning: 'All people are your near and dear ones. Don't forget what Jesus said when they tried to call him back to his mother and brothers. He pointed at his disciples and said: "Here are my mother and my brothers"' (p. 99).[17]

The impact of the marvellous meal spreads, not only to the guests around the table, but to everybody in the novel. Not least to Jakub, one of the central characters, whose development is especially significant. Jakub is the disillusioned intellectual who has seen through the miserable condition of the world and the deceitful nature of man; a nihilistic pessimist, he has been thoroughly disenchanted by the experience of being sent to prison by his erstwhile friends and communist party colleagues. He sums up his life credo in this disheartening statement to his protégée Olga:

I'll tell you the saddest discovery of my life: The victims are no better than their oppressors. I can easily imagine the roles reversed. You can call it a kind of alibi-ism, an attempt to evade responsibility and to blame everything on the Creator who made man the way he is. And maybe it's good that you see things that way. Because to come to the conclusion that there is no difference between the guilty and their victims is to reach a state where you *abandon all hope.* And that, my dear, is a definition of *hell* (p. 70).

At first sight Jakub's nihilism appears to be related to the morality of the novel: God's laughter echoes through the universe of the novel, showing that the concepts of good and evil, victim and perpetrator so dogmatically upheld by the agélaste are but relative quantities. But the relationship is only apparent. For here, the distorting troll splinter sticks in the pessimist's eye. Jakub's moral judgment is not suspended, but ratified and

---

17   As Banerjee points out, Bartleff's 'sexuality is expansive and many-sided', and as such matches his inclusive view of mankind: 'The quality of Bartleff's mind is as open and generous as his sexuality' (Banerjee 1991, 117-18). In this sense, one may add, a sort of junction is established between agapic and erotic love, traditionally looked upon as absolute opposites.

radicalised: *both* Anna Karenina *and* Karenin are judged. Hence the stigma of despair (*de-speratio*): to abandon all hope. 'And that, my dear, is a definition of *hell*.'

As we have seen, however, something happens as a result of Bartleff's miracle with the wine. Towards the end of the novel, when Jakub himself has – unknowingly – become a murderer, he achieves a new or rather deeper insight, though the recognition is essentially the same: all people are potentially murderers. But now the troll splinter in his eye has vanished, and the negative view has been replaced by a positive one:

The thought passed through his mind that he had been blaming people for something they could not help, something born in them, something they had to bear, like an incommutable sentence. And it occurred to him that he had no exclusive claim to nobility, that the greatest nobility was in loving people even though they were murderers (p. 205).

The perspective has been totally reversed, his radical all-including condemnation being replaced by a radical all-embracing love. Nobility lies not in considering all people murderers even when they have committed no actual murder, but in loving all people *even if* they are murderers. This is Jakub's acquired morality. It is Bartleff's morality. And it is also the morality of the novel itself.

And, so one might add: that, my dear, is a definition of *heaven*.

Bibliography

Banerjee, Maria Nemcova 1991. *Terminal Paradox. The Novels of Milan Kundera.* London: Faber and Faber.

Boisen, Jørn 2001. *Milan Kundera. En introduktion.* Copenhagen: Gyldendal.

Brown, Frank Burch 2000. *Good Taste, Bad Taste, and Christian Taste: Aesthetics in Religious Life.* New York: Oxford University Press.

Finkielkraut, Alain 1999. 'Milan Kundera Interview' [1982]. In: Peter Petro (ed.), *Critical Essays on Milan Kundera.* New York: C. K. Hall & Co., 33-44.

Grey, Francine du Plessix 1999. 'Journey into the Maze: An Interview with Milan Kundera' [1982]. In: Peter Petro (ed.), *Critical Essays on Milan Kundera.* New York: C. K. Hall & Co., 45-52.

Hass, Andrew W. 2003. *Poetics of Critique: The Interdisciplinarity of Textuality.* Hants (England) & Burlington, VT (USA): Ashgate.

Kundera, Milan 1984. *The Unbearable Lightness of Being* (Czech 1983). New York: Harper & Row.

Kundera, Milan 1991. *Life is Elsewhere* (Czech 1973). London: Faber and Faber.

Kundera, Milan 1996. *Testaments Betrayed* (French 1993). London: Faber and Faber.

Kundera, Milan 1997. *Slowness* (French 1995). New York: HarperCollins Publishers.

Kundera, Milan 1998. *The Farewell Party* (Czech 1978). New York: Alfred A. Knopf.

Kundera, Milan 1999a. *Identity* (French 1997). London: Faber and Faber.

Kundera, Milan 1999b. *Immortality* (Czech 1990). New York: HarperCollins Publishers.

Kundera, Milan 2005. *The Art of the Novel* (French 1986). London: Faber and Faber.

Kundera, Milan 2007. *The Curtain* (French 2005). London: Faber and Faber.

Løgstrup, Knud Ejler 1997. *The Ethical Demand* (Danish 1956). Notre Dame & London: University of Notre Dame Press.

Murdoch, Iris 1959. 'The Sublime and the Beautiful Revisited'. *Yale Review*, 4, 247-71.

Murdoch, Iris 1961. 'Against Dryness'. *Encounter*, 1, 16-20.

Porter, Robert 1981. *Milan Kundera – a Voice from Central Europe*. Aarhus: Arkona Publishers.

Robertson, Scott 2007. 'The Eighteenth-Century Novel'. In: Andrew W. Hass, David Jasper, Elisabeth Jay (eds.), *The Oxford Handbook of English Literature and Theology*. London: Oxford University Press, 431-47.

Rorty, Richard 1991. *Essays on Heidegger and others: Philosophical papers*, 2. New York: Cambridge University Press.

Roth, Philip 2001. *Shop Talk. A Writer and His Colleagues and Their Work*. London: Jonathan Cape.

STANDING ON THE SHOULDERS OF GIANTS WITH MY HEAD BETWEEN MY FEET

A MINISTER'S REFLECTIONS ON RECEPTION AND TRANSFORMATION IN THE FICTION OF MARTIN A. HANSEN

Jakob Nissen

The modern consensus is that the Bible does not contain the direct word of God in a sacred language and that the stories in the Bible are not in themselves holy. For this reason we are allowed to translate the Bible into Danish, English, German, French and so on, and in this sense the holy book can be seen – albeit not exclusively – as a work of literature.

The Bible begins with two different myths to explain how the world was created and contains four different Gospels with slightly different recollections of the life of Jesus. However, the Bible is not merely an historical account of times past. It is also a literary work that invites scholars to turn to works of fiction in an effort to understand the stories it contains.

This process has been going on for centuries. The Bible has been a source of inspiration to countless great artists: Dante, Michelangelo, Milton, Dostoevsky, to name but a few. Among the writers inspired by it we can include the Danish author Martin A. Hansen.

In this essay I present a brief introduction to Hansen's work, focussing especially on the way it combines Christianity and art. There is a tendency among Hansen's readers to focus on the negative aspects of this combination. I will attempt to focus on the positive.

Martin A. Hansen was born in 1909, and at his untimely death in 1955 he was one of the most prominent authors in Denmark. His two best known works are the novels *Lucky Christopher* and *The Liar*. The dominant theme in all his work is the struggle between the old world, dominated by tradition, and the new, modern world. Hansen was familiar with this struggle from his own life and times. Born and raised in a rural Christian environment, he moved to the city as a young man to train as a teacher. Living in the city meant becoming acquainted with a modern urban culture in which Christian beliefs were no longer taken for granted. Many years later, when he matured as a man and as an author, he would seek to reconcile Christianity and modernism.

Martin A. Hansen's work is infused with a deep knowledge of the Bible. He uses the biblical stories as a pattern for his own fiction, which reveals a constant preoccupation with his identity as an author and a Christian. In his diary he speaks of the possibility of becoming a priest for the nation (Hansen 1999: 25/4-1939). Later, having wavered in his faith, he found his way back to Christianity: not to his childhood faith but to a new understanding. For Hansen, being a Christian meant not simply adhering to tradition and the dogma of the church, but coming to terms with Christianity in one's own way, which included reading its critics, thanks to whom he found a renewed form of critical faith. In many ways Hansen's fiction represents a continuation of that process: his own attempt to do for others what had been done for him – to make Christianity once again come alive.

Martin A. Hansen's work testifies to the complexity involved in combining art and Christianity, to both of which he had a strong commitment. His fiction is strongly influenced by Christian belief, without falling into the category of preaching. In what follows I shall focus on the reception and transformation of the Gospel in Hansen's work by comparing two texts: his essay 'The Son of Mary' and his short story 'The Birds'. These are not the best known of Martin A. Hansen's works, but they serve well to convey his ideas on the Gospel and thus provide a good introduction to the Christian aspects of his authorship.

One of the key elements in the general reception and transformation of the Gospel is the element of norm, in both the religious sense and the sense of social convention. In comparing 'The Son of Mary' and 'The Birds', we are able to examine some of the differences between these two uses of the term and at the same time point to different ways in which religious and social norms interact within religion and literature.

The Son of Mary

The essay 'The Son of Mary' gives a useful exposition of Martin A. Hansen's general conception of Christian belief.

Hansen begins his essay by referring to the magicians of Antiquity who would reputedly bend forward and look between their own feet. From that angle the world seemed different; the laws of nature were turned upside down. Hansen's essay is autobiographical and recollects the time immediately after his departure from his parents' house. As a writer just starting out, he sought inspiration in the Bible, trying to read it with fresh eyes, as he would have read any other book for the first time. Like the ancient magicians, Hansen sought to 'stand with his head between his feet' and turn everything he knew upside down, but his first efforts were unsuccessful. In this early re-reading of the Bible he was still in thrall to conventional normativity. Too familiar with the edifying and dogmatic side of the holy book, he was unable to set tradition aside or to read the Bible other than in the manner his preconceptions dictated.

Instead he began to study the critics of the Bible, starting with the Danish-Jewish writer Georg Brandes, one of whose notable achievements had been to introduce Friedrich Nietzsche to a Scandinavian audience. In *The Legend of Jesus*.[1] Brandes treats

---

1   *Sagnet om Jesus.* My translation.

the Gospels as a legend in the same way as one would the legend of Wilhelm Tell or of Robin Hood, in other words as essentially fictional. Responding to Brandes' iconoclastic vision made it possible for Hansen to immerse himself in the Gospels again, but this time with the focus on Jesus as the son of Mary, rather than the son of God. For the first time the holy text became coherent to him as a truly magnificent story. Brandes did as the ancient magicians had once done: He turned everything upside down. Standing 'with his head between his feet', Hansen discovered that the normative way of reading the Bible no longer sufficed.

By reading *The Legend of Jesus*, Hansen found his own way to an understanding of Christianity. Another, perhaps more correct way of saying this is that he discovered he could read the Bible as literature. This offered him a way around the moralistic, edifying, religious normativity that governed the traditional understanding of the holy book. Hansen saw that this understanding was founded not directly on the Bible itself, but rather on the traditional interpretation of it. This insight enabled him to replace the conventional interpretation of the Bible with a religious norm, according to which everyone must find his own understanding of the Gospel. Hansen's own revelation, found within the Bible, was to see Jesus as both the son of Mary *and* the son of God.

As the son of Mary, Christ himself was a man. As such he was able to approach the outcasts of society, not hesitating to communicate with prostitutes and sinners. In Hansen's understanding, the gospels themselves are critical towards the conventional norms operating in Jesus' time, disseminating as they do a message that human decency has little to do with society's moral standards.

In Hansen's view, the conventional reading of the Bible was biased towards the social norms of the upper/middle class. Reading the Gospel as the story of Jesus, the son of Mary, revealed that its message was in fact far from the moralistic norms of the *petite bourgeoisie*. As he puts it in the essay:

The Gospel is strange, violent, terrifying at times, horrible to those who only have a taste for decency. What kind of people did Christ associate with? A decent home would surely bar these people. Whom is Christ correcting? – The supporters of Society (Hansen 1948, 106 – my translation).

Arriving at this point, Hansen sees the Gospel as a resource for use in his own writing. Yet not everyone can use the Gospel as a source for art. In his essay Hansen mentions two artists who were able to do so. One was Vincent van Gogh, who could paint Mary Magdalen as she was; neither pretty nor virginal, but simply a prostitute, marked by her hard life, and bearing the oil with which she would anoint Jesus.

The second Christian artist whom Hansen mentions is Dostoevsky. He could do with words what van Gogh could do with his brush. Hansen writes:

From sinners such as Dostoevsky and van Gogh Christianity has received sacrifice, devotion, faith and a mighty power: a capital that petty moralists devour (Hansen 1948, 107).

He concludes in the last paragraph of his essay:

If one sets out to read the gospels with a clear focus on Christ as the son of Mary, the words of the gospels become revitalised. Seen as the son of Mary, Christ breaks through all human norms. Then there is only one thing to say: And the son of God. You dare not shape him after your own poor soul. "Man and God": Forget the first of these terms and everything is turned upside down: the son of God is delivered into the hands of man, and made into a protecting spirit for decrepit prejudices (Hansen 1948, 107 – my translation).

The essay is interesting because it shows two different uses of the Gospel. The first is institutional, emerging rigidly and dogmatically from within the church, according to Hansen, and leaving little room for individual dissent or contributions. Here there is nothing for the artist to add. Christianity in this interpretation is a fixed set of beliefs with no room for change. The goal at hand is simply to make sure that Christianity remains free from interference, with nothing new or challenging to pollute the story of God. The Gospel is true not because you feel it to be so, but because everyone else tells you that it is. It belongs to rational thinking rather than the incomprehensibility of the divine. This is the kind of normativity that is legitimised by the sheer number of its followers, rather than by any deep reading or dissemination of the Gospel. Focussing on Jesus as the son of God also means seeing him as a truly moral example for each individual to follow. He is the incarnation of God's will and therefore his life is the ideal life. But if we focus too much on this godlike aspect of Jesus, we fail to see him as a man, who came to the sinners and the sick.

The second use of the Gospel is the artistic use exemplified by van Gogh, Dostoevsky and Hansen himself, in which the Bible is drawn upon as an inspirational source for art. In this understanding the point of departure is not Jesus the son of God but Jesus the son of Mary. Yet paradoxically, the reading of Christ as the son of Mary leads back, eventually, to a better understanding of Christ as the son of God. Meanwhile, the surplus meaning in the human nature of Jesus, understood as the son of Mary, leaves room for the artist. The relationship between art and Christianity in this context deserves special attention. Not only is the artist able to create works of art by listening to Christianity, but Christianity is also "created" and "recreated" through art. Understood thus, the artist is a sort of assistant to God, not changing the Gospel but making it understandable to contemporary audiences. In his own context, he recaptures the Gospel.

It could be argued that that there is something apostolic in this vision of the artist's role as someone who spreads the Gospel to his contemporaries. However, it is important to note that Hansen was reluctant to claim such a function in relation to his own works. He was alert to the dangers of fusing Christianity with art, seeing the risk of corrupting Christianity or even of turning the word of God into something diabolical. This conflict between art and Christianity is ever present in Hansen's works. His ideal was an exchange between the two, in which both would benefit and be enriched. Art would draw inspiration from the Bible, while Christianity, when combined with art, would be safeguarded against the pitfalls of inflexibility and rigidity, and be constantly renewed. This dream of mutual exchange between art and Christianity, touched upon in 'The Son of Mary', is also a theme of 'The Birds'.

The Birds

The combination of being a Christian and an artist never came naturally to Martin A. Hansen. Throughout his life and his career he struggled to combine the ethical demands of Christianity with the hard, lonely life of an artist. Most scholars focus on the negative elements of this conflict in Hansen's work. Yet there are positive sides to being at once a Christian and an author. The short story 'The Birds' was written in a period of Hansen's life when he saw great potential in combining the two sides of his quest.

The main character in 'The Birds' is Espen, a young man from the countryside. The short story begins with his resigning from his previous position as a farm labourer and becoming farmhand to a priest. The latter is disliked by his congregation; indeed he is known as the 'fool priest'. Still, Espen seeks employment with him precisely because he gives bad sermons. Espen cannot stay awake during a good sermon. He stays at the priest's for a period of time, even after the priest's wife dies. Prior to her death, the priest had taken the entire household out on a stormy night, on which she caught pneumonia. Before she dies she asks Espen to take care of her husband: 'A bird is living in his chest' (Hansen 1979, 111). After her death, Espen devotes himself to taking care of the farm. It is a tough job since the fool priest is completely incompetent with money. Espen manages until the moment when the priest starts drinking, having learned that his daughter is a woman of easy virtue.

This recourse to the bottle, and the priest's lack of popularity among his congregation, lead eventually to his being fired. At first, Espen decides to go back to his original employment, but he ends up changing his mind and deciding to stay with the priest. The two of them begin to wander round the countryside, the priest continuing to deliver bad sermons, while Espen provides for them both, finding them food and shelter. The story ends with the priest dying in hospital and Espen returning to his father.

In discussing the positive combination of art and Christianity in Hansen's work, it is relevant to pause over the name of the main character. Hansen used a lot of time and energy in selecting appropriate names for his characters. In this case the spelling 'Espen' (normally 'Esben') is unusual. One can divide the name into two syllables: *Es – Pen*. *Es* is of course the second person singular of the verb 'to be' in Latin: 'you are'. *Pen* means the same in Danish as in English, i.e. the writing instrument. So the actual meaning of the name Espen is: 'You are a pen' or in other words, 'You are a writer' (cf.

Bugge 2005, 36-37). This offers a new perspective on the meaning of 'The Birds'. It is not merely the story of a young farm labourer and a foolish priest. It is also an attempt to come to terms with the role of being a Christian author.

The priest's nickname is well earned. He *is* a fool, apparently incapable of surviving on his own or running his farm. He is a useless father and husband, his wife dying from his neglect. He is too trustful of his fellow human beings and is constantly exploited. The congregation finds his sermons boring. He ends up drinking too much and being fired by his superiors. He is in every conceivable way a foolish priest as well as a fool in general. And yet, nothing is what it seems.

In the course of the narrative it becomes clear that the priest, at first sight such a negative figure, is in reality a positive character who symbolises Christianity in this world.[2] Just before she dies, his wife says to Espen: 'Take care of him. He has a bird in his breast. Take good care of it' (Hansen 1979, 111). And at the end, when the priest dies, we are told that Espen has carved the image of a bird on the priest's Bible. The bird, then, connects the priest with the holy book.

In the light of Hansen's essay 'The Son of Mary', this connection is not surprising. A crucial point in Hansen's essay is that the Christian gospel offers a new normativity that is at odds with the prevailing bourgeois morality. Christianity is a revelation that turns everything upside down. The powerful are actually weak, and the weak powerful; the wise are foolish, and the foolish wise (cf. 1 Cor 1:17-25). Christian wisdom or truth is not transparent in ordinary human wisdom or truth. It may sometimes appear foolish or weak – unfit for worldly life. This is one of the most prominent aspects of Hansen's understanding of Christianity: that it always reveals itself in a different form than you would expect – as weak, foolish, or simply incomprehensible in terms of traditional social norms.

This aspect of Christianity also separates it from art. Art is always at least to some extent rational. It is born of man's ability to think about and experience the world around him; it represents his attempt to grasp the world and make it his own. In this way art and Christianity constitute opposite forces. The life of Jesus is God's attempt to tell man something he cannot think of himself, and there will always be a kernel of Christianity that remains inexplicable: one that human beings and human art cannot grasp. Still, there *is* one kind of art that grasps this incomprehensible element.

When the priest takes his family out one stormy night, he says: 'Now you're going to see God create a poem' (Hansen 1979, 109). And later in the short story, the priest refers to the storm as an occasion on which 'Homer's superior composed hexameters' (Hansen 1979, 111). Here it seems that God himself is in some way linked to poetry, literature and the other arts. Great artists, such as Homer, Dostoevsky and van Gogh have the ability to mediate Christianity and pass it on to others such as Martin A. Hansen. Even the critic Georg Brandes, though not a Christian himself, was able to

---

2   Depicting the Christian as a fool is not unheard of in literature. Dostoevsky notably did the same in his novel *The Idiot.*

make Christianity come alive to Hansen. It seems to be one of the advantages of art that it can serve to keep the Christian faith alive. Institutionalised Christianity has a tendency to turn into a moralistic religion that is remote from the original teachings of Jesus. Somehow the gifted artist is able not only to see through the corruption of Christianity, but to reveal this corruption to others and thereby open a way back to the original understanding of the gospel. The artist becomes a mediator of Christianity.

This casts light on the role of Espen in 'The Birds', as a kind of mediator for the fool priest. It is he who makes sure that the priest is able to deliver his bad sermons; he who continues to encourage the priest when the latter wants to give up; he who ensures that the farm is taken care of. In fact, he takes care of all practical matters so that the priest is able to deliver his sermons.

A different kind of normativity

'The Birds' is thus a short story that revolves around the relationship between art and Christianity. By itself it would seem to suggest that the only role for art was to be the servant of Christianity. But Hansen's work, and his own life, indicate that it plays a broader role in keeping Christianity alive and well. Hansen himself became a Christian through reading Brandes, whose work made him realise that the portrayal of Jesus in the Gospel calls for the suspension of conventional normativity. This discovery of the connection between art and Christianity is felt throughout his work, which evinces a longing for the past in which Christianity emerged as the truth, and a desire himself to become a priest or an apostle for the people. Hansen sought throughout his writing to give new meaning to Christian faith. The collection of short stories *The Partridge* is the best testimony to this endeavour.

The struggle between Christianity and art never ceased in Hansen's mind. Many scholars have suggested that this is why he stopped writing fiction some years before his death. Yet this struggle was the fuel for his work: it was what made him persist in his writing. His work offers a fascinating glimpse into his nature as an artist, as a man, and as a Christian in the years following World War II, and into the struggle between Christianity and modernity. But most of all, it offers an intriguing example of the Bible's continued role in modern literature and culture and of the way in which Christianity has been passed on through history, continuously received and transformed by individuals, passed on from person to person and from one generation to the next.

It was through another man's criticism of the Christian gospel that Hansen found his own path to Christianity. Brandes' work, in turn, was deeply indebted to Friedrich Nietzsche. One could say that for Hansen there were two different kinds of Christianity, two different kinds of norms for Christian faith: one that consisted in following conventional norms, and one that consisted in the imitation of Christ.

It was the conventional form of Christianity that Hansen knew as a child but abandoned when he left home. The form of Christianity to which he eventually returned was of a different kind. His first efforts to arrive at an independent reading of the Bible failed; at this stage he still carried the weight of tradition on his shoulders, and was unable to escape the conformity that had infiltrated Christianity.

Hansen's encounter with a rational critic of Christianity, in the form of Brandes, had a surprising effect. In Brandes' treatment of the Gospel as literary fiction, Hansen saw a way of transforming Christianity rather than destroying it. One could say that he took parts of Brandes' modern approach to religion and used it to free himself from the social normativity of the institutionalised church. Treating Jesus as the son of Mary helped him to transcend the dogmas of rigid religious thinking. But this approach also left Hansen open to a different kind of normativity. Reading the Gospel with a new emphasis on Jesus as the son of Mary, he arrived back at the notion that he was also the son of God: '.... And the son of God' (Hansen 1948, 107 – my translation). It was precisely Brandes' separation of conventional normativity from Christianity that appears to have enabled Hansen to perceive Jesus as the son of God. Christianity, for Hansen, was no longer constituted by the dogmas of the church or by the standard normativity often upheld by conventional Christians. Instead, it consisted in one's own understanding of the Gospel. It is the Gospel that speaks to the individual through time. The normativity of the church was replaced by the revelation of Jesus as the son of God, and thus by a new norm that offers a personal kind of Christianity.

Rather than dwell on the traditional story of Jesus, the son of God, wandering in the vicinity of Jerusalem preaching, healing and doing wonders, Martin A. Hansen revitalised Christianity by bringing the story into the here and now. He saw it not only as the story of Jesus, the son of God, but also as the story of Jesus, the son of man, and hence as the story of every man. In his works, Christianity came alive in the contemporary world, offering not only a narrative of the past but one about people he knew in the present day – including himself. Christianity was thus no longer bound to tradition.

In espousing this new form of Christianity, Hansen showed his reluctance to accept unconditionally the traditions and dogmas of the church, but he never sought to leave the Gospel behind. On the contrary, he believed that each generation should discover the Gospel anew, and that each individual should find his or her own way to Christianity – not as a conventional religious movement, but as a personal, revealed message from God.

This view of an individually-discovered Christianity also casts new light on Hansen's work. Just as Brandes had helped reveal the true Christianity behind the denominational church, so Hansen hoped that his works could function as an eye-opener to other people. Literature was not to replace the Bible, but offered a means to discover the truth in the Bible. If the Bible could be freed from dogmatic interpretation and institutional conventions, each man and every age would also be liberated to discover it in his/her own way.

Bibliography

Bugge, David 2005. *Medusas søn*. Copenhagen: Anis.

Hansen, Martin A. 1947. *Agerhønen*. (1955). Copenhagen: Gyldendal.

Hansen, Martin A. 1948. *Tanker i en skorsten*. Copenhagen: Gyldendal.

Hansen, Martin A. 1979. *Against the wind: Stories by Martin A. Hansen. With an introduction by H. Wayne Schow:* New York: Ungar.

Hansen, Martin A. 1999. *Dagbøger I-III*. Copenhagen: Gyldendal.

Receptions and transformations of the Bible in philosophy

GENERAL REFLECTIONS
WRESTLING WITH THE TEXT

Marie Vejrup Nielsen

Within the broader issue of the relationship between Christianity, modernity and postmodernity, lies the specific question of the relation between biblical texts and the modern world. The issue is of interest to theologians and philosophers engaged in the traditional hermeneutical quest for a connection between the contemporary reader and texts from the distant past.

This problem of historical distance between text and reader is one of the central points in the development of philosophical thought on the normativity of the biblical texts 'today'. It was famously formulated by G.E. Lessing (1729-1781) as the problem of 'the foul wide ditch' (der garstige breite Graben) in his text *Über den Beweis des Geistes und der Kraft* (*On the Proof of the Spirit and the Power*) (1777) concerning the foundations of religious belief. The biblical texts describe scenarios in which miraculous events take place, but even if we grant that such things might have happened then, why should such distant, historical episodes hold any normativity for us today? For Lessing, as an enlightenment thinker, the issue at stake was the clash between the content of these stories and the claims of reason, on which he himself put such emphasis. The problem, which Lessing expressed so clearly, emerged out of new insights into the biblical texts, based on critical analysis. This critical attitude towards the biblical texts developed from the Enlightenment onwards into a new awareness of historical context. Historical critics looked at biblical texts in much the same way as they would look at any other text, asking the same questions: Who wrote these texts and what was their world like? What can be said about the various textual and oral traditions that have influenced them? Yet, while this historical-critical approach offered new ways of understanding the texts, it also contributed to the problem of distance.

Theologians and philosophers over the centuries have struggled with this issue, coming up with a variety of solutions as to how it might be possible to form a connection after all: one that both acknowledges yet overcomes the problem of distance, for example by appealing to a common human existence that transcends contextual differences. Others have seen the modern and postmodern approaches to biblical texts as an attack on their view of Christianity and have responded vigorously to any attempts to diminish the explanatory power of the Bible. This conflict has played out within Christianity not only in the varying interpretations of the Bible as a normative text, but also in what might be called the "culture wars" of 20th century Western societies. One such "war" can be seen in the clash (mainly in the USA, but increasingly elsewhere) between conservative, Christian creationists, who advocate the literal use of the Bible as an explanation of our origins, and evolutionary scientists, who insist that children be taught the Darwinian account of evolution. Christian creationists insist on the primacy of the Bible as a set of normative texts, denying any pluralism of interpretation and resisting any critique of these texts from both inside and outside Christian circles.

In Denmark, too, cultural conflict has entered these discussions, observable for example in the debates during the winter of 2007 where it emerged that a significant number of male colleagues 'disapproved' of female pastors. Some newspapers claimed that those who were against female pastors were being 'faithful to the Bible'. Others, in favour of female pastors, argued that they were just as 'faithful'; they were simply interpreting the same texts in a different way. Yet who decides not only how such texts should be interpreted, but *which* biblical texts are relevant here? Examples such as these serve to show that the discussion is still alive, not only within theological circles, but more generally within society itself, and reminds us that different groups may adopt different relationships towards the Christian texts.

Such debates raise the question: What role should the biblical texts play in our world today? Are they obsolete remnants from the past, now best forgotten? None of the thinkers presented in this section would agree with that analysis. All of them argue in their various ways that biblical texts can be received and transformed in a contemporary context, but that we are no longer naïve enough to accept these texts directly. We engage with these texts with two possible ends in view: either in order to make them meaningful for readers today (the position of Kierkegaard and Løgstrup), or else, on the contrary, to demonstrate that they can today no longer be thought of as viable sources of information on the world (the position taken by Richard Dawkins and E.O. Wilson). The issue of reception and transformation – of how the texts should be received and how this affects both texts and readers – is central to all of the writers discussed in this section, albeit in different ways.

Although the thinkers presented in the three articles that follow present a wide range of attitudes towards the biblical texts, they do in fact share a number of features. First of all, each is wrestling with the problem of the relationship between the texts in question and modern society. Some take up a combative attitude, seeking to banish the biblical text and replace it with another view of human beings and the world we live in; others are engaged in a constructive endeavour to establish a viable connection between text and contemporary reader. It is clear that all the thinkers dealt with here share a critical attitude towards the Bible, ranging from a dismissal of the text altogether, to a position more concerned with reaching its deeper meaning and bringing it to light through new ways of reading. These various perspectives share another common feature: a high degree of selectiveness not only in choosing to focus on particular texts from the Bible, but in singling out certain sections of these texts for special attention, while leaving other areas in the dark. Normativity is the issue: The very fact that these texts are being engaged with points to their normative status. Through their struggles with the biblical texts the authors highlight a tension relating to the normativity of the biblical text today; on the one hand their interest in the texts indicates that the latter do indeed play a normative role, but on the other their struggles – whether expressed through combat or dialogue – underscore the fact that this normative status is constantly being challenged from a variety of angles.

So there are common strands here. But there are also a number of issues that set these thinkers apart from each other. First of all, there is the long time span involved, stretching from Søren Kierkegaard in the mid-19th century through K.E. Løgstrup in the mid-20th, and on into the 21st century with the works of Richard Dawkins and E.O. Wilson. Second, the writers concerned come from a variety of disciplinary backgrounds. Kierkegaard and Løgstrup are from the more classic disciplines of philosophy and theology, in which discussion of the Bible is evidently not out of place, whereas the fact that we find the reception and transformation of the Bible being discussed by evolutionary biologists such as Richard Dawkins and E.O. Wilson is perhaps more surprising. A third difference concerns purpose and aim: behind the engagement of these thinkers with the texts there are often very different motivations. Kierkegaard and Løgstrup both approach the Bible with the intention of finding there something that relates to them in their own context. For example, in Kierkegaard's reception of the Book of Job, we find an almost loving relationship between text and reader. The reader embraces and is embraced by the text and thus transformed by it. Yet at the same time Kierkegaard also shows us the ambivalent relationship between text and reader, with the reader sometimes disregarding the demands the text makes on him or simply ignoring its message. Kierkegaard wants to shake us out of our complacency. He takes as his premise that the biblical texts have become so domesticated in our culture that we may have become blind to their challenging potential.

Løgstrup is critical towards many elements of the New Testament, yet at the same time aims to find something true and genuine behind their trappings. Truth is not there on the surface, but must be teased out by the critical acumen of the contemporary reader; only then can a genuine relationship between the text and the reader be established. And while he suggests that the task of finding the true message of the texts is easy enough as soon as the right key is in place, the young Løgstrup nevertheless acknowledges that we are confronted with layers in any biblical text that do indeed resist our understanding. In her article on Løgstrup Marie Møller ends by proposing an alternative approach to Løgstrup's, though one that is equally positive in its search for what is genuinely meaningful in the biblical texts. Both Kierkegaard and Løgstrup explore the ways in which we can continue to find normative guidance in the biblical texts by linking them to the fundamental issues of human existence. E.O. Wilson and Richard Dawkins, by contrast, engage with the texts in order to displace them, entering them for a contest in which there will only be one winner. Yet at the same time they too display a fascination with the biblical texts, with their language and with the power of narrative in general.

One overarching idea relating to the issue of normativity unites all the positions presented in this section: namely the view that the biblical texts are texts about what it means to be human. Both Kierkegaard and Løgstrup overcome the gap between the archaic text and the contemporary reader by concentrating on what these texts can tell us about human existence and about the fundamental issues that are relevant to every human being at any time. Through his reception and transformation of the story of Job, Kierkegaard connects the modern reader to the text by raising the question of the meaning of suffering, addressed by Job and his friends in very different ways. Likewise, Løgstrup is interested in the humanity displayed by Jesus in the Gospels; he sees this as the essential message of these texts and one that is relevant to any reader who reflects on what it means to be human. The evolutionary biologists, on the other hand, engage in their conflict with the texts precisely because they see them as having had such a powerful, yet malign, influence on our understanding of human nature, an influence that they are determined to overturn. They recognise that the image of humanity presented in narratives such as that of Job's confrontation with his Creator has powerful resonances in their own culture; by choosing to spend time and energy in combating these stories, they pay tribute to the normativity of the biblical text as a narrative about human existence.

It goes without saying that the writers in question are all trying to instil a certain attitude towards the text in their readers, rather than simply musing over these questions for their own sake. They want to convince, whether by showing their readership the features of the ideal reader, as Kierkegaard does, or by excavating the true message of the text, as Løgstrup does, or else, as Dawkins and Wilson do, by trying to undermine the readers' faith in the biblical texts as a source of understanding about human beings and their place in the world. All are keenly aware of their readers, thereby placing themselves within the dynamics of reception and transformation, showing through their own writings how they think the biblical texts should be received and transformed.

All in all, the section presents three intriguing positions, each of which wrestles with the text, struggling with it in an attempt to bring it into a right relationship with today's readership, or to bring the modern reader into the right relationship with the texts. All the writers recognise that these texts are potent sources of knowledge concerning what it means to be human, although they differ in their notions as to the role of the biblical texts in peoples' lives today. The relationship envisaged might be any of three things: a constructive interaction between the ideal reader and a benign text (Kierkegaard), the critical examination by a reader aware of what the various layers of the text may hide (Løgstrup), or, finally, the aggressive denial of the text as a meaningful communication with readers today (Dawkins and Wilson). Yet although their views may differ on the right relationship between text, reader and contemporary culture, all the writers in question display an eagerness to get involved with the stories and characters, the meanings and messages, of the texts they are concerned with. They are all genuinely intrigued by the power of these stories, and see the task of addressing them as central to their own literary and scholarly projects. Whether their attitudes towards the biblical texts are positive or negative their engagement points to the continued normative status of the Bible. But normativity for them does not mean unchallenged authority. The texts broached by the writers in question are never accepted in a naïve or straightforward manner, but placed before us as texts that we need to wrestle with, texts that do not fit simply into our lives in the world today. The challenge is to place them in critical interaction with readers who take the task of reading seriously.

So: reading and interacting with these texts is not something to be taken lightly: it involves a challenge that all the thinkers presented in this section are acutely aware of, whether or not the outcome is a complete denial of the texts or an attempt to connect them critically with our own time. Nor is the process of reading these texts just a neutral pastime: it not only informs, but *trans*forms the reader, who in turn transforms the text he or she is grappling with. This has important implications when these texts are seen – as all the commentators presented here see them – as key resources for our understanding of human existence: how we should live our lives, how we should understand our place in the world and how we can live with the fundamental conditions of our existence such as suffering and loss. The texts need to be wrestled with precisely because they are texts about what it means to be human. In short, they matter to us, irrespective of whether we engage with them in order to find truth or, alternatively, to examine them critically and maybe even finally discard them.

'MY DEAR READER'
KIERKEGAARD'S READER AND KIERKEGAARD
AS A READER OF THE BOOK OF JOB
RECEPTION AND TRANSFORMATION IN
THE WRITINGS OF KIERKEGAARD

Iben Damgaard

What does it mean to be a good reader? Kierkegaard addresses this question both when he encourages his reader to engage in dialogue with his own text, and when he discusses how to read the Bible. However, Kierkegaard does not only write *about* reading – his writings are themselves imbued with readings of the Bible. He stresses his reader's freedom in the appropriation of his writings, and this corresponds with the way he himself acts as a reader of the Bible, since he rewrites biblical texts remarkably freely. He continually insists that his own writings are written by an author without authority; in contrast to the Bible, which speaks with authority. But the emphasis on the authority of the Bible does not prevent him from creatively reworking biblical texts, since this is a way of dealing with the dialectical and dialogical element that is crucial in the appropriation of any text whether it has authority or not.[1]

This article explores the interplay between Kierkegaard's reflections on reading and his own readings of the Bible by focusing on one particular biblical figure. Through a detailed analysis of Kierkegaard's reading of Job, we will investigate the reception and transformation of the Bible in Kierkegaard's writings.

It is well known that Kierkegaard's authorship consists of two distinct groups: the books written under different pseudonyms, and the collections of upbuilding discourses that were published in Kierkegaard's own name. The upbuilding discourse takes its point of reference in a biblical quotation that it seeks to shed light on. At first sight, the Bible does not apparently play the same pervasive role in the pseudonymous writings. On closer inspection, however, it turns out that the Bible is present in quite subtle ways in many of the pseudonymous writings as well.

We will explore this through a close reading of the reception of Job in the pseud-onymous work *Repetition*. *Repetition* was published on October 16th, 1843 under the name of the pseudonymous author Constantin Constantius, and only two months later Kierkegaard returned to Job in an upbuilding discourse with the title: 'The Lord Gave,

---

1   Cf. *Concluding Unscientific Postscript to Philosophical Fragments*, volume 1, 35. I discuss this question of author-ity in greater detail in: 'Kierkegaard's Rewritings of Biblical Narrative' in *Kierkegaard and the Bible*, Aldershot, United Kingdom: Ashgate (forthcoming). On the issue of authority, see also Jolita Pons 2004, 39f.

and the Lord Took away; Blessed Be the Name of the Lord'. The discourse wrestles with the praising figure of Job in the first chapter of the Book of Job in contrast to *Repetition*, which focuses on the protesting figure of Job who is used as a figure of identification by a suffering young man in the midst of a life crisis. The differences in the way Job is portrayed in the pseudonymous and the upbuilding text respectively provide a rich example of the play with a diversity of genres and points of view that characterises Kierkegaard's dialogue with biblical figures.

The young man as a reader of the Book of Job

The subtitle of *Repetition*: 'A Venture in Experimenting Psychology', calls attention to the experimenting character of the book. The category of repetition denotes not only a paradigm of thought, but also a mode of existing. So the nature of repetition is communicated not directly through a philosophical treatise, but indirectly through a psychological experiment that mixes different genres and confuses, teases and provokes the reader to question how to make sense of repetition. Theological fragments of the category of repetition as a Christian category of a renewal of life in the encounter with God[2] are interwoven with parodic anecdotes of everyday repetitions, autobiographical reflections on Constantin's failed attempt to repeat an earlier journey to Berlin, and the fictitious story of a poetic young man who leaves his girlfriend and becomes passionately engaged in reading the Book of Job.

In a direct address to 'My dear Reader', Constantin announces that 'it is an art to be a good reader' (R, 225)[3]; and *Repetition* can in fact be interpreted as a book about reading, since the young man's passionate reading of the Book of Job provokes us to consider what it takes to be a good reader.

The nameless young man is initially presented as a friend of Constantin, but at the end of the book Constantin suddenly admits that he has invented the young man as an imaginary figure to explore the psychological meaning of the category of repetition. The story can be narrated in a few words: a young man falls deeply in love with a young girl who also loves him, but he is so absorbed in a backward mode of recollection that he cannot marry her. According to Constantin, his fatal mistake is that he is at the conclusion of the relationship at the moment when it is about to start, for the girl is merely: 'the occasion that awakened the poetic in him ... She had made him a poet – and precisely thereby has signed her own death sentence' (R, 138). The young man becomes increasingly depressive the more he realises that he is unable to marry her, and in the end he simply leaves her without a word of explanation. From his hiding place in Stockholm, the runaway man sends a series of eight letters to his friend Constantin. These letters reflect his intense reading of the Book of Job, and we

---

2   Cf. Niels Nymann Eriksen, *Kierkegaard's Category of Repetition* for a very convincing reconstruction of the meaning of the category of repetition.

3   I refer to Kierkegaard's Writings in the Hong and Hong Translation and use the following abbreviations: R for *Repetition*, EUD for *Eighteen Upbuilding Discourses*, and WL for *Works of Love*.

will therefore examine them closely in the following exploration of the young man as a reader of Job.

Job as a spokesman

In the second letter Job already plays a pivotal role for the young man caught in an overwhelming life crisis. He reads with existential passion, and he uses Job to find comfort and meaning in his own painful situation.

Job! Job! O Job! Is that all you said, those beautiful words: The Lord gave, and the Lord took away; blessed be the name of the Lord? Did you say no more? In all your afflictions did you just keep on repeating them? Why were you silent for seven days and nights? … When all existence collapsed upon you and lay like broken pottery around you … did you immediately have this interpretation of love, this cheerful boldness of trust and faith? … Do you know nothing more to say than that? No, … you did not disappoint men when everything went to pieces – then you became the voice of the suffering, the cry of the grief-stricken, the shriek of the terrified, and a relief to all who bore their torment in silence, a faithful witness to all the affliction and laceration there can be in a heart, an unfailing spokesman who dared to lament "in bitterness of soul" and to strive with God (R, 197).

The young man criticises the fact that Job's initial words of praise have become such a matter of course that they are used as empty consolation by 'professional comforters', who find them appropriate to say to a suffering person 'just as they say "God bless you" when one sneezes!' He wonders how Job was able to perform this interpretation of love and trust in the midst of his suffering; and he emphasises that Job said something that is left out by these professional comforters, for after his seven days of silence Job gave voice to lamentation and complaint and dared to strive with God. The young man quickly leaves the patient Job of the first two chapters of the Book of Job and calls attention instead to the figure of Job in the dialogue speeches after the prose prologue. At this point Job critically questions the meaning of life and suffering when he confronts the empty wisdom of his friends and summons God to appear in court and show himself for what he really is. This is what makes Job such a powerful spokesman and model for the young poet in despair:

Speak up then, unforgettable Job, repeat everything you said, you powerful spokesman who, fearless as a roaring lion, appears before the tribunal of the Most High! Your speech is pithy, and in your heart is the fear of God even when you bring complaints, when you defend your despair to your friends who jump like highwaymen to attack you with their speeches, even when you, provoked by your friends, crush their wisdom under foot and scorn their defence of the Lord … I need you, a man who knows how to complain so loudly that he is heard in heaven, where God confers with Satan on drawing up plans against man … Speak loudly. To be sure, God can speak louder – after all, he has the thunder – but that, too, is a response, an explanation, trustworthy, faithful, original, a reply from God himself, which, even if it crushes a man, is more glorious than the gossip and rumours about the righteousness of Governance that are invented by human wisdom (R, 198).

Job's friends defend God's righteousness by arguing that Job's suffering must be a punishment from God because of some secret sin. This argument is based on the assumption that God rules on the basis of a moral law of reward and retribution. But against his friends, Job insists that he suffers despite the fact that he is innocent. The young man continually puts the emphasis on Job's attack on his friends, and he thereby addresses the question that he himself is struggling with in his letters, i.e. whether he is guilty or not for having left the girl. He cannot come to grips with the ambiguity of his guilt, as he himself explains in his third letter:

My whole being screams in self-contradiction. How did it happen that I became guilty? Or am I not guilty? Why, then, am I called that in every language? What kind of miserable invention is this human language, which says one thing and means another? ... Even if the whole world rose up against me, even if all the scholastics argued with me, even if it were a matter of life and death – I am still in the right. No one shall take that away from me, even if there is no language in which I can say it. I have acted rightly (R, 200).

The young man is caught in restless self-contradiction because he feels innocent since he cannot see how he could have avoided leaving the girl. On the other hand, since language embodies conventional values of society, language judges him guilty for having broken the engagement. Language thereby figures as a parallel to Job's friends. He insists that he cannot express his condition in any language, but nevertheless uses a lot of words to ensure that even if the whole world is against him, he will – like Job – maintain that he is in the right! In practice, however, he does not – like Job – engage in dialogue with friends. On the contrary, in fact – he makes sure that his friend Constantin does not know where he is hiding and cannot answer his letters, and he thus avoids communication and defiantly withdraws from the world in his solitary readings of Job. He is 'nauseated by life', and he expresses this in an outcry of absurdity that echoes Job's laments:

Who am I? How did I get into the world? Why was I not asked about it, why was I not informed of the rules and regulations but just thrust into the ranks as if I had been bought from a peddling shanghaier of human beings? How did I get involved in this big enterprise called actuality? Why should I be involved? Isn't it a matter of choice? And if I am compelled to be involved, where is the manager – I have something to say about this. Is there no manager? To whom shall I make my complaint? (R, 200).

The young man's questioning the meaning of life calls to mind the lament in Job's first long speech, in which his longing for the world of death is contrasted with the miserable reality of his present condition in a series of exclamatory 'why' questions: 'why did I not die at birth (Job 3:11)[4], Why does he[5] give light to the sufferer (Job 3:20) … to one who cannot see the way, whom God has fenced in?' (Job 3:23).

It is not the patient Job of the prose prologue but the critical figure of the passionate and poetical speeches that the young man – and perhaps his modern reader – uses as a figure of identification. The young man's passionate questioning of the meaning of life echoes the lament of Job. They are both structured around exclamations of why the 'I' came into this world, and both express an existentialist feeling of meaninglessness: life appears futile and aimless. The parallel, however, make us aware of an important contrast: the young man can find no one to answer his questions, and he asks for a 'manager' [dirigent] to whom he can address his complaint. Job, however, never questions whether there is a 'manager', and his questioning of why he was born into a life of suffering, in which his way[6] in life has been obscured by God, is directed against God.

Job as clothing and alcohol

The fourth letter gives us a passionate evocation of what the reading of Job means to the young man. He describes how he constantly reads Job in new ways, and he poetically narrates how he gets up at night, illuminates the whole house, opens his window and cries out Job's words into the world! Although he has read the Book of Job again and again, it is always new to him and he keeps interpreting the specific points in 'the most diverse ways': 'It is impossible to describe all the shades of meaning and how manifold the meaning is that he has for me. … Every word by him is food and clothing and healing for my wretched soul' (R, 204). The young man plunges himself into the words of Job and completely gives himself up to the text. He has a hunger for Job's words, which calm him when he is restless and awaken him when he has given in. Metaphorically, he describes Job's words as clothing and food for his wretched soul, yet it turns out that alcohol might be an even more appropriate metaphor:

Like an inebriate, I imbibe all the intoxication of passion little by little, until by this prolonged sipping I become almost unconscious in drunkenness. But at the same time, I hasten to it with indescribable impatience. Half a word – and my soul rushes into his thought, … more swiftly than lightning seeks the conductor does my soul glide therein and remain there (R, 205).

The young man is completely absorbed in Job's words. He surrenders himself to the text without reserve. He repeats Job's words again and again, but he does not transform them

---

4   The biblical quotations are taken from *The Holy Bible* in the New Revised Standard Version.

5   The standard translation renders it: 'why is light given to one in misery', but I am quoting instead from the translation in Habel 1985, 99, for in his literal translation, the 'he' as subject of the opening verb points at God as the subject. This possibility has been chosen in other translations, for instance the Danish standard translation: 'Hvorfor giver Gud lys til de elendige'.

6   In wisdom literature, the Hebrew word 'derek' – way – means the conduct of life and personal destiny, so we might as well render it as: 'purpose in life' (Habel 1985, 111f).

into an existential practice in real life – a textual repetition has replaced an existential repetition, as pointed out by Joakim Garff (Garff 1995, 134). The young man plunges himself into the text with 'indescribable impatience' and loses himself in a state of self-oblivion and intoxication that blinds him for the decisive return to the sobriety of ethical action. He reads with existential passion, but his way of losing himself in the text appears as aesthetic self-deception (Pattison 1997, 295f.).

When the young man metaphorically describes Job's words as clothing for his wretched soul, the reader may perceive the ironic reversal of the way Job points to the fragility of the fundamental nakedness of the human condition, for we may question whether the young man merely dresses up in Job's poetic words in order to conceal the true nature of his own condition. By the end of the letter, the young man seems to discover this incongruity between Job and himself: 'these words I make my own. At the same time, I sense the contradiction and smile at myself as one smiles at a little child who has donned his father's clothes' (R, 206).

Job as figure of repetition

In his fifth letter, the young man accepts the consequence of this discovery. He regards himself as being liberated from a rage of fever, and he does not sink into the text as before, but rather engages in calm and sober reflections on what Job makes us aware of. The young man praises Job because he 'witnesses a noble, bold confidence that knows what a human being is … in him is manifest the love and trust that are confident that God can surely explain everything if one can only speak with him' (R, 208).

The young man imagines a fainthearted person, who does not have Job's perseverance and therefore submits to the friends' argument that his misfortune is caused by his sins and that he therefore ought to repent and beg forgiveness, after which all will be well again. Such a fainthearted person may adopt his friends' belief because he 'vaguely conceives of God as a tyrant, something he meaninglessly expresses by promptly placing him under ethical determinants' (R, 207). An understanding of God in ethical determinants turns God into a tyrant persecuting a human being according to a law of retribution. Job is praised precisely because he 'knows how to avoid all cunning ethical evasions' (R, 210). Job maintains his trust in God despite his friends' attempt to explain the unexplainable by explaining God and God's actions by referring to a moral law of retribution and thereby reducing God to a God that can be measured on a human scale (Müller 1969, 203).

The young man focuses on the protesting figure of Job, who he does not see as 'a hero of faith' but rather as 'the whole weighty defence plea on man's behalf in the great case between God and man' (R, 210). Job is approached through the category of an 'ordeal' [Prøvelse], which is transcendent and places an individual in a 'personal relationship of opposition to God' (R, 210), so that he cannot allow himself to be satisfied with an ethical explanation like the one his friends are always trying to impose on him. The young man focuses again on the cruelty in Job's friends' insistence that

Job's suffering is his own fault, and this is taken up again later by Kierkegaard, who elaborates on it in different journal notes, for instance the following note on the Book of Job from 1851:

The significance of this book is really to show the cruelty which we men commit by interpreting being unhappy as guilt, as crime. This is essentially human selfishness, which desires to avoid the earnest and disturbing impression of suffering, of what can happen to a man in this life – therefore in order to protect ourselves against this we explain suffering as guilt: It is his own fault. O, human cruelty!

Job is concerned with proving himself right, in a certain sense also in relation to God, but above all in relation to his friends, who instead of consoling him torment him with the thesis that he suffers because of guilt (*Journal and Papers* # 1536, Pap X,4, A 396).

In his journals, Kierkegaard argues that the human cruelty that Job's friends embody is an expression of the selfishness that does not want to face what may happen to a human being in this life and therefore makes up an explanation through which we seek to shield ourselves against the suffering that disturbs our peace in life and our naïve image of God as the guarantor of justice and success in this life. The young man's reflections on Job's friends thus turn out to have a remarkable resemblance with Kierkegaard's own journal notes on Job.

In the sixth letter, the young man briefly deals with Job's encounter with God, who finally speaks to Job from within the thunderstorm at the end of the Book of Job. The young man asks:

Was Job proved to be in the wrong? Yes, eternally, for there is no higher court than the one that judged him. Was Job proved to be in the right? Yes, eternally, by being proved to be in the wrong *before God*. So there is a repetition, after all. ... When did it occur for Job? When every *thinkable* human certainty and probability was impossible (R, 212).

I take this to mean that whereas on a human level Job was always innocent and thus in the right in contrast to his friends, he was – like every human being – in the wrong before God. God transcends the moral order and contradicts any human calculation of the probable. He gives and takes but not in a way that we as human beings may wish, expect or explain. In his encounter with God, Job lets go of his demand for an explanation, and he thereby transcends the moral order and relates to God as the source of unknown possibilities – which is what repetition is about.

Reading as repetition

In the seventh letter, the focus shifts again from Job and back to the young man, who is impatiently awaiting a thunderstorm and a repetition like the one Job finally experienced. The young man insists that this repetition will 'make me fit to be a husband.

It will shatter my whole personality – I am prepared. It will render me almost unrecognizable to myself' (R, 214). Constantin then interferes to warn the reader that the young man suffers from 'a misplaced melancholy': 'He is waiting for a thunderstorm that is supposed to make him into a husband, a nervous breakdown perhaps' (R, 216). When the reader has read the young man's final letter immediately after Constantin's intervention, he is inclined to agree with Constantin, for the young man writes:

She is married – to whom I do not know, for when I read it in the newspaper I was so stunned that I dropped the paper and have not had the patience since then to check in detail. I am myself again. Here I have repetition; I understand everything (R, 220).

The young man understands everything; the reader, however, is left confused since all the young man's theological reflections on repetition are thrown away like a worn-out garment when the girl's marriage is suddenly understood as repetition. Constantin remarks that the young man uses the occasion to withdraw from actuality in order to live in an ideal world of poetry. As I see it, Constantin is right in this. The young man ends up with a parodic repetition.

His perspective in life and his way of acting have not been transformed through his reading of Job. When he reads about the girl's marriage, he immediately flings himself into an imaginary world of poetry as expressed in his final poetic outcry: 'The beaker of inebriation is again offered to me …three cheers for the dance in the vortex of the infinite, … three cheers for the cresting waves that fling me above the stars' (R, 222). His impatient plunge into the words of Job that he was sipping like 'an inebriate' is now echoed when he plunges himself into poetic possibilities, and he is once again sipping the 'beaker of inebriation' until complete self-loss in the intoxication of the poetic, which has nothing to do with the embrace of this finite life with all its sorrows and responsibility that characterise Job's repetition in faith. The young man lacks patience – he stands impatiently on one foot before definitively taking flight into the dizzying vortex of the infinite – whereas the ethico-religious, according to Kierkegaard, is all about becoming sober and finding 'the firm footing of actuality' [Virkelighedens Fodfæste] (WL, 163). The young man's reflections on Job do not make him question whether there might be some self-deceit in his impatient way of justifying himself through Job. But is this necessary in order to be a good reader?

Let us explore whether Constantin gives us guidelines to what it means to be a good reader. In his final letter to his 'dear Reader', he polemises against the hurry of his age, when no one realises that it is an art to be a good reader and it takes time to become one. He does not, however, directly say what it takes to be a good reader, but indirectly and negatively he approaches the issue by mentioning a few examples of bad readers. He exposes the way in which different readers will read the book only to look for a confirmation of their own personal life view. Another example of bad reading is the distanced, objective reviewer that merely tries to make the text fit into conventional aesthetic categories. Constantin confides that he has written his book in such an 'inverse' way that 'the heretics are unable to understand it', inasmuch as 'it is not a ready-made uniform that fits every musketeer' (R, 225). *Repetition* is full of enigmatic gaps, and this disruptive, open form obstructs the (bad) reader, who only wishes to rush into the text and wear it as a uniform, because *Repetition* does not fit the reader smoothly but rather calls for the reader's response. We look in vain for positive guidelines in *Repetition* as to what it means to be a good reader. It only gives us a brief catalogue of bad readers that does shed some – albeit negative – light on reading.

In *Eighteen Upbuilding Discourses* from the same period, Kierkegaard is much more explicit about what it takes to be a good reader. In his discourse on Job, Kierkegaard advocates an existentially and ethically oriented reading of Scripture with the emphasis on the need to move from text to action. The art of being a good reader thus implies that the reader examines himself in the light of the text. The text calls the reader's self-understanding into question in order to transform his way of living and acting. In this way we may speak of reading as repetition – i.e. the transformation of the text to existential practice, and it is precisely this existential repetition that the young man evades. He does not use his creative and rich reflections on the Book of Job to examine whether he is deceiving himself, but rather uses them to maintain that he is in the right because he is a parallel figure to Job. Because of this unwillingness to let the text question him, he lacks the earnestness needed in the art of being a good reader.

Kierkegaard emphasises that reading requires our imagination, which opens up the horizon of the possible and makes us perceive other ways of being in the world that are projected in the text. But through negative examples of readers such as the young man who loses himself in an imaginary dream-world, Kierkegaard points to the complicated dialectics at stake in reading between *imagination* and the *will* to discover our own illusions in a quest for true self-understanding.

The Upbuilding Discourse: Job as prototype

In Kierkegaard's preface to the upbuilding discourse on Job, he declares that he sends the text out to find 'that single individual, whom I with joy and gratitude call *my* reader, that favorably disposed person who receives the book … gives it meaning, and transforms it into much' (EUD, 107). *Reception* involves *transformation*, since the meaning to be understood in the text is only fully realised in the reader's actualization of it in his own existence. The reader is expected to transform the text into action, and this is stressed throughout the discourse when Kierkegaard reminds the reader of the task of responsible decision and self-appropriation.

The discourse focuses exclusively on the first chapter of the Book of Job. It takes its point of reference in the words of Job: 'The Lord gave, and the Lord took away; blessed be the name of the Lord'. Like the young man, Kierkegaard remarks that we have heard these words repeated so often that they have become a matter of course for us, and this is what he sets out to deconstruct in his discourse. He contrasts Job with a series of figures that represent despairing and defiant ways of relating to sorrow and suffering, and through these disanalogies to Job we are led to discover anew what is at stake in Job's response to his misfortune and thereby also challenged to ask ourselves how we would respond in that situation. This rhetorical strategy of presenting the reader with the biblical text by rewriting it in different versions is very characteristic of Kierkegaard's reception – and transformation – of the Bible both in the upbuilding discourses and in some of the pseudonymous writings, especially *Fear and Trembling*, which opens with four different rewritings of the story of Abraham and Isaac, Gen 22:1-19.[7]

The discourse on Job is structured in four parts: a prologue that distinguishes between what Job said and what he did; a narrative preamble that rewrites the first chapter of the Book of Job; the main part, which consists of an exegetical analysis of Job's words; and an epilogue of admonition.

In the prologue, Kierkegaard points out that Job is a teacher of humankind not because he left us a teaching but because he left himself as a 'prototype' [Forbillede]. His significance 'by no means consists in what he said but in what he did'. So, what did he do? He not only said the words that have since become a proverb, but he 'acted upon it', since he said these words of worship just when he had lost everything he treasured, and *this* is what makes his assertion itself an action. If he had said the words on another occasion, then Job would have been forgotten, for it is not the words themselves but their performative character as worship of God (Eriksen 2000, 43) despite the tragic circumstances that makes Job a prototype.

The discourse moves on to a rewriting of the first chapter of the Book of Job, but leaves out the dialogue in heaven between God and Satan (1:6-12). We meet the old, blessed Job whose joy in life was his children's joy. He is sitting peacefully in the quiet security of joy, and then suddenly everything is shattered when one messenger after another arrives to report the destruction of all his fortune culminating in the death of his many children. Job's sorrow, says Kierkegaard, 'did not make use of many words, or rather he did not say a single one; his appearance alone gave witness that his heart was shattered. Could you want it any other way?' (EUD, 114). Kierkegaard himself immediately answers his question by presenting a contrasting figure to Job. He imagines a person who makes himself insensitive to human emotions: 'does not the person who takes pride in not being able to sorrow on the day of sorrow have the shame of not being able to rejoice on the day of joy, either?' (EUD, 114f.). Kierkegaard stresses that Job surrendered to sorrow – not to despair, and this distinction anticipates a crucial claim in *Works of Love*: 'I do not have the right to become insensitive to life's pain, because I *shall* sorrow; but neither do I have the right to despair, because I *shall* sorrow' (WL, 43). It is implied that the person addressed is suffering because he has lost the beloved; and the question is then whether the sufferer in despair seeks to shield himself from the loss by giving up love and making himself immune to the pain, or whether he in sorrow perseveres in and through love. In sorrow Job was able to confess:

---

7   I have investigated Kierkegaard's rewritings of the Bible more detailed in Damgaard 2007a and Damgaard 2007b.

'Naked I came from my mother's womb, and naked shall I return ... The Lord gave, and the Lord took away; blessed be the Name of the Lord' (EUD 115). This leads to the main part of the discourse, which presents an exegesis of Job's famous saying that has become so domesticated that we are no longer surprised and puzzled by it.

Would we not expect, Kierkegaard wonders, that if a man loses everything he treasured, he would focus not on what he has been given, the *gift*, but on the loss, since we would expect that the loss would overwhelm him so much that he could only speak of the loss? Kierkegaard goes on to explore figures that give in to despair and defiance and burning restlessness unable to bear the loss, and notes that we would never finish if we were to talk about the despairing reactions to misfortune that occur so often in this world. He thus returns to Job, who takes his point of departure not in the loss but in the gift, in the thankfulness that the Lord had given him all the blessings that have now been taken away from him. Job maintains: 'the bold confidence in faith' [Frimodigheden i Troen], so Kierkegaard sees him as the voice of comfort that 'trembles in pain and yet proclaims joy' (EUD, 122). This voice of comfort guides the troubled one to find joy even in the depths of sorrow.

This leads Kierkegaard to the epilogue of the discourse in which he addresses the reader through constant questions and admonition. Kierkegaard assures us that the discourse applies to the reader whether he has been tried in life or not, and in a final admonition the reader is told to examine himself closely to discover whether he seeks to evade the task that is embodied in seeing Job as a prototype. For instance, the reader might delude himself into thinking that Job's words are only applicable to an extraordinary situation like the one Job experienced, and that if something similar happened to himself the terror itself would give him the strength to develop this 'humble courage' [ydmyge Mod] (EUD, 123) of faith that Job embodies. Kierkegaard reminds the reader of Job's wife, who did not bear the loss as Job did but rather advised Job to curse God and die. Kierkegaard thereby encourages the reader to earnest and honest self-examination: 'learn from Job to become honest with yourself so that you do not deceive yourself with imagined power, with which you experience imagined victory in imagined struggle' (EUD, 123).

Closing words

Kierkegaard's discourse deals only with the first chapter of the Book of Job, and even leaves out the dialogue in heaven when Satan challenges God to test Job (Job 1:6-12). The discourse focuses exclusively on the praising figure of Job, who embodies the humble courage of faith. We may wonder why Kierkegaard writes a discourse on Job that does not even mention the lamenting and protesting figure of Job, who was the pivotal figure in the young man's letters. But it is quite characteristic of Kierkegaard's reception of the Bible that he highlights a particular problem that he wants to shed light on and then twists and turns it to look at it from constantly new perspectives without taking into consideration how the concrete piece of text relates to its biblical context – in this case the rest of the Book of Job. We may find it crucial to reflect on how to interpret the Book of Job as a whole, but the aim of Kierkegaard's discourse is rather to build up the reader by making him discover anew the courage at stake in Job's praise, and then the protesting figure of Job is used to pursue other issues in *Repetition*.

At first sight, the two approaches to Job are extremely different. In the upbuilding discourse, Job is constantly juxtaposed with alternative, imaginary figures that lack the courage of faith, and this is linked to a direct questioning of the reader to examine himself to find out whether he has this courage. *Repetition* focuses instead on the protesting figure of Job, who is used as a figure of identification by a poetic young man in the midst of an overwhelming life crisis. He sees Job as a spokesman for the innocent sufferer, who questions the righteousness of God and attacks the argument of Job's friends that God rules on the basis of a moral law of reward and retribution. In the young man's letters, Job's questions about the meaning of life are repeated and re-contextualised in the young man's quest for identity in a modern world without God. But since he is unwilling to let the text question and examine him, he ultimately fails in the art of being a good reader, since according to the upbuilding discourse this requires patient self-examination and the transition from reading to action.

However, through different literary devices and focuses of interpretation both readings of Job seek to deconstruct the fact that the Book of Job has become so domesticated in our culture that we are no longer surprised and personally challenged by Job's response to suffering. It is thus worth noticing that even though the young man does not say much about Job's initial praise, the little that he does say actually anticipates what we later learn about the praise in the upbuilding discourse; for the young man wonders how Job was able to maintain his interpretation of love and boldness of trust and faith in the midst of his suffering, and this is a key to what is at stake in the upbuilding discourse. The two approaches to Job thus *complement* rather than contradicting each other. It therefore makes sense when Kierkegaard in his journal notes that his discourse on Job attempts to depict in a more calm and edifying way what *Repetition* had depicted with unsettling passion.[8]

Both approaches to Job are quite characteristic of Kierkegaard's reception and transformation of the Bible, for he takes his point of departure in the assumption that our belonging to the Christian tradition has made biblical texts so familiar to us that we read them as harmless pieces of cultural heritage and have become blind to their challenging potential. When we know the stories by heart, it is too easy to ignore the fact that they require our ethical involvement and our transformation of the text to existential practice. It is too easy to ignore the fact that it is an art to be a good reader, and that it takes not only time but also self-examination to become one!

This is why Kierkegaard plays 'stranger with the old and familiar' (WL 210) biblical text as we have seen it in the rewritings that present disanalogies to Job in the upbuilding discourse, as well as the narratives of fictitious readers of the Bible like the

8   Pap. VI B 98,52.

young man, who provokes the reader to consider what it takes to be a good reader of the Bible, as we have seen it in *Repetition*. Through a rich variety of literary devices and perspectives Kierkegaard attempts to produce an alienating distance to the biblical text that forces us to see it anew on the one hand, and proximity and contemporaneity with the biblical text on the other since we are constantly encouraged to ask ourselves how *we* would react if *our* existence lay like broken pottery around us.

Bibliography

Damgaard, Iben 2007a. 'Kierkegaard og Bibelen'. In: Sigfred Pedersen (ed.), *Skriftsyn og Metode*. 2nd ed. Aarhus: Aarhus University Press, 170-194.

Damgaard, Iben 2007b. 'The Danger of "the Restless Mentality of Comparison". Kierkegaard's Parables of the Lily and the Bird'. In: Niels Jørgen Cappelørn, Hermann Deuser (eds.), *Kierkegaard Studies Yearbook 2007*. Berlin / New York: Walter de Gruyter, 193-208.

Eriksen, Niels Nymann 2000. *Kierkegaard's Category of Repetition: A Reconstruction*. Berlin / New York: Walter de Gruyter.

Garff, Joakim 1995. *"Den Søvnløse" Kierkegaard læst æstetisk/biografisk*. Copenhagen: Reitzels Forlag.

Habel, Norman 1985. *The Book of Job. A Commentary*. London: SCM Press.

Kierkegaard, Søren 1967-1968. *Journals and Papers* (eds.) Hong & Hong. Bloomington & London: Indiana University Press.

Kierkegaard, Søren (1843) 1983: *Repetition*, Kierkegaard's Writings, VI, Tr. Hong and Hong, Princeton University Press.

Kierkegaard, Søren (1843-44) 1990. *Eighteen Upbuilding Discourses*, Kierkegaard's Writings, V, Tr. Hong and Hong, Princeton University Press.

Kierkegaard, Søren (1846) 1992. *Concluding Unscientific Postscript to Philosophical Fragments*. Kierkegaard's Writings, XII,1, Tr. Hong and Hong, Princeton University Press.

Kierkegaard, Søren (1847) 1995. *Works of Love*. Kierkegaard's Writings, XVI, Tr. Hong and Hong, Princeton University Press.

Müller, Paul 1969. 'Søren Kierkegaards forståelse af teodicéproblemet, belyst ud fra hans skildring af Job-skikkelsen'. *Dansk Teologisk Tidsskrift*, 32, 199-217.

Pattison, George 1997. 'If Kierkegaard is Right about Reading, Why Read Kierkegaard?' In: Niels Jørgen Cappelørn, Hermann Deuser (eds.), *Kierkegaard Revisited*. Berlin / New York: Walter de Gruyter, 291-309.

Pons, Jolita 2004. *Stealing a Gift: Kierkegaard's Pseudonyms and the Bible*. New York: Fordham University Press.

FINDING THE TRUE JESUS?

RECEPTION AND TRANSFORMATION OF THE JESUS FIGURE IN THE HOMILETICS AND SERMONS OF LØGSTRUP[1]

Maria Louise Odgaard Møller

Introduction

Knud Ejler Løgstrup (1905-1981) is one of the twentieth century's greatest Danish thinkers. He was a theologian and a philosopher, and during his long and active life he served as a parson and later joined the Faculty of Theology at Aarhus University as a professor of ethics and philosophy of religion. During his lifetime his thinking on ethics, philosophy and theology was the object of much controversy and extensive debate, a situation which continues today. He is best known for *Den etiske fordring*, his seminal work on ethics from 1956 (*The Ethical Demand*, Løgstrup 1997).

The topic of this article is Løgstrup's reception and transformation of the image of Jesus found in the gospels. My understanding of the term 'reception' is the presentation of the Jesus figure that Løgstrup arrives at, based on the method he uses in his reading of the texts. The 'transformation' of the Jesus image in the gospels must be seen in continuation of this; the new interpretative formation that Jesus undergoes in Løgstrup's thinking results in a Jesus who is reduced in relation to the image presented in the gospels. The wider purpose of this article is to examine to what degree, and in what way, Løgstrup regards the Bible as normative in his reading and treatment of biblical texts with a view to his sermons. Løgstrup himself does not apply the concept 'normative', but speaks of the way in which the gospel scriptures can be said to be 'authoritative'. However, in Løgstrup's usage, the term 'authoritative' can, by and large, be equated with the term 'normative', since Løgstrup links it closely to the concept of truth: only when there is a historical truth to be found in what the texts tell us can they be valid and applicable to people today. And this is precisely how the normative can be defined: that which has and retains validity because its content can be defined as 'true'. In the following I shall therefore use the terms 'authoritative' and 'normative' synonymously.

When Løgstrup speaks of 'the historical method' and 'historical truth', his terminology cannot simply be taken to refer to the historico-critical method and the historico-scientific truth in the Bible's accounts that this latter method seeks to establish. Løgstrup has certainly subsumed the historical Jesus research into his image of Jesus, but it is in the light of the inspiration taken from Rudolf Bultmann's existential interpretation in particular (Bultmann 1926) that Løgstrup's 'historical method' must be understood. Rather than searching for the strictly historico-scientific facts concerning the his-

---

1   This article was translated by Heidi Flegal.

torical character Jesus of Nazareth, it is a matter of arriving at a historico-existential understanding of the life that Jesus the human being lived, and what it means to us today. However, many of Løgstrup's arguments in his book *Prædikenen og dens tekst* (*The Sermon and Its Text*) inevitably call to mind historico-critical methodology and its efforts to reach the 'true' historical person Jesus of Nazareth that lies 'behind' the gospel texts, not least because Løgstrup unambiguously talks about peeling away the different layers of the text, allowing one to 'find and establish the truth about what happened and was said' (Løgstrup 1999, 54). Løgstrup's 'historical method', and his talk of 'historical truth', can thus be seen as positioned midway between the historico-critical methodology and Bultmann's existential Jesus interpretation (see Løgstrup 1999, 9-37; 39-65).

The focus of this article is the period 1936-1943, during which Løgstrup served as the pastor of two small country parishes on the island of Funen in southern Denmark. Besides writing a sermon for each Sunday of the ecclesiastical year, Løgstrup also compiled *Prædikenen og dens tekst*, in which he explains his methodological reflections upon how the gospels can be said to be authoritative and how they should be read, not least when one is working on a sermon.

Løgstrup's sermons and his slender volume on homiletics give quite an illuminating portrayal of his perception of the Jesus figure during that period of Løgstrup's life and work, and of his attitude towards the normative status of the Bible. He deals first and foremost with Jesus the *human being*, focusing almost exclusively on his life and works. His crucifixion and death play a minor role, and Løgstrup's interest in the resurrection is almost infinitesimal. As we shall see later on, one of the main reasons for this is that Løgstrup wrote his work on homiletics as part of an ongoing controversy with what he polemically referred to as 'Barthian scripture theology', which, according to Løgstrup, pays homage to a 'theophanic Christology'. By this he means that all of the gospel scriptures are read based on the presupposition that the special thing about Jesus was, above all, that he was divine. If the texts are read based on this presupposition, the original message in the proclamation of Jesus is distorted; and rather than being a *human being* who lives completely differently than we do, Jesus becomes a *demigod*. This distortion of the original gospel message is found not only in 'Barthian scripture theology'. According to Løgstrup, it is also found in the writings of the evangelists themselves. Løgstrup thereby takes a highly critical stance towards the idea that the Bible, taken in its entirety as one work, should have any normative status. On the contrary, he declares that the Bible contains many examples of texts that cannot be said to be historically true, and which therefore must be rejected as non-normative. This is why a wrestle with the texts is necessary, making a historico-critical effort to peel away the falsified layers of the gospels that contain theophanic Christological statements, allowing the true message in the proclamation of Jesus, and the truth about him as a person, to become clearly evident.

In the following we will look at how Løgstrup intends this to take place, and at the Jesus image that Løgstrup believes to be the true and unfalsified image. In addition, taking Paul Ricoeur's biblical hermeneutics as my starting point, I will outline an alternative to Løgstrup's approach and to his image of Jesus, additionally discussing whether the two different methods can be perceived as qualified proposals for a contemporary normative reading of the Bible today.

Løgstrup's reception and transformation of the Jesus image in the gospels

Løgstrup calls the method that must be used to reach behind the gospel texts and reveal the original image of Jesus 'the historical method'. This method can be used in the reading of these texts because they themselves are historical accounts of Jesus, the man and his life and works here on Earth. If we then approach these texts as historical accounts, we must meet them with the questions that most readily spring to mind: 'Genuine history (…) will understand the meaning of the events in themselves, as human life – a meaning that is only uncovered if the historian poses real, human questions to these events' (Løgstrup 1999, 43).

The gospels are not merely historical accounts, but also testimonies relating to the words and works of God. This makes it relevant to ask whether these testimonies are true or false – a question which can be answered through the 'historical method'. Regarding the goal of historical criticism, Løgstrup explains: 'But what is the goal of historical criticism? Why are the accounts taken as testimonies? Because one wishes to find and establish the truth about what happened and was said' (Løgstrup 1999, 54). It is only after burrowing back into the historical truth in a text that one can perceive the text as authoritative. In Løgstrup's work the historical truth is what is linked to the true testimony, and so there is a strict correspondence between verifying the contents of a text as historically accurate and true (a true testimony), and the potential for regarding this text as authoritative; as normative. In opposition to this situation, Løgstrup regards the presence of theophanic Christological falsifications in the gospels as layers in the text that we can completely disregard today, since they are solely an expression of the evangelists' subjective theological convictions and personal faith. Their historical truth cannot be traced or verified, which means that they cannot be perceived as authoritative. In Løgstrup's usage, the concepts of 'authority', 'normativity', and 'true' historicity therefore become almost identical.

When characterising Jesus, Løgstrup concentrates almost exclusively on his words and deeds – that is, on the human life he lived. Løgstrup finds it extremely important to be aware that the gospels smuggle in passages that betray the original intention of the words and deeds of Jesus. What Løgstrup does, then, is to set up this original intention as the primary norm in the reading of the texts, at the expense of the gospels themselves. Løgstrup distinguishes between, on the one hand, the original intention of the words and deeds of Jesus, which one must find the way back to using the historical method; and, on the other, the evangelists' intention of proclaiming Jesus to be divine. Through such theophanic Christology, the intention of the gospels falsifies the original intention of the words and deeds of Jesus, which was to proclaim the kingdom of God. While the evangelists (according to Løgstrup) seek to get this message across by presupposing a divinity in Jesus that ostensibly enabled him to work supernatural wonders, predict events far into the future, and thus live a life rooted in a completely different world than ours, the message of the kingdom of God presented in Løgstrup's understanding of Jesus is solely associated with his humanity. There is a very intimate connection between the message Jesus proclaims and the life he lives: 'The message in the proclamation of Jesus is that without consideration, he *lives and proclaims* life itself, the created life, life in the kingdom of God' (Løgstrup 1999, 84 – my emphasis).

It is solely the content of Jesus' words and deeds that we must take note of – and not the way in which he said or did them. The apparently miraculous and supernatural nature of his works must, in other words, be disregarded. What can bring us to see that he is the son of God is not any external sign or feature that he bears, but the content of his proclamation and the clarification of what carried him through the life he led. Regardless of who he met, spoke to and kept company with, the content of his words and deeds had one particular overarching idea. According to Løgstrup, both the words of Jesus, which most often means his parables, and his deeds, which most often mean the wonders he worked, are characterised by the concepts of mercy, untroubledness, giving, forgiveness, and service. Løgstrup intends to completely excise the miraculous aspect of the miracles. The point is not to see, in Jesus, a worker of wonders, a vision-ary dreamer, and in doing so be led to the idea that he must be divine. The point is to see the mercy in what he does.

Particularly 'mercy' and 'untroubledness' are mentioned countless times, both in Løgstrup's sermons and in *Prædikenen og dens tekst*. These concepts constitute the core of the message of Jesus, his way of living, and his humanity. And the way of showing this mercy was simply to *live* it. Throughout Løgstrup's presentation there is a correspondence between the message of Jesus regarding the kingdom of God as a kingdom of mercy and the way Jesus lived. Jesus both proclaimed and lived the life of the kingdom of God, the created life, *because* he lived in mercy: 'His life was really the way that life is – before the destruction – as created by God: life in mercy for the human being, life in connectedness to our fellow man, life in giving, life in forgiveness (…)' (Løgstrup 1995, 159). And only in this way – by living completely in mercy – does he reveal God. For Løgstrup, the revelation is solely linked to the humanity of Jesus, whereas his death on the cross and his resurrection do not play any role in this context.

Examples from the sermons

To sum up Løgstrup's view, the litmus test of whether a text can be said to recount authentic words or deeds of Jesus, and thus can be considered as historically true and therefore normative, is whether the spoken word or the deed done reflects unilateral mercy and untroubledness. *Mercy* is the original intention behind the words and deeds of Jesus. If a work is not done solely to alleviate the need of the other, but instead to demonstrate the divinity of Jesus, then the account of this work must be rejected as historically untrue. This is the case, for instance, in the story of the woman at the well, John 4:13-26, on which Løgstrup bases the sermon he delivered on Whit Monday of 1942. He spends much of this sermon explaining why the story can *not* be taken to be historically true. One reason he gives is that the story intimates that Jesus had some sort of advance knowledge of the woman's marriages, previous and present. This makes Jesus a mind-reader and a miracle-maker, which from Løgstrup's perspective means that a theophanic Christology has been smuggled into the text, which must in turn reveal it as a story invented by the evangelist. Instead of dealing with how Jesus mercifully and spontaneously helps the people he meets, this story sets out to prove that Jesus is divine, by endowing him with supernatural abilities (see the sermon on Whit Monday, 1942; unpublished).

The same considerations appear in connection with the parables. Several of the parables in the gospels cannot be attributed to Jesus himself, since the image of God that they portray simply cannot be in accordance with the God that Jesus reveals by living fully and completely in mercy, untroubledness, forgiveness and service. One example of this is found in Matthew 22:1-14, in the parable of the wedding feast. Here, according to Løgstrup, the evangelist added some of his own deliberations to the original account because he could not easily accept the image of God that the parable would otherwise project, namely an utterly merciful and inviting God.

The author could not make do with Jesus' story about the inviting and ever-inviting God and the receiving and ever-receiving, evil and good, lowly human beings. For him this was too simple. And then he added on the examining God (…) (Løgstrup 1999, 113).

Again we see how Løgstrup puts his presupposed conception of the true intention in Jesus' proclamation ahead of the authority of the gospels, enabling him to determine that texts or parts of texts are historically untrue, and hence to declare them non-normative.

It is evident that both in *Prædikenen og dens tekst* and in some of his sermons, Løgstrup quite explicitly formulates statements on the potential historical veracity of various texts. By contrast, his approach to the texts that deal with the death and resurrection of Jesus is much less clear-cut. The reason is that when it is time for Løgstrup to deliver a sermon on this issue, for instance on Easter Sunday, he has a tendency to completely sidestep the theme of resurrection. Often he simply has his Easter sermons deal with something completely different, such as – again the favourite theme – the life, words, and works of Jesus. This is most clearly evident in his sermons for Easter Sunday in 1940 and 1941. The main topic of his 1940 Easter sermon is how the way Jesus lived was completely different from the way we live, because 'That is the enigmatic thing about Jesus' life, that he had no "I", the way we have an "I"' (Løgstrup 1995, 153). Our 'I' is the thing that makes us live in a constantly forward-oriented interest seeking to achieve results. We ruminate on, and constantly worry about, our performances and therefore about the value we believe can be accorded to our lives. Unlike our lives, the life of Jesus was characterised by joy, love, and an untroubled approach. Jesus had no 'I' that could worry, because he was life itself. That is why, in the very last line of his sermon, Løgstrup can say – despite everything – that 'in Jesus Christ it was life that rose from the dead' (Løgstrup 1995, 154). We see that this Easter sermon is completely focused on the life that Jesus lived, whereas resurrection – understood as the resurrection *of life* – is only mentioned briefly, and at the very end.

It is more the exception than the rule for Løgstrup to deal with the death of Jesus. An explanation of why Jesus had to die is, once again, given solely in the light of the way he lived his life. Løgstrup presents this interpretation in a sermon he gave on Christmas Eve in 1938 (Løgstrup 1995, 115-118). He depicts how we today have destroyed God's creation by living in 'the self-invented delight in power, and delight in possession', whereas Jesus lived in quite the opposite, 'in God's created delight in the fellow man'. But precisely because Jesus lived in a completely different way than us, he had to die: 'And because Jesus defied our destruction of God's creation, for that reason we crucified Him.' The crucifixion was not the necessary sacrifice that God had decided upon as atonement for our sins. According to Løgstrup, the circumstance that the crucifixion thus brings about atonement and salvation is something that happens quite surprisingly, and upon Jesus' request during the hours of his crucifixion: 'If my life, as an example, could lead them to salvation by way of emulation, then let my crucifixion lead them to salvation by way of forgiveness. And God said "yes" – because his son asked this of him.' So we see that when Løgstrup finally deals with the significance of the crucifixion, he does so in a controversial and untraditional interpretation, according to which God's action and intervention in Jesus' death on the cross is not obtained until Jesus requests it. Furthermore, it is exceptional in Løgstrup's sermons to see the crucifixion and death of Jesus interpreted as the locus of salvation and atonement. In most other places, atonement is linked to the humanity of Jesus. Because Jesus entered into the fallen world, himself guilt-free, his life and humanity could become salvation for us: 'God magnified Jesus by allowing the co-assumption of guilt, into which he entered in his humanity, to apply to everyone who believes in his name' (Løgstrup 1995, 105).

Løgstrup's image of Jesus – a reduction

According to Løgstrup, the original and unfalsified image of Jesus seems to be the image of a human being who lived in a completely different way than we do. A human being who (by living fully and wholly in mercy and untroubledness) reveals God, the kingdom of God, and created life as it was intended for us, from the beginning, from the creator's hand. A human being who in every word and every deed proclaims mercy and forgiveness, and who is totally preoccupied with alleviating the need of his neighbour and living in interconnectedness with his fellow human beings. Jesus was God's son, but not God; he was not divine. In his parables and in his works of wonder there is no sign that he is a (demi)god. All we can see is that he lived a very different life than ours; we who live in complacency, hunger for power, self-invented morals – in sin. And it is only by wondering at his peculiar humanity that the thought can occur to us that he is God's son. He was crucified by the people of this world for living his own curious life, even though precisely this life, and possibly also his death, brought about salvation – forgiveness for the destruction of life and of God's creation – for those very same people. Whether he rose from the dead, and if so what meaning this would have, no one can say. We only know that Jesus was a very special person who once lived among us, long ago, and who by living the way he did revealed God as merciful and forgiving.

Løgstrup's reception and transformation of the image of Jesus in the gospels is, above all, a reduction. Løgstrup draws his image of Jesus by one-sidedly focusing on the part of the gospels that has to do with his life and works in Galilee, while disregarding both the stories of the background of Jesus and the story of Easter. By means of a method that he himself calls 'historical', Løgstrup has transformed the Jesus of the gospels into a one-sided figure whose life, words, and deeds in Galilee are all that matters. Concepts such as mission, selection, atonement, and triumphing over death by resurrection from the dead have nothing to do with Løgstrup's Jesus. And in Løgstrup's writing it cannot be hinted, either, that Jesus was chosen by God from the beginning, or that he was God incarnate, or Christ the anticipated Saviour, for Løgstrup focuses solely on Jesus the *human being* and on the particular life he lived. We can conclude, then, that Løgstrup has assimilated and received the gospel-based image of Jesus in his sermons and in his homiletic work *Prædikenen og dens tekst* in such a way that he drastically and selectively crops the evangelical accounts of Jesus. And therefore Løgstrup's image of Jesus can only be said to agree with the image in the gospels to a very limited extent.

Outlining an alternative to Løgstrup's approach: Ricoeur's biblical hermeneutic

Even in his own time, Løgstrup's homiletic method and his perception of Jesus were criticised from several sides. His methodology was characterised as naïve, and hence his Christology as poor, lacking the most important element: the resurrection. I cannot embark here upon this criticism, instead I shall use the remainder of this article to outline how, by means of Ricoeur's biblical hermeneutics – which is a modern alternative to Løgstrup's approach in particular, and to the historico-critical method in general – it is possible to read biblical texts and retain their normative nature. Based on this method I shall also consider an alternative to Løgstrup's image of Jesus.

The French philosopher Paul Ricoeur (1913-2005) was particularly fascinated by hermeneutics, of which biblical hermeneutics were a part. He, like Løgstrup, was interested in finding out how the Bible can be said to be 'normative' in the sense 'valid and true', and how biblical texts ought to be read. Like Løgstrup, he turned against an orthodox (scripturalist) reading of the Bible, which straightaway perceives every-thing in the Bible as authoritative and thereby refrains from posing critical questions. Furthermore, Ricoeur shares with Løgstrup an interest in reaching back to something 'original' in the texts, although as it will become clear in the following, when using this word Ricoeur means something quite different from Løgstrup (see Ricoeur 1979, 74f.). And so, although at the outset these two thinkers have quite a lot in common, their paths quickly diverge when it comes to the issue of methodology. As we have seen, the early Løgstrup is very keen on a version of the historical method that can be said to occupy a position midway between the historico-critical methodology and Bultmann's existential interpretation. At the time Løgstrup wrote *Prædikenen og dens tekst* and the sermons dealt with above, this approach, and the historico-critical methodology in general, were still a part of the new movement within Bible scholarship. Ricoeur, however, with his biblical hermeneutics, was more interested in how biblical texts can be read and perceived as normative, even when *disregarding* a historico-critical approach to the texts. Taking no interest in the potential historical veracity of the texts, Ricoeur attempted to propose how both the individual texts and the Bible in its entirety can be valid for us today.

Hermeneutics is a philosophical discipline. The reason Ricoeur finds it so important to apply this particular method when reading *biblical texts* is that they claim to enounce something that is true. In other words, the religious discourse professes to be norma-tive: '(…) philosophy is implied in this inquiry because this kind of discourse does not merely claim to be meaningful, but also to be true' (Ricoeur 1995, 35). It is clear, then, that this interest in investigating what is true in, or in relation to, biblical texts is some-thing Ricoeur and Løgstrup have in common. However, in Ricoeur's view, the special thing about biblical texts is that they are *poetic* texts. The truth one finds in such texts is different from the truth in the usual scientific, philosophical, or – as Løgstrup sees it – historical sense. The reason is that the statements presented in a poetic, and in this case religious, text can neither be verified nor falsified, in part because the statement is cut off from having an ostensive function in the context of the currently existing reality. So biblical texts do not necessarily refer to anything in the currently existing reality, or to any historical event. So how can they still profess to enounce something that is true; something that is valid for and applicable to people living today? Ricoeur tackles this question by examining the reference of the text, which precisely has to do with the issue of its normativity. Here, Ricoeur introduces the concept he calls 'the world of the text' (Ricoeur 1995, 41), employing the distinction that the mathematician and philosopher G.F.L. Frege makes between a text's immanent meaning (*Sinn*) and its reference to reality (*Bedeutung*):

The sense of the meaning is the ideal object that is intended. This meaning is purely immanent to discourse. The reference is *the truth value* of the proposition, its claim to reach reality (Ricoeur 1995, 42 – my emphasis).

It is in the reference of the text, then, that its *truth value* must be found. A special condition for the reference of the poetic text is that it is dual; it is a *split reference*. What the poetic text does is that it initially suspends the language's immediate reference to reality (*the first-order reference*), and then subsequently reinstates a new meaning on a figurative level (*the second-order reference*) (Ricoeur 1995, 42). What is characteristic of this other level, created by the religious text – *the world of the text* – is that it can open up new life opportunities for the human being. In Ricoeur's analysis, the text's immediate reference to reality takes a long route, beginning with the suspension of the first-order reference, then moving onto the establishment of the second-order reference and the world of the text, to which the concept of truth – the poetic truth – is linked. This poetic truth has the capacity that by speaking about the world of the text, it can re-describe reality and thereby be world-opening to the reader. And it is by virtue of this capacity that poetic texts – and hence biblical texts – can be regarded as having a normative quality. For in Ricoeur's view, this type of truth, this second-order reference, is more original and fundamental than the first-order reference, to which only a descriptive function can be ascribed. The latter solely has to do with 'the manipulable objects of our everyday environment' (Ricoeur 1995, 222), whereas the former refers to 'our many ways of belonging to the world before we oppose ourselves to things understood as "objects" that stand before a "subject"' (Ricoeur 1995, 222). If we accept this distinction that Ricoeur makes between a first and second-order reference, we can see that Løgstrup only has an eye for the first-order reference, which has to do with how extensively and in what way the texts have a direct connection with the currently existing reality, which, in Løgstrup's case, would be in a historico-descriptive sense.

According to Ricoeur, the second-order reference embodies an element of revelation. As a poetic text, it does so in a 'nonreligious, nontheistic, nonbiblical sense of the word' (Ricoeur 1995, 222), because it deals precisely with that dimension of the text that can re-describe reality for the reader, and thus has a world-opening effect. The text *reveals* this new world to the reader; a world that can describe, more fundamentally than anything else, what it means to be a human being belonging in the world. When we are dealing with biblical texts, however, 'revelation' also has an additional religious dimension. In that case, the new world that the text opens to us has a very particular designation: 'The proposed world that in biblical language is called a new creation, a new covenant, the Kingdom of God, is the "issue" of the biblical text unfolded in front of this text' (Ricoeur 1979, 103). Moreover, obviously, the special thing about biblical texts is that they have one reference in common: God. This reference is important to, and constituting for, both the Bible's immanent text universe and the second-order reference it has: the world of the text.

Something that is particularly important for the reference 'God' is the dimension that is added by Christ's death and resurrection. According to Ricoeur, the Bible cannot be read with a view to finding verification of statements such as 'God exists', or in a quest to go back and find a 'historically true' Jesus behind the early congregations' confessions that he, and he alone, was the resurrected Christ. For Ricoeur, the resurrection is the very essence of the Bible, and if anything it is the resurrection as a key concept that adds a new and decisive significance to the concept of 'God'. Ricoeur's starting point, and the entire basis of his talking about the biblical texts' presentation of God, is indeed the resurrection; whereas Løgstrup never reaches that point because his primary focus is reaching back to a historically verifiable core in the gospel accounts of Jesus. Furthermore, Ricoeur is acutely aware that biblical texts are, first and foremost, *statements of faith*. The gospel scriptures express the first Christian congregations' confession of their faith in the man known as Jesus of Nazareth being Christ, the resurrected Saviour, and as such the son of God. What Løgstrup attempts to do – to read 'behind' these statements of faith – is not possible, since it is not possible to eliminate the 'faith filter'. In other words, the historical Jesus cannot move to the foreground as an isolated figure through the reader's attempt to excise the resurrected Christ.

Normativity, reception and transformation – two different approaches

As previously described, it is possible to outline a Ricoeur-based image of Jesus, even though Ricoeur himself never took up this precise topic as the main focus of his hermeneutic reflections on biblical texts. The following presentation must therefore be seen only as an indication of the sort of Jesus image that appears when one takes an approach to biblical texts that is 'hermeneutic' in the Ricoeur-inspired sense outlined above.

The resurrection is Ricoeur's initial point of view when he talks about Jesus and his significance. The resurrection not only adds to the Jesus figure a new and decisive meaning, but also generally adds a completely new dimension to the concept of God. It is therefore not possible in Ricoeur's understanding to clearly distinguish between talking about God and talking about the resurrected Christ, who, in turn, cannot be separated from talking about Jesus of Nazareth. Whereas Løgstrup concentrates on interpreting the significance of the life, words and deeds of Jesus, Ricoeur is concerned with interpreting the significance of the resurrection, which he refers to as 'the heart of the Christian kerygma' (Ricoeur 1979, 158). With Ricoeur, the key to a hermeneutically motivated reception and transformation of the image of Jesus in the gospel lies in the interpretation of the resurrection. And the key concepts that must be linked to an understanding of the resurrection are freedom and hope.[2] The resurrection must firstly be seen in association with the Old Testament concept of 'promise'. It is not sufficient, however, to say that the resurrection has exhausted the category of 'promise' by fulfilling it. According to Ricoeur, 'the meaning of the Resurrection is in its future' (Ricoeur 1979, 159), and rather than focusing on the 'already' meaning of the resurrection, Ricoeur is interested in unravelling its meaning of 'not yet'. This is where hope comes into the picture. The resurrection of Jesus Christ makes it possible

---

2   Here Ricoeur establishes an explicit link to Moltmann 1965 (see Ricoeur 1979, 155-182).

for people to step inside the category of hope; the hope of resurrection from the dead. This is a new 'creation *ex nihilo*' (Ricoeur 1979, 159), which in the hermeneutic reading of the biblical text as a poetic text reflects light back onto the world that the text opens to its reader by means of its second-order reference. It is precisely in the category of hope that the biblical text can re-describe reality. And out of hope springs *freedom*: 'What is freedom *in the light of* hope? I will answer in one word: it is the meaning of my existence in the light of the Resurrection' (Ricoeur 1979, 159). Thus, the resurrection of Christ can add hope and freedom to human existence, and it is in extension of this that the gospel accounts about Jesus of Nazareth must be read. Ricoeur's image of Jesus is therefore quite fundamentally defined by the accounts of the resurrection, which reflect light back onto the other texts about Jesus. Ricoeur can justify this reading by being aware, from the very outset, that everything written in the Bible – not least the accounts in the gospels – are statements of faith. The elements of historically true accounts and the elements of faith statements from the earliest congregations are impossible to distinguish from one another. That is why the resurrection is an absolutely decisive and fundamental concept in the gospels – and therefore also for the image of Jesus. A Ricoeurian image of Jesus therefore has the resurrection as its precondition, its starting point and its ultimate goal, which is why, for Ricoeur, a representation of Jesus that completely disregards the resurrection is not even remotely possible.

Compared to Løgstrup's approach to biblical texts, Ricoeur's method can, above all, be said to be broad and opening. He looks for diversity in the way the texts speak of God, while Løgstrup's main concern is finding the unity in the message of Jesus, which he believes constitutes the core in his original intention. Løgstrup cuts and crops, whereas Ricoeur includes everything. Moreover, Løgstrup actually cuts and crops using a method that must ultimately be considered dubious in terms of its historical quality, and therefore also in terms of its objectivity. One must, instead, consider Løgstrup's method as a thoroughly subjective proposal for the norm one can establish in reading the texts of the gospels. Løgstrup entirely links historicity to the so-called 'original intention' in the message of Jesus, namely mercy. It is this concept – rather than any genuine interest in what can, quite factually, be held as historically true in the gospel accounts of Jesus – that is the litmus test for Løgstrup's quest for the original message in the proclamation of Jesus, and for the truth about him as a person. It is therefore extremely difficult to characterise his method as 'historical', and due to the method's distinctly subjective nature it would be difficult, if not impossible, for anyone other than Løgstrup himself to use it. In the light of this Løgstrup's methodological approach, and therefore also his image of Jesus, must ultimately be rejected as an untenable proposal for a normative reception of the gospel-based image of Jesus: His reading of the texts can simply not be claimed as valid and applicable for anyone apart from himself, because 'mercy', used as the guiding principle in reading the texts, is a concept that is difficult to define unambiguously. It cannot serve as a generally applicable methodological starting point. And the result of Løgstrup's subjective and narrow approach is that his image of Jesus is drastically reduced compared to the image of Jesus given in the gospels.

In contrast to this, Ricoeur's Jesus is, essentially, the resurrected Christ. The importance of the resurrection lies first of all in how it reflects the light of new interpretation back onto the other accounts of Jesus in the gospels, and secondly how it opens a new world for the reader, a world characterised by the concepts 'hope' and 'freedom'; an opening that is enabled by a hermeneutically motivated approach to biblical texts as poetic. A Ricoeurian image of Jesus is therefore not a reduction of the evangelical image in the gospels. It is, rather, a very particular interpretation of Jesus that is, to a very great extent, contained in the gospels themselves, namely the interpretation of Jesus of Nazareth as the resurrected Lord and Saviour; as Christ. It is certainly fair to say that this image of Jesus is in greater accordance with the gospels' image of Jesus than Løgstrup's is, and thus Ricoeur's reception and transformation of Jesus is quite a credible proposal for how the accounts of the gospels, and their proclamation of Jesus as Christ, can be claimed to have a normative (in the sense 'valid') meaning for us today. By means of his method, Ricoeur enables himself to carry out a normative reading of biblical texts; a reading that is not narrow and subjective, but which makes it possible for other readers to take over his method. Ricoeur's method is, in short, generally applicable.

The overall conclusion is that having two different perceptions of the concept of 'normativity' and applying this concept to the Bible will lead to two very different receptions and transformations of the gospels' image of Jesus. As this investigation shows, it is reasonable and valid to emphasise Ricoeur's biblical hermeneutics and propose it as a highly qualified basis on which to carry out a modern normative reading of the Bible, and also to suggest Ricoeur's image of Jesus as a tenable new interpretation of the Jesus image of the gospels – whereas the same cannot be said of Løgstrup's self-styled 'historical method' and the drastically reduced image of Jesus in which it results.[3]

Bibliography

Bultmann, Rudolf 1926. *Jesus*. Berlin: Deutsche Bibliothek.

Løgstrup, Knud Ejler 1995. *Prædikener fra Sandager-Holevad*. Elsebeth Diderichsen and Ole Jensen (eds.). Copenhagen: Gyldendal.

Løgstrup, Knud Ejler 1995a. *Metaphysics*, 2 vols. Milwaukee, WI: Marquette University Press.

Løgstrup, Knud Ejler 1997 [1956]. *The Ethical Demand*. Notre Dame: University of Notre Dame Press.

Løgstrup, Knud Ejler 1999. *Prædikenen og dens tekst*. Niels Henrik Gregersen & Jan Nilsson (eds.). Copenhagen: Gyldendal.

---

3   Løgstrup's view of the Jesus figure changes and evolves throughout his writings. Resurrection, for instance, comes to play a decisive role in his later works. In that connection, Løgstrup emphasises *hope*, which brings his view of the resurrection and its significance closer to Ricoeur's (see Løgstrup 1995a, vol. 1).

Løgstrup, Knud Ejler. *Unpublished sermons.* The Løgstrup Archive, Faculty of Theology, Aarhus University.

Moltmann, Jürgen 1965. *Theologie der Hoffnung.* Munich: Chr. Kaiser.

Ricoeur, Paul 1979. *Essays on Biblical Interpretation* (ed. Lewis S. Mudge). Philadelphia, PA: Fortress Press.

Ricoeur, Paul 1995. *Figuring the Sacred – Religion, Narrative, and Imagination.* Minneapolis, MN: Fortress Press.

ANSWERING JOB'S CHALLENGE
RECEPTION AND TRANSFORMATION
IN EVOLUTIONARY THEORY

Marie Vejrup Nielsen

Biblical texts are utilised and referenced in a multitude of ways in our culture today. The references appear in various forms ranging from direct references to a character or quote from the Bible to the more indirect use of intertextual references or allusions through symbols and artefacts, such as the Apple logo (an apple with a bite taken out of it).

This article will examine one specific and perhaps unexpected framework for contemporary biblical reception and transformation, namely books about evolutionary biology written for a general public by evolutionary scientists. Through my reading of works about evolutionary biology I have been struck by the involvement with literature, biblical as well as other genres. The many references to and the use of narratives motivated me to take a close look at those evolutionary scientists who draw upon biblical texts in their work. This article is primarily the result of my studies on the work of evolutionary biologists E.O. Wilson and Richard Dawkins. They have been prominent in the discussions about evolutionary theory in the 20th century, and continue to be so today. Together they introduced the discipline of socio-biology in the 1970s and 1980s with the aim of spreading the scope of evolutionary theory to social behaviour in humans and other animals.

Dawkins has contributed to public awareness of evolutionary theory significantly through a long list of best sellers, many of which have caused controversy both inside and outside academic circles.[1]

This article does not claim that evolutionary biologists draw on biblical texts in general, but instead it offers a specific study of the occurrence of biblical references in the publications of two evolutionary biologists deeply engaged in communicating their insights to the general public. The article is a presentation and discussion of how and why these specific scientists include biblical material in their books. A study of this particular dimension of the reception and transformation of biblical texts in contemporary culture offers insights into aspects of current biblical normativity which have not received much attention prior to this publication.

The presentation will include three themes related to the examination of the reception and transformation of biblical material. First, it is necessary briefly to discuss the context of cultural conflict between evolutionary theory and conservative Christian

---

1   Dawkins 1986, Dawkins 1989 [1976], Dawkins 1995, Dawkins 2000, Dawkins 2004, Dawkins 2006, Dawkins, Shanks 2004, Wilson 1998, Wilson 2000 [1975], Wilson 2002, Wilson 2004 [1978], Wilson, Caplan & et al. 1978.

groups as the historical background for the recent work by Richard Dawkins in particular. Second, the general phenomena of intertextuality will serve as a background for comparison with the reception of biblical material in order to see if there are special features to be considered in relation to this reception. To do so, I shall discuss the use of narrative language of agents and plots within science to introduce my thesis that narrative language serves as an aid in the communication of difficult scientific insights to a general public. As part of the examination of the reception of biblical material, a third theme will be presented: Wilson's involvement in what might be called a 'narrative challenge' to traditional religion in the light of the recognition of the power of narratives to transform people's lives. Finally, the article will use the work of Stephen Prickett to examine Dawkins' and Wilson's attitudes towards narratives.

Biblical reception

When one reads the books of Richard Dawkins and E.O. Wilson, it is striking how many references are made to biblical texts. This is even more striking when one considers the brutal conflict they are involved in with Christianity specifically and religion in general. This conflict influences the way in which these evolutionary biologists receive and transform biblical narratives.

A context of conflict

Christian theology and the Darwinian theory of evolution have been in contact from the onset of Darwin's thoughts. The interpretation of the nature of this contact, whether it was one of conflict or a more complex co-existence with a variety of responses, informs the discussions among historians of science and current reflections on the conflict that have recently surfaced between conservative Christian groups and evolutionary biologists, such as the conflicts Richard Dawkins has been involved with against school boards wishing to include creationism or Intelligent Design in science curricula. Many of the recent conflicts concern the issue of school curricula, and a succession of court cases have ruled on whether other ideas about the creation of life should be taught alongside evolutionary theory. These court cases started with the infamous 'Scopes Monkey Trial'[2] in 1925, involving a teacher who had taught evolutionary theory, and they continue today. There have been some spectacular victories for the conservative Christians as well as defeats, and the battle continues. At first the conflict took place between creationists and evolutionary biologists, but in recent years attacks on evolutionary theory have been launched by members of the Intelligent Design movement (ID). The main difference between these two types of criticism of evolutionary theory

---

2   For further reading on the subject of the Scopes trial and its complicated history, Edvard J. Larson's book is recommended (Larson 1997). Other works that address the issue of the reception of Darwin's ideas and the controversy they caused are (Dennett 1995, Richards 1987).

is that traditional creationism sets the biblical creation story against evolutionary theory and sees The Book of Genesis as a literal description of the creation of life; whereas ID claims to represent an alternative scientific perspective, arguing for some kind of purposeful intelligent designer behind the processes of life. This is primarily done by stressing alleged flaws in current evolutionary science. ID proponents often wish to emphasise the difference between traditional creationism and ID, for instance by refusing to identify intelligent design with any specific creator god. Still, they are perceived as religiously motivated opponents of evolutionary theory and deemed unscientific by many.[3] This conflict is situated within a larger cultural conflict in the USA between a conservative, Christian wing and a liberal wing, often represented by people very critical of religion.[4] Many features of the current conflict originate in this North American context, but the attack on evolutionary theory has spread from the USA and from Christian circles into Islamic communities for instance, cf. the resolution issued by the Council of Europe on 'The dangers of creationism in education' (Resolution 1580, October 2007).[5] This resolution emphasises the importance of keeping creationist views out of science curricula in Europe. Richard Dawkins has been heavily involved in the conflict in the USA, which has shaped his increasingly fierce attacks on all kinds of religion, as well as his support of a new term for the non-religious. He suggests replacing the term 'atheist' or 'non-religious', which have a negative ring to them, with 'bright', which connotes the enlightenment and thoughts on how reason should expel religion.

Evolutionary biology and the involvement with literature and narratives

Before moving to a presentation of the reception of biblical texts, another theme will be addressed: The inspiration from literature as well as a general inspiration from narratives. Recent works by Wilson and Dawkins show an abundance of references to novels, short stories, poems and ancient myths, all of which make the books easy and enjoyable to read and facilitate the dissemination of difficult scientific insights to those outside scientific circles. The best example of this use of narrative is Dawkins' book *The Ancestor's Tale – a Pilgrimage to the Dawn of Evolution* (Dawkins 2004). The whole structure of this book is inspired by Chaucer's *Canterbury Tales*, in which a group of pilgrims share stories. In Dawkins' book the reader is taken on a pilgrimage into the past, and through a series of stops at the junctions of evolution, more and more pilgrims join the pilgrimage, all the way back to the beginning of life. The pilgrims are joined by all other life forms from higher primates to bacteria, all of which have a story to tell us about life. The book is full of narrators, and the author only plays the role of host to these narrating voices. This feature of references to literature can be found in E.O.

---

3   For more information on the Intelligent Design movement and presentations of the arguments from both inside and outside their own circles, see Dawkins & Shanks 2004, Dembski 1999, and Dembski, Behe & Meyer 2000. For a Danish perspective on the issue see Hammersholt Christensen & Harnow Klausen 2007.
4   Dawkins 2006, Harris 2005, Harris 2006.
5   See http://assembly.coe.int/Main.asp?link=/Documents/AdoptedText/ta07/ERES1580.htm.

Wilson's recent work, where he quotes poets such as Yeats, Joyce, and Sappho (Wilson 2004 [1978], 3, 69, 200). Both scientists are very good at establishing a connection between science and contemporary culture in a variety of ways. And it might be plausible to think that their reception and transformation of biblical texts would resemble their general, well-educated use of poets and novelists en masse. However, we shall see how the use of 'Eve' within evolutionary biology as well as the direct confrontation of biblical texts such as the Book of Job indicates that other issues are at stake in their reception and transformation of biblical texts and characters.[6]

The narrative language used by Wilson and Dawkins is yet another issue which is important in relation to the general scope of evolutionary biology and narratives. Dawkins in particular has found himself at the centre of attention due to the language he chose to describe evolutionary theory in his first bestseller; *The Selfish Gene* (Dawkins 1989 [1976]). In this book the genes seem to come alive. They have intentions and ambitions of their own, they roam around as main agents in the book, and even take on the role as our creators as can be seen in a famous paragraph from the book: 'The argument of this book is that we, and all other animals, are machines created by our genes' (Dawkins 1989 [1976], 2).

By coining the term 'selfish gene', Dawkins struck gold in labelling the scientific content he wanted to present and in appealing to the general public. Nevertheless, he also laid the foundation for a debate that primarily dealt with the question of how popular science writers use metaphors. The philosopher Mary Midgley criticised Dawkins for what she considers an unwarranted, ideological use of science (Midgley 1979, 1983, 1992, 2002). His choice of language has set him on a never-ending task on explaining what he meant by 'selfish'. Dawkins comments on this in his endnotes from 1989, calling such criticisms 'over-literal misunderstandings' (Dawkins 1989 [1976], 268), and he claims his right to use what he calls 'sloppy language' that might confuse or irritate some, but helps translate difficult scientific information. Dawkins proposes the possibility of translating back and forth between the 'real' scientific level and more 'sloppy' language. However, what he does not address is the fact that there is nothing 'sloppy' about his language. It is in fact narrative language, which gives us a clue as to why it is so tempting to use it even though it causes problems.

This is precisely the feature of Dawkins' work that H.P. Abbott addresses in the article 'Unnarratable Knowledge: The Difficulty of Understanding Evolution by Natural Selection' (Abbott 2003). Here Abbott discusses the issue of the narratability of the theory of evolution by natural selection. He points to how vital and central narratives are to human understanding, and even goes so far as to speculate on how phenomena that are not narratable may simply not be understandable (Abbott 2003, 143). And evolution by natural selection is precisely this kind of non-narrative information because it entails neither agents nor plot, so it is also difficult to grasp for most people. The

---

6   Gillian Beer has examined the relation between literature and Darwin's work, and offers an analysis of Darwin's works as literature (Beer 1996, Beer 2000).

challenge for evolutionary theory is the wide barrier caused by the lack of narratability between the knowledge that evolutionary scientists have about biological life and the knowledge of the general public.[7]

But there is a way out of this problem: the transformation of the non-narrative into narrative by adding what is missing, namely agents and plot. And this is exactly what Dawkins does through his 'sloppy' language:

Be warned that if you wish, as I do, to build a society in which individuals cooperate generously and unselfishly towards a common good, you can expect little help from biological nature. Let us try to *teach* generosity and altruism, because we are born selfish. Let us understand what our self-ish genes are up to, because we may then at least have a chance to upset their designs, something that no other species has aspired to (Dawkins 1989 [1976], 3).

We have the power to defy the selfish genes of our birth and, if necessary, the selfish memes of our indoctrination. We can even discuss ways of deliberately cultivating and nurturing pure, dis-interested altruism – something which has no place in nature, something that has never existed before in the whole history of the world. We are built as gene machines and cultured as meme machines, but we have the power to turn against our creators. We, alone on earth, can rebel against the tyranny of the selfish replicators (Dawkins 1989 [1976], 200-201).

Suddenly we have a story with agents, selfish genes and the 'we' of humanity, and with an amazing plot in which humanity is able to rebel against evil creators and attain a better world. It is a story complete with heroes and villains, antagonists and protago-nists. We find a similar narrative imagination in the work of E.O. Wilson, where the theories of evolution are transformed by narrative language and structures into a story of how humanity has caused the breakdown of the eco system. However, it may be able to save the planet through its special abilities. Here, humanity is faced with the choice of being the villain or the hero of the story (Wilson 2002).[8]

Abbott examines this narrative involvement in relation to the conflict between Christian fundamentalists and evolutionary biology. He points to how the religious narrative has a cognitive advantage over the scientific material, simply by being a nar-rative, thereby making it easier to convey the message within (Abbott 2003, 153). We shall see in the following that Wilson is acutely aware of this cognitive advantage of religion, and that he tries to remedy the lack of convincing narratives in evolution-

---

7   Abbott seems to stress that the move to narrative is illegitimate as a narration of what is in itself unnarratable. David Herman discusses this issue in his article in the same book. Herman points out that all narratives are constructions based on the unnarratable (Herman 2003, 170). The unnarratability of natural phenomena does not in itself block the human tendency or ability to construct narratives. Hayden White's theories on tropology in historiography also relate to the issue of the narratability of the non-narrative (White 2000).

8   In the work of evolutionary scientist Lynn Margulis we find yet another narrative of humanity within a scientific theory, where we meet another hero, namely Gaia, the biosphere. I have explored these examples of narrative involvement by scientists in relation to Christian narratives of human nature in the dissertation *Being Human – Crisis and Solution in Grand Narratives of Humanity – The Doctrine of Sin in Dialogue with Evolutionary Biology.* Forthcoming in Studies in Philosophical Theory, Peeters, Leuven.

ary theory. Abbott sees narrative language as a tool to enable better understanding of scientific theories, but a close look at the use of biblical texts will reveal that more is at stake than this educational purpose. Dawkins and Wilson are locked in an ideological battle in which narratives play a central role.

Creation received and transformed

The reception and transformation of biblical material within evolutionary biology can be divided into two groups: the antagonistic use, with biblical texts being pitted directly against evolutionary biology and evolutionary biology being used to correct or even make the biblical text redundant; and a more neutral use, with biblical texts being referred to as part of the general cultural context of the scientists without any intention of wanting to criticise religion.[9] The following paragraph will examine examples of both neutral and antagonistic reception of biblical texts with an emphasis on the antagonistic use within the work of Dawkins and Wilson.

In relation to the conflict surrounding evolutionary theory, it is particularly interesting to look at the reception and transformation of the creation stories of Genesis as well as other biblical texts addressing creation. It is the theme of creation in general, and the creation of humankind specifically, which has been at the centre of many conflicts between evolutionary theory and other conceptions of humanity. The portrayal of human nature presented by evolutionary biology and socio-biology is not only at the core of conflicts between evolutionary biology and creationism and ID, but was also debated in the initial conflicts between evolutionary biology and social sciences and humanities. This debate raised issues about free will and ethics, and caused accusations of male chauvinism and racism (for instance) within evolutionary biology and its conception of human beings (Lewontin, Rose & Kamin 1984).

Adam and Eve transformed

However, there is one example of a neutral use of biblical material which points to some problems concerning the reception of biblical texts in this field. Within evolutionary theory 'Mitochondrial Eve' has become a standard expression for the most recent common female ancestor.[10] It is possible, through evolutionary science, to trace a line back to our most recent common female ancestor because mitochondria

---

9   This use of such a distinction in relation to a general reception and transformation of biblical texts was brought to my attention by Professor Bent Flemming Nielsen, University of Copenhagen, in relation to a joint lecture on non-biblical stories of Jesus throughout history. For a presentation of a scale of reception and transformation spanning from retelling of the Bible via further writing and rewriting to counter writing, see David Bugge's General Reflections in this volume.

10   Mitochondria perform the function of transforming organic materials into energy that fuels the cell. Mitochondria were originally independent bacteria that joined in the making of the cells, and therefore have their own DNA. This makes it possible to track the genetic ancestry of mitochondria separately from the DNA of an individual. See article by A.C. Wilson, R.L. Cann, S.M. Carr, M. George Jr., U.B. Gyllensten, K. Helm- Bychowski, R.G. Higuchi, S.R. Palumbi, E.M. Prager, R.D. Sage, and M. Stoneking 1985, 375-400.

are only passed on through the maternal lineage. By following this particular trail we find 'Mitochondrial Eve' in evolutionary theory. Similarly, it is possible to track the so-called 'Y-chromosome Adam' along the line of the hereditary line Y-chromosomes. By choosing names connected to the first human couple as they are presented in Genesis, evolutionary biologists faced a series of problems connected to the use of language and metaphors in general and the use of biblical material specifically.

This is evident in Richard Dawkins' book *The Ancestor's Tale*, in which Dawkins sets up a whole series of disclaimers around the use of 'Eve' and 'Adam' in evolutionary theory, including these words added within parentheses: '(creationists please refrain from deliberate misquotation)' (Dawkins 2004, 54). This comment is followed by a list of associations to avoid when we read the names. First, he points out that there are many other ways of finding a most recent common ancestor in the genetic sense, all of which would lead us to different points in time on the evolutionary scale. 'Eve' is found by travelling only from mother to mother, and 'Adam' by travelling from father to father, but we might choose any number of ways to combine these and find other important most recent common ancestors. Second, he wants to emphasise that the evolutionary Adam and Eve were not a couple. They probably lived very far apart in time. And third, he says, these names are not of specific individuals, but are titles that can be reallocated because it is the current common gene pool that is our starting point for finding the most recent ancestors, and if some elements of this gene pool die out the title of most recent common ancestor will change position as well.

These reservations remove the well-known features belonging to the Adam and Eve of Genesis 2. They are no longer a couple, they are not the source of common off-spring to populate the earth, and they are not specific human individuals.[11] Instead, they are something completely different: honorary titles given to a specific phenomenon of evolutionary biology based on modern genetics and the tracing of DNA. They are a part of the scientific lingo. But this begs the question: why add this layer of confusion to the theory, especially a layer connected to the Judeo-Christian creation story which has traditionally been used in opposition to evolutionary theory? Why not simply avoid the use of 'Eve' and 'Adam' if a series of disclaimers are required before this terminology is released for use by the general public?

There are no simple answers to this, but it is possible to outline some features of this more neutral use of biblical material and its subsequent dilemmas. First of all, one of the reasons for using the terminology is of course to facilitate quick understanding of what we are talking about. This applies primarily to the internal use of such termi-nology among scientists. They know the scientific content of the terms in question, and may therefore experience fewer problems than Dawkins because he is addressing the general public and cannot rely on science to correct the many 'wrong' associations

---

11   This could lead us into a discussion of the function of the creation myths of Genesis, for example the issue of whether Adam and Eve are individuals or just titles/descriptions of a function such as 'first female' etc. The aim here is to emphasise how the features of the narrative characters 'Adam' and 'Eve' lose all their characteristics within the original narrative framework as well as the features associated with the use of these characters.

he lists. The fact that it is helpful to use the terminology of 'Eve' and 'Adam' points to the cultural context of the development of evolutionary biology: a Western, Christian culture, in which any talk of common ancestors quickly leads to associations to the biblical story of the creation of humankind.

The normativity of the characters from the creation story seems not to have been lost through the general secularisation of the West. As a culturally important text, the creation story still functions as a point of reference. Most people within a Western context immediately understand that 'Adam' and 'Eve' have something to do with our origins, even if they do not think of themselves as particularly Christian. It is this common ground to which evolutionary biologists wish to connect in order to facilitate their communication. However, some problems obviously occur when scientists take these names out of their original context and give them a new meaning. The name 'Eve' calls upon the many layers of meaning connected to the narratives of Genesis 2-3 as well as the meanings set within the context of each recipient. The associations these names evoke are not easy to control, and Dawkins realises this to some extent as can be seen through his attempt at damage control. The use of 'Adam' and 'Eve' in evolutionary biology and the problems it has caused can be compared to the use of other characters not affiliated with religion but still belonging to the common cultural context. In evolutionary biology, the term 'tin man genes' is used to signify genes responsible for instructing the cells to make hearts in both drosophila and mice (Dawkins 2004, 423). The name is taken from the character of the Tin Man in the story of *The Wizard of Oz*, who was in search of a heart, thereby making a meaningful reference at least to an US audience, since this particular narrative has a special place in North American culture. This use of the Tin Man has not caused the same discussions as the use of 'Adam' or 'Eve', although there are as many points at which it would be wrong to infer from our knowledge of the story of the Tin Man to our understanding of what is meant by the tin man gene. Apparently, the use of the biblical narrative and its normative status cause more difficulty than other cultural texts, even when the use of biblical material is neutral. This is of course not surprising considering the conflict situation between evolutionary science and conservative Christian groups, a context which becomes even more apparent once we look at the direct confrontational use of biblical texts within evolutionary biology.

Genesis confronted

When we look at the more antagonistic uses of biblical texts and references, set within an open conflict between Christian groups and evolutionary biologists, we find a variety of uses of the biblical material on creation. First of all, there is the title of one of Dawkins' early books, *River out of Eden*, from a time when Dawkins has clearly not yet turned so aggressively towards religion, but still offers a transformation of the text reference (Dawkins 1995). The rivers running out of Eden in Genesis 2:10 are transformed into images for the genetic development of life as rivers of genes flowing through time and individuals. This imagery offers a reception and transformation of biblical material which points to how Dawkins sees the evolutionary description of the development of life as one which has made any Christian description of the development of life redundant. The rivers out of Eden are now rivers of DNA flowing through all life. In a quiet take-over, biblical material is adopted and transformed into a purely scientific understanding of life which still draws on the language and imagery as common points of reference.

When we look at one of E.O. Wilson's early texts, we find a direct confrontation between evolutionary biology and Genesis, not as a battle between the creation story and science, but surprisingly as a battle between narratives. In 1978 Wilson launched a narrative challenge to traditional religion. Science, and evolutionary science in particular, is able to replace traditional religion as the basis for our understanding of ourselves as well as a basis for moral guidance:

It [scientific materialism] presents the human mind with an alternative mythology that until now has always, point for point in zones of conflict, defeated traditional religion. Its narrative form is the epic: the evolution of the universe from the big bang of fifteen billion years ago through the origin of the elements and celestial bodies to the beginnings of life on earth. The evolutionary epic is mythology in the sense that the laws it adduces here and now are believed but can never be definitely proved to form a cause-and-effect continuum from physics to the social sciences, from this world to all other worlds in the visible universe, and backward through time to the beginning of the universe (Wilson 2004 [1978], 192).

Evolutionary science can offer an epic to replace the flawed myths of religion. Even if the epic of evolution might not be provable in every detail, it is still based on scientific fact to a much larger extent than any other epic of creation. So it offers a more accurate understanding of human nature and a better point of departure for guidelines as to how we should live our lives. For Wilson, traditional religion is the chief rival of scientific naturalism, and the latter is pronounced the winner of the battle. Religion is defeated by evolutionary biology both in the negative (by removing the content and power of religion) and in the positive (by offering a new myth). The goal of science, according to Wilson, is not only to destroy other mythological world views, but to produce its own.

Wilson mentions that this new epic is disadvantaged compared to traditional religion because it cannot base itself on some divine authority. Yet it has the strength of honesty based on its scientific background, a new and (in Wilson's view) truer authority. The power understood as the ability to tell stories for people to live by can now be utilised by evolutionary biology. This is similar to what Abbott clearly saw in Dawkins' use of narrative: those who can tell stories have an advantage. Wilson realises and responds accordingly. If science is not in itself able to tell stories, it must transform its language in order to do so. It must become narrative, otherwise religion will win.

This challenge is the subject of the last chapter of the book, with the telling title: 'Hope' (Wilson 2004 [1978], 195-209). Wilson diagnoses the situation of his contemporaries and states that we face a problem: all other myths have failed, but at the same time we need the power of these narratives to live by because otherwise we will see 'a loss of moral consensus, a greater sense of helplessness about the human condition and a shrinking of the concern back toward the self and the immediate future' (Wilson 2004 [1978], 196). Without these grand narratives, the epics of creation, we have no basis for long-term vision, which we need in order to solve the problems of humankind. Scientific explanations do not suffice, because they leave us without the necessary guidelines for life.

Wilson predicts that a biology of ethics will emerge from socio-biology, and that this will enable us to choose a better understanding and therefore more stable moral code based on evolutionary science (Wilson 2004 [1978], 196). Although initially evolutionary biology seemed to have robbed humanity of all its foundations for ethics, humanity has actually gained a new and sound foundation. We can learn who we are as humans by looking at our evolutionary past, where we find that natural selection has favoured 'selfishness and tribalism' (Wilson 2004 [1978], 197); but at the same time, when we view evolution from the long-ranging perspective, we can 'envision the history and future of our own genes' against a background of the entire human species. According to Wilson, we can achieve an honest view of our past and use this in order to transform society. After presenting this view of the new foundation for ethics, Wilson returns to his interest in narratives, now in relation to what he calls our 'mythopoeic drive'. This drive is part of our human nature, a propensity for narratives and linked to the power which narratives have over us. This mythopoeic drive can be 'harnessed to learning and the rational search for human progress if we finally concede that scientific materialism is itself a mythology in the noble sense' (Wilson 2004 [1978], 201). This is not just any narrative:

The evolutionary epic is probably the best myth we will ever have. It can be adjusted until it comes as close to truth as the human mind is constructed to judge the truth. And if that is the case, the mythopoeic requirements of the mind must somehow be met by scientific materialism so as to reinvest our superb energies (Wilson 2004 [1978], 201).

Wilson quotes J.B.S. Haldane: the new epic is 'far more awesome than the first chapter of Genesis or the Ninevite epic of Gilgamesh' (Wilson 2004 [1978], 202). The first chapter of Genesis has fallen, mainly because science has proved it wrong, and religion has fallen because science is now able to explain it through evolutionary theories. Still, humanity will not have to live without the great stories of Genesis or the epic of Gilgamesh.

This challenge to traditional religion has many interesting aspects, but in this article the main point to notice is that Wilson attempts to adopt what he sees as the main function and form of the creation story of Genesis: that the Genesis account functions as a framework of meaning, and that it has the form of an 'epic'. Wilson seems to place the Genesis story on the same level as the scientific description to some extent: they are both explanations of the world; but whereas the scientific description is true, the religious description is not.[12] At the same time, he accepts the function of the myth as something more than a description. It is a myth, a source of meaning and thereby the source of ethics and values for human life. He wishes to use science to replace both of these elements, thereby crossing the commonly recognised boundary between the scientific and the narrative set up by many researchers within narrative research.[13]

This becomes the model for Wilson's ambitious work, which is aimed not at the creation of a new religion based on science, but instead at the creation of a new epic which can facilitate a takeover of the positive function of religious narratives. In other words, making a foundation for ethics which functions the same way religion does but without having to deal with the problems of the religious narratives (i.e. their wrong descriptions of the world). In his reception of Genesis, Wilson has chosen an understanding which seems to match an understanding found among fundamentalist Christians: that the story of Genesis is a description of creation itself, and that it has the form of an epic, a grand myth which people can live by. Because he sees the Genesis account of creation in the same way as the fundamentalists do, the epic can fall due to new and better descriptions and its function as an epic can be copied and infused with a much better content based on evolutionary science. Wilson accepts the authority of these texts and thereby contributes a negative recognition of their normativity. Wilson does not express any understanding of developments in the studies of biblical texts within various disciplines, and nor does he discuss theories of myth in general. He counterpoises what he sees as the religious view of these texts with what he proposes as the true alternative in a conflict scenario, where only one can be left standing because they are competitors for the same territory.

When we move on to another text which addresses the issue of humanity in relation to its creator and the rest of creation, we will see the sincerity of Wilson's project expressed even more clearly.

Empowered Job

Wilson presents us with a reception and transformation of the book of Job. He offers a new framework for this story in which we no longer have to stand like Job, who was awestruck because God had challenged him to explain the inexplicable: God's creation. In the Book of Job, Job asks God for an answer in the midst of all the suffering and receives a response which Wilson describes in the following way: 'Recall how God lashed Job with concepts meant to overwhelm the human mind' (Wilson 2004 [1978], 202). Wilson continues to quote from the Bible at length, ending with God's words 'Have you comprehended the vast expanse of the world? Come, tell me all this, if you know' (ibid.) (Job 38:4).

---

12   Wilson does not address the fact that Genesis offers more than just one creation story.
13   See for example Barbour 1990, Bruner 2002.

These final words, intended to emphasise the relation between humanity and its creator (how can human beings ever understand the vastness of creation?), are chosen by Wilson because in his view this is precisely where the change has occurred. In Wilson's view we can now answer the challenge to 'come and tell', because evolutionary biology has given humanity a comprehension of life: 'Jehovah's challenges have been met and scientists have pressed on to uncover and to solve even greater puzzles' (ibid.). It might be that God's words silenced Job, but now we can answer.

Dawkins expresses a similar view of how the world has changed after this discovery, and in this description we find the hero of this change standing out clearly:

Living organisms had existed on earth for over three thousand million years before the truth finally dawned on one of them. His name was Charles Darwin. To be fair, others had had inklings of the truth, but it was Darwin who first put together a coherent and tenable account of why we exist. Darwin made it possible to answer the curious child whose question heads this chapter [Why are people?]. We no longer have to resort to superstition when faced with the deep problems: is there a meaning to life? What are we for? What is man? (Dawkins 1989 [1976], 1).

This scientific discovery has brought on a fundamental change in the understanding of life, and it has made the traditional religious narratives superfluous as descriptions of life and obsolete as myths, as stories which offer a meaningful framework for human existence. To Wilson there is a direct link between the truth value of the statements and their usage as guidelines for life. Humanity no longer has to accept some divine authority as its creator. Through science it can gain knowledge of how life works. The answer to the deep questions does not belong to religion or philosophy – it lies within evolutionary theory.

In his challenge to religion, Wilson displays a keen awareness of what Abbott called the cognitive advantage of religion through narratives, and he aims to meet the challenge by making the unnarratable narratable. Dawkins does not go into this meta-discussion of creating an alternative myth based on science, but his work is overflowing with narrative features, fulfilling the task that Wilson set out.

Conclusion

This article set out to explore some of the themes and issues related to the reception and transformation of biblical material in selected books on science. The use of biblical material has been outlined through examples of both a neutral and a directly confrontational use of these texts. Both of these categories occur in the work of Dawkins and Wilson within a framework in which the involvement with literature as well as with the telling of stories has become apparent.

The presentation of the way biblical material is utilised sheds some light on why it is used at all. First of all, the use of biblical material points to the cultural context of these scientists, who assume that these texts are known to their readers. Wilson just says 'recall', before he quotes the Book of Job, without even mentioning chapter and verse. They are addressing an audience in whom familiarity with biblical texts is expected alongside familiarity with the main works of literature in general. Second, their involvement with narratives, both the narration of the 'unnarratable' and the narrative challenge of the evolutionary epic, reflects the fact that they have a strong sense of stories as a tool for understanding. This is expressed throughout their books, and is part of their success. Third, the antagonistic use of the texts reveals how their thoughts have been shaped by conflict with religious groups. This has shaped not only their aggressive tone towards religion in general, but seems to be reflected in their understanding of biblical texts. To some extent, Wilson and Dawkins seem to have adopted the textual approach of their opponents.

They place biblical texts against scientific insights and compare them, and they wish to take over the power of religion established through narratives by constructing new epics. They see myths as having a truth claim similar to that of science in the same way that fundamentalist Christians do. Their view of these texts seems to be shaped by their adversaries, causing them to completely neglect all the perspectives on these narratives found within theology, literary and religious studies, thereby presenting a view of myth which seems just as fundamentalist as that of the religious people they wish to overcome. They do not opt for a more post-modern approach, in which the power of any text with a claim to ultimate authority can be defused by reference to the 'death of grand narratives' or the plurality of local stories vs. the one, global narrative.[14] Instead, they engage in a battle of grand narratives in which only one can be left standing, thereby affirming the normative status of text. They create a scenario in which 'the Bible' is opposed to 'science' in an ideological battle between two world views in the same way that traditional creationists have done.

Literary scholar Stephen Prickett offers an analysis of the confrontation of narratives from both religion and science through his use of the dichotomy of irony and fundamentalism as approaches to the status of the grand narratives of both fields. Using Prickett's terminology we can categorise Dawkins, Wilson and the creationists as representatives of a fundamentalist position with one true grand narrative, whereas an ironic position would be to accept the plurality of global narratives in our current context and our inability to ever find the ultimate and 'true' narrative to live by. Wilson, Dawkins and the conservative Christians share a notion of strong normativity when it comes to biblical texts, and neither of them recognises the insights of the academic studies of texts throughout the last centuries.

The reception of biblical material within the work of Dawkins and Wilson is of interest as a special area of reception and transformation of the Bible which has not received much attention until now. It is also of interest as a cultural phenomenon in relation to the cultural conflicts between conservative religious groups and modern Western culture which have occurred in a multitude of ways around the turn of the

---

14   Lyotard 1984; Prickett 2002.

millennium not only within Christianity, but also in many of the world religions. Many of these controversies are related to the discussion of texts and their normativity in contemporary society, and raise many questions with far-reaching consequences for both those inside and outside the various religions: Does the Bible match modern science when it comes to describing the world? What is the status of the Koran in relation to Western culture? It has been stated many times that religion has returned in our contemporary society, and with this return of religion the normativity of texts as part of ideological conflicts has become a recurring theme. Accordingly, the use of biblical material by evolutionary scientists involved in a war on religion should be seen as one aspect of the return of religion just like the return of fundamentalist approaches within a variety of ideologies based on religion as well as science.

Bibliography

Abbott, H. Porter, 2003. 'Unnarratable Knowledge: The Difficulty of Understanding Evolution by Natural Selection'. In: David. Herman (ed.), *Narrative Theory and the Cognitive Sciences*. Stanford: CSLI Publications, 143-162.

Barbour, Ian G., 1990. *Religion in an Age of Science*. London: SCM Press.

Beer, Gillian, 1996. *Open Fields: Science in cultural encounter*. Oxford: Clarendon Press.

Beer, Gillian, 2000. *Darwin's Plots*. Cambridge: University of Cambridge Press.

Bruner, Jerome, 2002. *Making Stories – Law, Literature, Life*. Harvard: Harvard University Press.

Dawkins, Richard, 1986. *The Blind Watchmaker*. Essex: Longman Scientific and Technical.

Dawkins, Richard, 1989 [1976]. *The Selfish Gene*. Oxford: Oxford University Press.

Dawkins, Richard, 1995. *River Out of Eden – a Darwinian View of Life*. London: Weidenfeld & Nicholson.

Dawkins, Richard, 2000. *Unweaving the Rainbow – Science, Delusion, and the Appetite for Wonder*. Boston, Mass: Houghton Mifflin.

Dawkins, Richard, 2004. *The Ancestor's Tale – A Pilgrimage to the Dawn of Evolution*. New York: Mariner Books/Houghton Mifflin Company.

Dawkins, Richard, 2006. *The God Delusion*. Boston, MA: Houghton Mifflin.

Dawkins, Richard & Shanks, Niall, 2004. *God, the Devil and Darwin – A Critique of Intelligent Design Theory*. New York, N.Y.: Oxford University Press.

Dembski, William A., 1999. *Intelligent Design – The Bridge Between Science & Theology*. Downers Grove, Illinois: Varsity Press.

Dembski, William A.; Behe, Michael J. & Meyer, Stephen C., 2000. *Science and Evidence for Design in the Universe (Proceedings from the Wethersfield Institute)*. San Francisco, Cal. Ignatius Press.

Dennett, Daniel C., 1995. *Darwin's Dangerous Idea – Evolution and the Meanings of Life*. New York: Simon & Schuster.

Hammersholt Christensen, Torben. & Harnow Klausen, Søren (eds.), 2007. *Darwin eller intelligent Design*. Copenhagen: ANIS.

Harris, Sam, 2005. *The End of Faith: Religion, terror, and the future of reason*. New York: W.W. Norton & Co.

Harris, Sam, 2006. *Letter to a Christian nation*. New York: Knopf.

Herman, David, 2003. 'Stories as a Tool for Thinking'. In: D. Herman (ed.), *Narrative Theory and the Cognitive Sciences*. Palo Alto, Stanford University: CSLI Publications, 163-192.

Larson, Edward J., 1997. *Summer for the Gods – The Scopes Trial and America's Continuing Debate over Science and Religion*. Cambridge, MA: Harvard University Press.

Lewontin, Richard C.; Rose, Steven & Kamin, Leon J., 1984. *Not in Our Genes – Biology, Ideology and Human Nature*. New York: Pantheon Books.

Lyotard, Jean-Francois, 1984. *The Postmodern Condition: A Report on Knowledge*. Minneapolis: University of Minnesota Press.

Midgley, Mary, 1979. 'Gene-juggling'. *Philosophy*, 54, 439-458.

Midgley, Mary, 1983. 'Selfish Genes and Social Darwinism'. *Philosophy*, 58, 365-365-377.

Midgley, Mary, 1992. *Science as Salvation: a Modern Myth and its Meaning*. London: Routledge.

Midgley, Mary, 2002. *Evolution as Religion*. London: Routledge.

Prickett, Stephen, 2002. *Narrative, Religion and Science – Fundamentalism versus Irony, 1700-1999*. Cambridge: Cambridge University Press.

Richards, Robert J., 1987. *Darwin and the Emergence of Evolutionary Theories of Mind and Behavior*. Chicago: University of Chicago Press.

White, Hayden, 2000. 'An Old Question Raised Again: Is Historiography Art or Science? (Response to Iggers)'. *Rethinking History*, 4.3, 391-406.

Wilson, Allan C., Rebecca L. Cann, Stephen M. Carr, Matthew George Jr., Ulf B. Gyllensten, Kathleen Helm-Bychowski, Russell G. Higuchi, Stephen R. Palumbi, Ellen M. Prager, Richard D. Sage, and Mark Stoneking 1985. 'Mitochondrial DNA and two perspectives on evolutionary genetics', *Biological Journal of the Linnean Society* 26, 375-400.

Wilson, Edward O., Caplan, Arthur L. & et al., 1978. *The Sociobiology Debate – Readings on the Ethical and Scientific Issues Concerning Sociobiology*. New York: Harper & Row.

Wilson, Edward O., 1998. *Consilience – The Unity of Knowledge*. New York: Knopf/Random House.

Wilson, Edward O., 2000 [1975]. *Sociobiology the New Synthesis* (25th anniversary edn.) Cambridge, Massachusetts: Belknap Press of Harvard University Press.

Wilson, Edward O., 2002. *The Future of Life*. New York: Vintage Books/Random House.

Wilson, Edward O., 2004 [1978]. *On Human Nature*. Cambridge, Massachusetts: Harvard University Press.

PART III

*Receptions and transformations of
the Bible in religious communities*

GENERAL REFLECTIONS
ADDRESSED BY SCRIPTURE

Marianne Schleicher

Most definitions of scripture have as their vantage point that scripture claims to be revelatory (cf. Smith 1989, 21, 36, 41-42; Levering 1989, 58; Holdrege 1989, 181-182). Within a Jewish and Christian context such revelation is seen to contain the direct words of God or eyewitness accounts of his intervention in this world, which also signals some kind of address to mankind. Divine address seems to characterise the content of scripture according to Jewish and Christian reception.

Scripture connotes writing. Once the divine address has become fixed in writing, meaning is detached from the "historical" speech event, disconnected from the mental intention of the author, and granted semantic autonomy which again is countered by the opportunity for multiple readings (cf. Ricoeur 1976, 25-37). In religious communities, especially in ritual settings, this autonomy is used to struggle against the consequences of fixation in order to transform scripture into God's contemporary address of those present. In this way, it seems that a dialectical move is made from orality over writing to a retrieved orality when it comes to the use of scripture.

To exemplify this dialectical move, one could mention the way in which Exodus 3:10 renders God's address to Moses, including the divine command to lead the Israelites out of Egypt. Once the exodus narrative has become fixed in writing, it becomes the object of exposition where God's authorial concern for the Israelites in Egypt is suspended. At least from the early Rabbinic period and onward, Jews transformed the exodus narrative to signify God's constant willingness and ability to intervene in the course of history, while early Christians used the exodus narrative as a prism to understand the resurrection of Jesus as the new exodus of mankind.[1] These expositions became possible thanks to the fixed form in which the link between the author and the first addressee could be suspended. Still, Jews and Christians read the exodus narrative as divine discourse addressing their acute needs and concerns at the beginning of the Common Era. The same reading strategy is applied in modern religious communities, where the original speech event has to give way to the users' implementation of their own context in which orality is retrieved because modern Jews or Christians also want to be addressed by God or benefit from divine intervention. The general reflections in this section on the reception and transformation of the Bible in religious communities will suggest how the ritual setting and human psychology enable this transformation.

---

1   Cf. *Haggadah shel Pesach* and the Christian placing of Easter during the Jewish celebrations of Passover.

As a cultural text, scripture hosts and legitimises religious norms concerning belief and practices (cf. Assmann (2000) 2006, 42-43). These norms cannot be disseminated to the religious community unless scripture is either interpreted by the individual (this is quite uncommon among lay people), or disseminated by a religious expert through commentary. This is where sermons play an important role in Jewish and Christian religion because the homiletic exposition of scripture enables the religious expert, be s/he rabbi or vicar, to guide and control the congregants on how to feel addressed by the weekly biblical portions, now that the institution is up against the otherwise free range of individual associations.

The free range of individual associations is a factor to be taken into account. Recent studies indicate that such associations arise from the non-semantic properties of scripture such as ornamental writing, leather binding, recitation techniques and regulations concerning its physical handling. As symbols of previous uses, these non-semantic properties activate associations to cultural and/or personal memories. The primary function of these associations seems to be to establish transitivity between the normative tradition, the personal past and the congregant's contemporary reception and transformation of scripture (cf. Malley 2004, 41-48; 70-72).

In the remaining part of the Jewish or Christian service, where the biblical text is only hinted at or read aloud without any subsequent exposition, the ritual character of the service seems to provoke the suspension of the scriptural content. For instance, when congregants perceive the cantor's or the vicar's reading of scripture, they do not necessarily listen to the content. It is more likely that its phonetic property is used as a mental stepping stone leading to association – reminding them for instance of the way their mothers read or retold the Bible at home during their childhood. If this is the case, a link is created between the congregant's sense of belonging to his/her family and of belonging to the religious community. Such associations do not constitute a threat to the religious institutions. On the contrary, they seem crucial for the congregants' religious identification and community feeling.

The use of scripture in religious communities seemingly reflects the merging of several sign systems. It is due to this merging that I shall include the concept of inter-textuality, as coined by Julia Kristeva in 1966.[2] She never intended it to imply the banal detection of the presence of one literary source within the text in focus, although this has become the popular meaning of the term. What was at stake for her was to illustrate how every signifying practice, be it scriptural interpretation or response to its non-semantic properties, constitutes a field of transposition for various sign systems. The term 'inter-textuality' denotes this kind of transposition of one (or several) sign system(s) into another (cf. Kristeva (1974) 2002, 48). The signifying practice represents a language event, in which '[D]iachrony is transformed into synchrony … [It is] a dialogue among several writings: that of the writer, the addressee (or the character), and the contemporary or earlier context' (Kristeva 1980 (1969), 65). The writer, addressee, contemporary and ear-

---

2   Her paper, presented in 1966, was published three years later, cf. Kristeva (1969) 1980.

lier contexts constitute textual surfaces that intersect and make up a three-dimensional space, in which language alternates between three coordinates, cf. my model:[3]

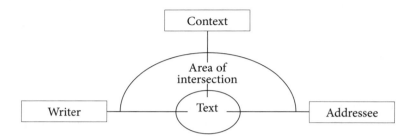

The text mediates on the vertical axis, for instance between the historical contexts of the writer and the addressee and the text itself. On the horizontal axis the text mediates between the writer and the addressee. The writer and addressee both share the words of the text, which structures diachronic relations into synchronic ones. This mediating function of the text is what Kristeva refers to as 'intertextuality' (cf. Kristeva (1969) 1980, 66).

Adding to the personal memories of the Jewish or Christian congregant which constitute one context of the addressee, the synagogue or church room constitutes another. The architecture and decorative symbols in the room become signifying markers that interfere with the reception of the biblical text. The Torah scroll including its ornaments connotes the Jerusalem Temple, where mediated access to God's holiness could be achieved. Christ on the cross is hung on the wall of every church so all Christians can become witnesses to and beneficiaries of his vicarious suffering. In other words, the Kristevan model of intertextuality helps us understand how (despite the historical distance to biblical events) the ritual room helps to transpose signs from the biblical past into the context of modern religious people, enabling them to feel addressed and affected.

The human psyche is particularly susceptible to this kind of transposition. To explain this, Kristeva develops her notion of intertextuality by including insights from psychoanalysis (cf. Kristeva (1984) 2002, 10, 13, 19; Kristeva (1974) 2002, 37). In her doctoral dissertation *Revolution in Poetic Language*, published in 1974, Kristeva describes what goes on during the signifying process in the human psyche when the inner drives of the individual clash with societal and biological constraints prior to the individual positioning himself through language. Common language or tradition does not take account of something so individual; and if common language or tradition were all that we had, we would not be able to articulate this clash. This is why as human beings we are in need of poetry, of literature. Poetic language is unique, says

---

3   This model has previously been presented in Schleicher 2007, 11.

Kristeva, because the poet creates poetry by revisiting that stage in the signifying process at which drives clash against constraints and remind the poet of where the drives really want to take him/her (cf. Kristeva (1974) 2002, 35-49). The Bible is literary in its character and articulates such clashes. One example to illustrate this fact can be found in the way King David, singer of psalms, expresses his distress:

My God, my God, why hast Thou forsaken me, and art far from my help at the words of my cry?
O my God, I call by day, but Thou answerest not; and at night, and there is no surcease for me.
Yet Thou art holy, O Thou that art enthroned upon the praises of Israel.
In Thee did our fathers trust; they trusted, and Thou didst deliver them.
Unto Thee they cried, and escaped; in Thee did they trust, and were not ashamed (Ps 22:2-6).[4]

God's protection of his ancestors and tradition's expectation of David to call onto God for help are contradicted by David's experience of God's absence. Reality is constraining vis-à-vis David's inner hope for deliverance, and this clash is articulated. Poetic articulation makes it possible for David to reposition himself within a tradition which does not offer adequate examples for identification.

David's repositioning is understandable in his context. However, once the Psalms were fixed David's reasons for such articulation were suspended, and over time listeners and readers have used his wording to reposition themselves in their contexts. This kind of repositioning is enabled thanks to the mental activity of transference, in which readers subconsciously remember how they benefitted from their mother's signification of the world and so find the courage to associate with any other person – a poet or a literary character – a potential signifying other whose signification can be incorporated as an attractive perspective (cf. Kristeva (1974) 2002, 43-45). While one may not have the courage to witness and articulate one's own clash between drives and constraints, the act of transference offers the perspective of an "other" who demands to be listened to and whose poetic articulation may be quite attractive in order to articulate one's own responses to the inner clashes of drives and constraints. Accordingly, sign systems stemming from the various positionalities of poet, character and reader are juxtaposed, even transposed into each other and provide one illustrative explanation of why congregants within a synagogue or church may feel personally addressed or feel like witnesses when listening to the Bible.

All three articles in this section deal with the fact that members of Jewish and Christian communities want to feel addressed by scripture. In my own article, p. 141-158, and from a descriptive point of view, I distinguish between Jewish uses of the Torah which promote the scriptural content, and uses in which personal or cultural memories are at play. I do this to illustrate how the various uses serve different functions and help maintain scripture in the mediating position of transmitting a divine

---

4   This translation is taken from the Jewish Publication Society's 1917 edition of the Hebrew Bible in English. It is available online at http://www.mechon-mamre.org.

address to the congregants. Nissen takes a normative stance when he adopts the vantage point that Christian congregants must be willing to be affected by the divine address embedded in scripture, as well as being willing to embody scripture to allow for a self-transformation through which the congregants will perform the scriptural ideals and commands, p. 159-171. Finally, Nielsen describes how the Danish Christian hymn book, intended for congregational singing, offers a poetic articulation which the congregants appropriate in order to form their communal response to God's address as formulated in the weekly Bible portions, p. 172-186. Dealing with the reception and transformation of the Bible in Jewish and Christian communities, this section focuses on what is probably the most central activity for religious identification.

Bibliography

Assmann, Jan 2006. *Religion and Cultural Memory* (2000). Stanford: Stanford University Press.

Holdrege, Barbara 1989. 'The Bride of Israel: The Ontological Status of Scripture in the Rabbinic and Kabbalistic Traditions'. In: Levering (ed.), *Rethinking Scripture*. Albany: SUNY Press, 180-261.

Kristeva, Julia 1980. 'Word, Dialogue, and Novel' (1969). In: *Desire in Language – A Semiotic Approach to Literature and Art*. New York: Columbia University Press, 64-91.

Kristeva, Julia 2002. *Revolution in Poetic Language* (1974). In: Oliver (ed.), *The Portable Kristeva*. New York: Columbia University Press, 27-92.

Kristeva, Julia 2002. 'My Memory's Hyperbole' (1984). In: Oliver (ed.), *The Portable Kristeva*. New York: Columbia University Press, 3-26.

Levering, Miriam 1989. 'Scripture and Its Reception: A Buddhist Case'. In: Levering (ed.) *Rethinking Scripture*. Albany: SUNY, 58-101.

Malley, Brian 2004. *How the Bible Works – An Anthropological Study of Evangelical Biblicism*. Walnut Creek: AltaMira Press.

Ricoeur, Paul 1976. *Interpretation Theory: Discourse and the Surplus of Meaning*. Fort Worth: Texan Christian University Press.

Schleicher, Marianne 2007. *Intertextuality in the Tales of Rabbi Nahman of Bratslav: A Close Reading of Sippurey Ma'asiyot*. Brill: Leiden.

Smith, Wilfred Cantwell 1989. 'The Study of Religion and the Study of the Bible'. In: Levering (ed.), *Rethinking Scripture*. Albany: SUNY Press, 18-28.

THE MANY FACES OF THE TORAH

RECEPTION AND TRANSFORMATION OF THE TORAH IN JEWISH COMMUNITIES

Marianne Schleicher

> 'There are seventy faces to the Torah: Turn it around and
> around, for everything is in it' (*Bamidbar Rabbah* 13:15)

This famous midrashic saying from the 12th century about the seventy faces of the Torah is usually taken to indicate not only the many possible meanings but also the infinite applicability of the Torah. Furthermore, the number seventy adds to the meaning of the saying in the sense that seventy is a symbolic number indicating completion or perfection within a Jewish context.[1] The conception of the Torah as complete and perfect is not only the result of its canonisation process, which took place in the centuries following the Babylonian exile. It is an ongoing process in which its relevance and applicability are constantly stressed and proved – a dynamic process of reception and transformation.

This article will argue that the general view derived from the canon debate that canonical texts must display closure as well as openness to remain canonical[2] does not suffice to explain 'the seventy faces of the Torah', or for that matter the ability of the Torah to remain uniquely privileged within Jewish communities. A distinction between scripture as a holy object and a holy text must supplement insights from the canon debate to explain the ongoing relevance and applicability of the Torah in Judaism.

Recent studies of scripture reveal that projections of personal and cultural representations influence the dominant part of scriptural use to such an extent that the term 'interpretation' would fail to describe the dynamics that secure its infinite applicability (Malley 2004). I label the projective activity 'artefactual use of scripture' because it treats scripture as an artefact whose textual content is basically ignored. Instead, scripture is treated as a symbol that can be manipulated to signify whatever individuals, collectives and institutions project into it. The projected meaning is subsequently associated

---

1   Seventy Jewish souls descended into Egypt, Gen 46:27. Seventy elders were chosen by Moses, *Talmud*, 'Sanhedrin' 17a. There were seventy members of the Sanhedrin, *Talmud*, 'Sanhedrin' 3b. King David lived seventy years, 2 Sam 5:4. There are seventy nations of the world, *Talmud*, 'Sukkah' 55b.

2   Jonathan Z. Smith writes: 'Where there is a canon we can predict the necessary occurrence of a hermeneute, of an interpreter whose task it is to continually extend the domain of the closed canon over everything that is known or everything that is. It is with the canon and its hermeneute that we encounter the necessary obsession with exegetical totalization' (Smith 1978, 23).

with (or subconsciously activated by) scripture's non-semantic, formal aspects such as binding and embellishment, spelling, recitation, quotation, storage and similar acts of ritual handling and regulation. Even religious interpretations that read scripture with the overt purpose of confirming the religious worldview already held within a religious community are matters of projection, and as such of artefactual use (Malley 2004, 73-81).

In those rare cases, however, when conscious attempts are made to analyse and gain access to the discourse of scripture, scripture is treated as a text. Going against post-modern claims that there is no such thing as a non-projective analysis of textual discourse, I draw upon Paul Ricoeur's approach to hermeneutics. He defines hermeneutics not in the popular but in the philosophical sense of the word as a matter of connecting:

two discourses, the discourse of the text and the discourse of the interpretation. This connection means that what has to be interpreted in a text is what it says and what it speaks about, i.e., the kind of world which it opens up or discloses; and the final act of 'appropriation' is less the projection of one's own prejudices into the text than the 'fusion of horizons' – to speak like Hans-Georg Gadamer – which occurs when the world of the reader and the world of the text merge into one another (Ricoeur 2003 (1975), 377-378).

Accordingly, I maintain that scriptural use can only acclaim the label 'textual use of scripture' if it rests upon interpretation proper. Interpretation is here understood as a hermeneutical use of the text that encourages the reader to consider whether the text's proposed religious worldview should be transposed into his/her own worldview. If so, the textual use of scripture will imply a fusion of the horizon of the text and the horizon of the reader, and as such transform the reader in the sense that the textual discourse demands a dynamic turn to either conscious appropriation or conscious refusal.

This article will argue that the artefactual and textual uses of the Torah are not mutually exclusive, but are activated in turn or simultaneously depending on the psychological, social and cultural needs of the user. It seems that artefactual use facilitates transitivity between the personal and cultural representations associated with scripture and current normativity at a subconscious level; whereas the textual use of scripture offers itself as a means of dealing consciously with the discourse of scripture when a crisis within a religious community makes it relevant to employ such a key normative text as a reservoir of advice on how to think, behave, situate oneself and remain within the boundaries of one's own religious tradition (Ricoeur 1979, 271-276).

The Torah as a holy object

If the scholarly conception of how the Torah is used rested upon the Torah's inherent claim to normative validity through interpretation, it would be easy to prove the existence of textual use in Judaism. The editing of the Torah and its transformation into a book conceived of as a holy text that requires exposition[3] could be substantiated intratextually through Deut 31:10-13 or through Ezra – scribe and teacher of the Torah in the middle of the 5th century BCE, cf. Neh 8:8. However, scholarship has to employ the hermeneutics of suspicion, for instance by looking for external sources that offer a less biased perspective on the actual use of the Torah in Jewish tradition.

When the Jerusalem Temple was destroyed in 70 CE, Jews no longer had access to a sacred place, an *axis mundi* where contact with God could be mediated. The Torah replaced the temple as the centre of cultic activity, as made evident in the Mishnaic and Talmudic specifications of how to make and handle the text of the Torah for liturgical purposes.[4] The saying in *Mishnah*, 'Pirkey Avot' 1:1 is one among many illustrations of this replacement. It encourages Jews standing in the oral tradition to 'make a fence round the Torah'. Segregating sacred space is a fundamental religious activity in that it marks the boundary between the sacred and the profane. When the temple was still standing it was constantly purified, i.e. segregated from profane matters. People officiating within it were equally purified from profanity, and the mundane world was fenced out of the temple precincts. The Mishnaic tractate 'Pirkey Avot' formulates this encouragement in its opening lines, so it is hard not to interpret this as an attempt to stress the very holy status of the Torah similar to that of the temple.

In early Rabbinic Judaism specifications are made for the non-semantic formal aspects of the Torah scroll which allow for easy recognition, and which define what is required for a Torah scroll to be perfect and complete. The holy status of the Torah depends on its textual passages being written in the Assyrian[5] script, on parchment, and in ink (*Mishnah*, 'Yadayim' 4:5). It also depends on the parchment being made of the skin of a clean animal. The hide must be prepared with the conscious intent of turning it into parchment for the Torah (*bTalmud*, 'Megillah' 19a). The parchment must be prepared on both sides (*bTalmud*, 'Shabbat' 79b) and cut into a square sheet, upon which lines must be ruled in columns leaving space for margins to surround and protect the holy letters to be written upon them. No vowels or accents are allowed if the scroll is to be fit for public reading. The sheets are then sewn together using threads made of the dried tendons of clean animals and 'the Scroll of the Law closes at its middle, there being a cylinder at each end' (*bTalmud*, 'Baba Bathra' 14a). These specifications provide guidelines to ensure the holy status of the Torah scroll.

To further the material distribution of the Torah as well as the bond between scripture and the individual, every man must write a Torah scroll for himself (*bTalmud*,

---

3   While the Torah stipulated norms for the behaviour of priests in the Jerusalem Temple, the authority of the Torah was challenged at least until 150 BCE by writings such as the Temple Scroll and the Book of Jubilees, cf. Cohen 2006, 175-177.

4   David Stern deals with the Torah as a liturgical Bible as well as a study Bible. He refers to the liturgical Bible as a 'quasi-holy artifact', cf. Stern 2003, 231. While I hold Stern's work in high esteem, I see no reason for him to modify this statement by using 'quasi', since the liturgical use he mentions is a full-blown matter of artefactual use of a holy object.

5   It is impossible to say if the rabbis knew that the Torah prior to the 5th century BCE was written in paleo-Hebrew letters, cf. Stern 2003, 234-235.

'Sanhedrin' 21b). If he is unable to write one, he can pay a scribe to do so (*bTalmud*, 'Megillah' 27a). Up to two mistakes per sheet are tolerable if corrected, and will not detract from the holy status of the Torah scroll. However, if there are three – some say four – errors on one sheet, the entire scroll must be put away in a *genizah*[6] (*bTalmud*, 'Menachot' 29b). Once written, inspected, accepted and in use for liturgical purposes, the Torah has to be chanted aloud using a special melody (*bTalmud*, 'Megillah' 32a).

In the Middle Ages, the status of the Torah as a holy object – or even sanctuary – is stressed by referring to it as *mikdashyah*; i.e. God's temple (Stern 2003, 233). The many specifications in the *Shulkhan Arukh*[7] for making, handling and reading the Torah in liturgical and study-related settings help to maintain this notion. This legal code from 1564 bases its specifications on the Mishnaic and Talmudic opinions mentioned above, but adds to them by making further meticulous regulations similar to those of ritual conduct.

A scribe – be he professional or lay – had to prepare himself mentally before writing a Torah scroll because of the numinous power of God's names in the Torah text. He had to say aloud that 'I have the intent to write the holy name' before doing so. The writing of the holy name was not to be interrupted, and it had to remain within the margins of the sheet as if they offered the holy writ some kind of protection. If an error occurred in the holy name or transgressed into the margins, the sheet had to be stored away in a *genizah* (*Shulkhan Arukh*, 'Yoreh Deah' 22).

The *Shulkhan Arukh* demands that the scroll is treated with great respect, that it must not be held uncovered. It is therefore covered with a Torah mantle in Ashkenazi Jewry, and in a Torah box in Sephardic Jewry. Nobody must touch it with dirty hands or take it into impure places. People must stand up when it is carried and cannot sit wherever it is resting. If a Torah scroll is beyond repair and/or unfit for public reading, it must be buried along with any defective accessories of the Torah scroll (*Shulkhan Arukh*, 'Yoreh Deah' 22), known as *keley qodesh*; i.e., holy vessels, typically made of silver except for the two wooden rollers (*ets hayyim*).

The accessories include a breastplate (*ephod*) connoting that of the high priest, containing the two pillars of the temple (Boaz and Jachin) on each side; the Torah pointer (*yad torah*), which prevents the reader of the Torah from touching the holy letters with his profane hand; the Torah crown/crowns (*keter/-im*), evoking messianic hope and God's kingdom, to be placed on top of the rollers; and the bells (*rimmonim*) similar to those carried by the high priest to warn ritually impure people that he was coming and that they would have to keep their distance. The tradition of making the Torah accessories probably arose as an opportunity for community members to remember and honour family members by donating such equipment to the local synagogue. In other words, the accessories not only transmit an aura of holiness associated with the

---

6   A storeroom in a synagogue in which worn-out, heretical or disgraced scrolls and books are placed to prevent their defective status from affecting the holiness of the ritual in which these objects were otherwise to be used.

7   The *Shulkhan Arukh* was written by Joseph Karo and serves as the normative code for orthodox Jewry even today.

Jerusalem Temple to the Torah scroll, but also serve as a means to create transitivity between this holiness and individual identities.[8]

Transitivity as a consequence of artefactual use

Once the holy status of the Torah has been established according to the above-mentioned specifications, another aspect of artefactual use emerges: transitivity. Transitivity is a term coined by Brian Malley to describe the functionality which occurs when associations evoked by the artefact create bonds between individual, collective and cultural representations and between the holy and the profane. The term seems particularly apt when looking at the accounts of Bent Melchior, the former chief rabbi of Denmark, whom I interviewed on 11th of October 2005. Melchior, who is himself the son of a chief rabbi, is telling me about the collection of scrolls in the Danish-Jewish community when he says:

Once someone donated a Torah scroll … A member of the community went to buy one, and he also donated the equipment for it by an artist named Arje Griegst, … On this shield it says that it was given on the occasion of [the 300th anniversary of the community] and that this man has given it in memory of my parents [Marcus and Meta Melchior]… Griegst is a great and skilled artist who has also made jewellery for the Queen and for Royal Copenhagen Porcelain. It was the only one that we took out this Saturday when someone in my family became bar mitzvah. I thought it was appropriate to use this shield.

The Torah shield reflects a member's recognition of Melchior's parents. Obviously, Melchior appreciates this recognition and the recognition even grows through associations to the artist Griegst, Queen Margrethe II and Royal Copenhagen Porcelain. Relations are being established which Melchior is proud of, and he is proud to transmit these relations to his grandson on his *bar mitzvah*. Establishing such relations is a matter of creating transitivity.

Melchior continues:

In there (he points in the direction of his living room) I have a crown for a Torah scroll, which we gave to my father … [We] bought it and had an inscription made for the occasion; and then when dad died, mum insisted that it stayed in our home. So now I have the problem of finding a place for it. … We have used it now and then in the synagogue when reading the last Torah portion, which is usually an honour given to the rabbi. So I took it to the synagogue to ensure that it was used.

By keeping a Torah crown in their homes, Melchior's mother and later on Melchior himself break the norm of keeping Torah equipment in the synagogue. But Melchior does not know what to do with such a holy object in the private sphere, even though

---

8   For more on these accessories, cf. Elbogen 1993, 359-363.

the family decided to keep it there. One can say that a holy artefact has been conquered despite the adjacent problems of handling it in a sphere that is not ritually pure. The problems increase if this artefact is a Torah scroll, and this became apparent when I asked the following question:

MS: If you had a Torah scroll made, could you then place it in your own home, or would it have to be kept in the synagogue?
BM: (Thinks) Well, it could stand in your own home, but then one would have to behave extremely respectably and wear a head cover in the room where it was. Actually, this room would have to be set aside for its mere presence.

In artefactual use, the accessories and the Torah scroll enable transitivity, not only between the individual, collective and cultural representations, but also between these three and the holy sphere. It seems that the numinosity of the holy sheds a sanctioning light on the established relations.

The Torah in between object and text

In my distinction between artefactual and textual use, it is very tempting to conceive of the Torah reading and sermons as examples of textual use. However, the actual uses reveal themselves to be in a kind of twilight zone.

The afore-mentioned passage in Deut 31:10-13 encourages a textual use of the Torah when Moses orders the Torah to be read every seventh year on Sukkot, the feast of the Tabernacles, in order to transmit an understanding of the commandments to contemporaries as well as the next generation, and in order to make sure that the legal content of the Torah was received among the people of Israel as its normative basis. It is indeed plausible to assume that the discourse in this Torah passage was respected and reflected upon. Once, however, the Torah reading became imbedded in a liturgical setting like the late temple and synagogue service (Cohen 2006, 64), the Torah reading attracted artefactual use as the following will show.

Readings every Sabbath probably developed from reading the Torah on high holidays and/or special Sabbaths, and was probably introduced before the middle of the third century BCE. At first these readings were not consecutive, but chosen freely (Elbogen 1993, 131-132). And everyone was permitted to read including women, children and slaves. But once regulations were made to secure a proper ritual conduct in the public reading of the Torah, only men could perform this holy act (Elbogen 1993, 139-140).

At the time of the Mishnah, it was stated that 'The reader may skip [from place to place] in a Prophet but not in the Torah' (Mishnah, 'Megillah' 1:5) to prevent any deviation from what was now customary: the triennial cycle of the Torah reading in Palestine or the annual cycle in Babylonia.[9] The annual reading cycle, divided into 54

---

9   Cf. bMegillah 31a-b; Cohen 2006, 64.

weekly Torah portions, became dominant in the Jewish world and began after Sukkot on Simchat Torah. Within the 54 pericopes, the beginning, transitions and end are marked verbally by saying certain blessings and amens. Such pericopes constitute phonetic characteristics that transform the text into an object of artefactual use. It becomes easily recognisable through sound alone and interferes with the overall textual discourse of the Torah, bracketing it into pieces that fit the present, liturgical context.

Since the Middle Ages, Torah readings have taken place on Mondays, Thursdays and Saturdays and constitute the core activity of synagogue service. They are surrounded by the reading and recitation of Biblical psalms, prayers and blessings, all to be found in the *Siddur,* the Jewish Prayer Book that emerged in edited form from the 9th century and onward (Elbogen 1993, 140).

The Torah scroll is stored inside the synagogue in the Torah cupboard (*aron ha-qodesh,* the Holy Ark), which faces Jerusalem. So in Europe it is situated on the eastern wall of the synagogue. Over the cupboard in the central Copenhagen synagogue a sentence is engraved: *de'a lifney mi ata 'omed* (be aware in front of whom you are standing). Together, the Hebrew name of the cupboard, the direction towards Jerusalem, and the engraved sentence heavily connote the Jerusalem Temple – and even the Holy of Holies, where the *Shekhinah,* the divine presence, used to dwell.[10] The architecture of the synagogue points to and stresses the holy status of the Torah, leaving the congregants and this analyst with the impression that the Torah functions as a metonymy of God.[11]

In Greek mystery cults, the central ritual activity orchestrates a revelation of the holy object. In a synagogue service, the Torah reading reflects a similar revelatory process which makes sense given its holy status derived from its inherent claim to contain the words of God because God speaks in Genesis, Exodus, Leviticus and Numeri, while Moses renders God's commandments in Deuteronomy. Once this holy object in the shape of a scroll is taken out of the cupboard, it is dressed in its garb/ box and with its holy accessories and then greeted before it is carried to the *bimah,* an elevated platform where it must never be left alone and from where it must be read. The reading of the Torah is divided into three parts to be recited by a Cohen, a Levite and an Israelite. Together they represent the entirety of Jews, which means that symbolically speaking all Jews take part in the recitation. After the Torah reading has finished, the scroll is held up and presented to the congregation, after which it is rolled up and redressed and then accompanied to its place in the cupboard (*Shulkhan*

---

10   For a similar opinion, cf. 'Ark of the Law', *JewishEncyclopedia.com* 2002 as of 7 January 2008. Still, this article is aware of the hesitance of the Mishnah to compare the synagogue with the temple. The Mishnah uses not the word *aron* but *tebah* for the cupboard, connoting the arks of Noah and Moses.

11   David Stern shares this impression, but with respect to the textual use of the Torah. To him, the Torah serves as a metonymy of God; i.e. that every word of God represents a part of God. When the Torah is seen as a metonymy of God, the prohibition against graven images (Ex 20:3) has consequences for interpretation because one fixed interpretation of a scriptural verse would equal an engraving of God. In this way, the multiple meanings of the Torah pay tribute to the transcendence of God, cf. Stern 1987, 619. See also Holdrege 1989, 180-261.

Arukh, 'Orakh Hayyim' 8). All in all, the act of Torah reading seems to involve revealing the holy artefacts. Reciting and listening to the Torah as a phonetic object signifies the culmination of synagogue worship and ensures transitivity between the holy sphere and the congregants.

Jewish homiletics owes a lot to Neh 8:1-9. In these verses Ezra points to the Torah as the central text to be read aloud and to be expounded. Later on in early Judaism, the study of the Torah was considered a mandatory act of divine worship (Cohen 2006, 53), although no evidence exists of public Torah exposition until the 1st century CE when Philo and various books in the New Testament report that 'synagogue services featured the sermon, the explication of the meaning of the sacred texts' (Cohen 2006, 64). An expounder of the Torah was called a *darshan*, derived from the Hebrew root *d-r-sh*, which signifies 'to search out [the will of God]'. This kind of preaching took place in public – in synagogues, private schools and academies – particularly on Friday evenings and Sabbath afternoons, but also privately at weddings and funerals. The literary genre *midrash* developed from these Torah expositions. Some of the earliest sermons of the rabbis were edited to provide teachers and preachers with examples of how to interpret scripture, especially its *halakhic* material; i.e. its legal content (Stern 1987, 616). These expositions can be found in *Mekhilta, Sifra* and *Sifre*, all of which are *halakhic midrashim* on Exodus, Leviticus, Numeri, and Deuteronomy, edited between 70 and 220 CE. Expositions of the *aggadic* or narrative, content in the Torah, especially Genesis, were edited between 400 and 1200 CE. Among these, *Genesis Rabbah* resembles a verse by verse exegesis, while *Leviticus Rabbah, Pesikta d'Rav Kahana, Deuteronomy Rabbah, Tanhuma, Numeri Rabbah II, Pesikhta Rabbati,* and *Exodus Rabbah* are homiletic midrashim (Rod-Salomonsen & Winther 2001, 161). In other words, based on this knowledge one could be led to believe that Jewish homiletics represented a matter of textual use. However, demands of relevance and applicability force the homiletic activity away from a clear focus on the discourse of the Torah text into the twilight zone between artefactual and hermeneutical use.

The homiletic midrash is characterised by a particular rhetorical structure that may have been commonly used by preachers as a way to recapitulate the initial verse of the weekly Torah portion (the *seder* verse) to open the sermon (Stern 1987, 617). A homiletic midrash would begin with a proem (*petihta*), including a 'distant' verse taken from any part of Jewish scripture to comment on the *seder* verse. The 'distant' verse and the *seder* verse are seemingly unrelated. However, the *petihta* creates a series of exegetical bridges between the 'distant' verse and the *seder* verse to connect these 'through their common imagery in order to make its own rhetorical point' (Stern 1987: 617). A rhetorical structure like this facilitates the application and pursuit of two principles: the principle of omnisignificance, which emphasises that every part of the Torah is meaningful; and the principle of the unity of God's address, with seemingly inconsistent or contradictory parts or verses being drawn together to prove and stress the coherence of the divine message.[12] When the basic rhetorical structure supports and furthers such principles, a move is made away from textual use towards the projective artefactual use in what was supposed to be expositions of the Torah.

In the Middle Ages, the sermon exhibited new rhetorical structures to expound the Torah. In the Sephardic world Biblical, Talmudic and Midrashic quotations were expounded together in the sermon by letting one quotation explain the preceding quotation, only to let the last one interpret the weekly Torah portion itself. At this stage, the preacher would be the rabbi who made sure that the exposition was directed to match the concerns and interests of the congregants. The rabbis would preach in the vernacular, but in those cases where these sermons were published they would be edited and translated into Hebrew.[13]

In the Ashkenazi world, the liturgical poems (*piyyutim*) that expounded the link between the prayers and other texts in the *Siddur* had prolonged the synagogue service to such an extent that there was no room for sermons. Adding to this, Ashkenazi rabbis seemed more concerned with studies of *halakhah* than the religious and moral edification of the congregation through sermons. Sermons were only held by the rabbis three times a year[14] in a way that excluded lay attention. Instead, lay people welcomed the new figure of the itinerant preacher, known as the *maggid*, who gained success by addressing the needs of the Jews in his expositions of the Torah, especially in the rural districts of Eastern Europe.[15]

Due to the Jewish enlightenment movement, known as the *haskalah*, the *piyyutim* were eliminated from the synagogue service and replaced by sermons in the vernacular, which helped to edify the congregants (who in return welcomed this kind of address). The first to produce modern, enlightening sermons in the Ashkenazi world was Moses Mendelssohn. The modern Jewish sermon was moulded to fit the Protestant model and became the preserve of the rabbi. Jewish reform rabbis in Berlin found guidance (for instance) in Friedrich Schleiermacher, who attended the rabbis' sermons in order to supervise them on how to improve their preaching. However, Jews of a more orthodox inclination trying to safeguard the boundaries of their religious identity looked to the old rabbinical accounts of how to preach.[16]

In Eastern Europe, which had remained more or less unaffected by the Enlightenment, the Musar movement arose in the 19th century and spread from here to the USA. As a religious revival movement it looked to the sermon as an obvious genre for

---

12 Cf. Stern 2003, 237-238; 243; 250. The intensified search for coherent worldviews in the early Middle Ages makes midrash develop into other literary genres and lose its close link to the *derashah* or sermon.

13 Cf. 'Homiletics', *JewishEncyclopedia.com* 2002 as of 10 January 2008.

14 These were *shabbat ha-gadol*, *shabbat teshuvah*; and the eve of the Day of Atonement.

15 Cf. 'Homiletics', *JewishEncyclopedia.com* 2002 as of 10 January 2008.

16 Cf. Jacobs 2004, 5-6. Jacobs reserves the term 'sermon' for the obviously personal and spontaneous address of a live congregation, while the term 'homily' is to be reserved for the formal and structured kind of scriptural exegesis that only differs from scholarly interpretation in that the preacher is conscious of his homily being based on personal experience or personally motivated studies of the Torah, cf. Jacobs 2004, ix-x.

addressing ethical matters, and for hell-fire preaching against moral corruption and neglect of the commandments (Jacobs 2004, 7).

Today, a Jewish sermon is based on the weekly Torah portion or that part of the Prophets that is read immediately after the Torah scroll has been replaced in the cupboard. The average length of a sermon is 20 minutes. Some are based on manuscripts, while others are spoken extemporaneously. The themes of the sermons match the day of the sermon in question, whether this is a high holiday, a special occasion in the personal lives of the congregants, or a time when the congregants are affected by urgent issues of communal or universal import (Jacobs 2004, 9-10). Here, transitivity is created between present concerns and the Torah. The present concerns dominate in this use, where the Torah is treated as something between object and text.

Homiletics is now a discipline to be learned in the rabbinic seminaries. However, students and teachers have a tendency to regard homiletics as inferior to other rabbinic disciplines, which is one of the reasons why Louis Jacobs[17] argues for the importance of homiletics as a key discipline in the rabbinic seminaries in his book *Jewish Preaching – Homilies and Sermons*. Jacobs explains this slightly condescending attitude towards preaching by pointing to the underestimation of the congregants' interests in theology. He writes:

[I]n an average Jewish congregation nowadays one is likely to find a number of hungry souls who are merely irritated by appeals to Jewish pride or loyalty but who have an intense desire to know what Judaism is, who are well aware of what Judaism would have them do, but are puzzled as to what it is that Judaism would have them believe (Jacobs 2004, 13).

As an experienced preacher, Jacobs is aware that he has to be on 'the lookout for definite, concrete experiences in his own life and that of his congregation to serve both as pegs on which to hang theological ideas and as actual illustrations of how these ideas are to be used' (Jacobs 2004, 14). Naturally, in order not to lose a mourning congregant, theology must give way for pastoral care and a recognition of the severity of the loss sustained (Jacobs 2004, 14). Similarly, modern Jewish theology has to face the task of aborting, modifying or demythologising the literal meaning of a scriptural verse to avoid losing sophisticated believers (Jacobs 2004, 20). Again, it is clear that the need for relevance makes the preacher compromise his (otherwise hermeneutical) intent to look to the Torah as a text to find normative formulations on Jewish beliefs.

The Torah as a text?

The question remains as to where one can find examples of textual use. Based on the thoughts of Jan Assmann, who claims that cultures of writing (unlike oral cultures) encourage the establishment of institutions that ensure literacy and interpretative skills

---

17   Louis Jacobs (1920-2006) was a famous English theologian and rabbi, representative of Conservative Judaism.

(Assmann 2006 (2000), 43), I shall look for textual use in educational institutions that enable and favour such qualities within the Jewish populace.

Even though the commandment to study and explain the Torah[18] was essential in Second Temple Judaism, Torah study and exposition were not skills acquired in schools but rather something that depended on parental instruction. Parental instruction enabled Jews to keep this commandment. Families probably gathered in private homes on Sabbaths to study the Torah, unless they were able to travel to the Jerusalem Temple. In the Diaspora, Jews gathered in communal prayer houses for the same purpose. Those Jews who actually chose to specialise in Torah exposition would join a disciple circle around a master and learn from him in his *bet midrash* or house of instruction, as shown in Ben Sira 51:23. But this 'school', the first evidence of the institutionalisation of higher education in Judaism, would exist only as long as the master concerned remained active (Cohen 2006, 114-117).

In Early Rabbinic Judaism, the *bet midrash* became a private but permanent school-like institution in certain localities, while master-disciple relations continued to dominate in other areas. During the existence of the patriarchate (ca. 200-415 CE), the patriarch appointed rabbis as school instructors in Syria and Palestine and also tried to place them in other important positions such as synagogues and local courts. However, the synagogues remained centres of folk piety until the 7th century, and until then the schools were important to the patriarch in his attempt to secure the dissemination of rabbinic theology and praxis to all Jews (Cohen 2006, 213-215; Stemberger 2000, 80). The question remains as to what extent this institutionalised Torah study favoured the discourse of the Torah over early rabbinic theology; i.e., treated the Torah as a text and not as an object of projective activities that was open to manipulation.

The highest institution for education including Torah exposition and jurisprudence was the rabbinic academy. It originated in what Stemberger regards as the internment camp for Roman prisoners of war in Yavneh (Stemberger 2000, 78). Once these prisoners of war were released, they passed through the towns of Usha, Bet Shearim, and Sepphoris to finally establish a permanent rabbinic academy in Tiberias, headed around 200 CE by Judah haNasi, the first patriarch and the redactor of the *Mishnah*. Here, rabbinic students were trained prior to their ordination, the so-called *semikhah*; i.e., the laying on of the hands. The same institutional development takes place in Babylonia around the court of the exilarch and the two academies in Sura and Nehardea; with the latter being replaced by Pumbedita in 259.[19]

The rabbinic students studied the entire Hebrew Bible. Together with the Prophets and the Writings, the words of the Torah:

served as the prism, the lens, through which the Rabbinic sages looked at and refracted their conception of the world. ... [However, the rabbis] knew the Bible as a text they had heard, memorized,

---

18   Cf. Deut 6:6-7; 31:10-13; Neh 8:8.
19   Cf. *Mishnah*, 'Sanhedrin' 4:3-4; Stemberger 2000, 81-82.

and carried around in their heads as a memorized text rather than as one they had read and studied in a scroll and therefore remembered in its spatial context on a writing surface (Stern 2003, 235).

In other words, the early rabbis used a large amount of their cognitive capacity to memorise the Torah instead of freeing some mental space for critical reflection upon its content.[20] Adding to this, the memorised sentences were often quoted in isolation from the intratextual discourses of the Torah to legitimise the early rabbinic theology. Again one wonders if it is possible to speak of studies that furthered (or at least were based on) textual uses of the Torah in these academies; or if the Torah text was only recalled to substantiate or legitimise the postulates of the rabbis, making the 'academic' use of the Torah a matter of projective artefactual use as well.

Once the rabbis and rabbinical students in the academies engaged in debating and recording their legal expositions of the Torah in particular, known as *midrash halakhah*, a shift towards textual use occurred. *Midrash halakhah* designates the activity of verifying the legal praxis by identifying its source in the Torah and by interpreting the Torah as proof of its authenticity. Rabbi Hillel and Rabbi Ismael collected seven and thirteen rules respectively to safeguard rabbinic Judaism against random interpretation of those legal Torah passages that dealt with everyday life in a setting where the temple was no longer standing, and where foreign rule in what was now called Palestine prevented the legal content of the Torah from forming the normative basis of society. Rabbi Akiva focussed not only on the details of the Torah verses, but insisted that 'every passage which stands close to another must be explained and interpreted with reference to its neighbour' (*Sifre*, Num. 131). This attitude reflects a certain interest in understanding the discourse of the Torah text prior to its reception and transformation in a new historical context. Furthermore, the ideal of keeping as close as possible to the plain meaning; i.e. *peshat*, of a biblical verse came to influence all subsequent midrashic activity through this sentence in the Babylonian Talmud: 'a verse should not lose its literal sense' (*bTalmud*, 'Shabbat' 63a).[21] Because of this sentence, a *peshat*-oriented exposition came to be considered more valuable than a *derash*-oriented one, where meaning was applied to the biblical verse to ensure that it made sense (Halivni 1991, 9). In other words, it seems that the academies at least encouraged and trained their students in the textual use of the Torah.

In the Middle Ages, Jewish children would be potentially prepared for engaging in the textual use of scripture through the school system. A male child between 5 and 13 years of age would attend a private school, a continuation of the master-led instruction in a *bet midrash*, or if his parents were without means he could attend a *Talmud Torah*; i.e. a school for Torah studies, financed by the local Jewish community. The curriculum included Classical Hebrew, the *Siddur*, the *Torah* and the *Talmud*. After having completed this compulsory education, some boys were sent to a *yeshivah*, an institution for

---

20   Cf. Assmann 2006, 21, 101-121.
21   See also *bTalmud*, 'Yevamot' 11b; 24a.

higher education, where the halakhic material of the Talmudic tractates and the legal codes were studied. When these students were not attending lectures, they were expected to study with a *havrutha*; i.e. a friend, to help them develop their argumentative skills in duo. Boys who were not as fortunate as to be sent to a *yeshivah* had to study *halakhah* for at least one hour every day. These boys often met and studied together prior to the evening service, or on Shabbat. Finally, adults still had the opportunity to join a disciple circle around a master to become professional teachers of the Torah. By the end of the 18th century, Talmud academies of more than 400 students arose and eventually developed into the rabbinic seminaries that we know of today.[22] Though the textual use of scripture is very rare, Jewish communities have made this activity possible by always providing its adherents with sufficient reading skills and knowledge of exegetical rules.

The function of the rare cases of textual use

The function of textual use becomes evident when we look at the philosophical and poetic contributions within Jewish tradition. Jewish *kalam* (dialectical theology) as represented for instance by Saadya Gaon (882-942), head of the academy in Sura, introduced the concept of rationality to the study of scripture (Stroumsa 2003, 71-90). Yet, Saadya was unwilling to base Jewish religion on rationality alone:

> If the doctrines of religion can be discovered by rational inquiry and speculation, as God has told us, how can it be reconciled with His wisdom that He announced them to us by way of prophetic revelation and verified them by proofs and signs of visible character and not by rational arguments?[23]

Saadya answers his own rhetorical question by saying that God took account of human inabilities, lack of patience and disposition for doubts by giving the Torah to mankind. The eyewitness accounts of Moses are there for everyone to read and to hold on to until one is able to deduce knowledge about God based on sense perception, reason and inference. The literal wording in the Torah about divine revelation was to be taken at face value, something that Maimonides of the 12th century could not accept.

Maimonides never disputed the divine origin or the complete and perfect status of the Torah,[24] but he did warn against literal understandings of the descriptions in the Torah (Maimonides 1981, 140). The very transcendent nature of God constitutes an argument against anthropomorphic understandings of God or immanent descriptions of the Messianic age, for instance, as they were current among traditional rabbis. 'Everywhere in Scripture that He is portrayed as having bodily attributes such as walking, standing, sitting, speaking and their like – all these are figures of speech' (Maimonides 1981, 152),

---

22   Cf. Trautner-Kromann 2001, 203-204. See also 'Education', *JewishEncyclopedia.com* 2002 as of 1 February 2008.
23   This quotation is taken from Saadya's introduction to his *Book of Doctrines and Beliefs* written in 933, cf. Neusner & Avery-Peck 2001, 136.
24   Cf. the eighth and ninth fundamental principle in Maimonides 1981, 155-156.

which is why a rational Jew will have to engage in allegorical readings in order to transform the Torah into applicable and meaningful scripture. What Maimonides does in his attempt to secure a rationality-based understanding of the commandments is to point to the ontological difference between God and mankind as it is described in the discourse of the Torah in order to transform the norms for Torah exposition as practised within traditional Judaism. This is an example of the textual use of scripture applied in a time of crisis to counter the reign of naïve, traditional rabbis. Maimonides says:

> As God lives, it is this class of thinkers that destroys the splendour of the Torah and darkens its brilliance. And they pervert the Torah of God into saying the opposite of what it intends to convey … If only they would remain silent since they do not understand (Maimonides 1981, 140).

Textual use of the Torah is not entirely an academic and philosophical enterprise. In literature and arts, the discourses of scripture are taken seriously as the voices against which alternatives are formulated. Shlomo ibn Gabirol (1021-1070) made 152 quotations from the Bible in his 40-stanza hymn *Keter Malkhut*, which could invite the assumption that he only made artefactual use of the Bible. But the quotations invoke a dialogue between the dominant discourse of the Bible legitimising God's judgements, and the alternative discourse within the Bible portraying God's obligation to show mercy. Gabirol is arguing for a theology of mercy to replace the dominant theology of reward and punishment as the only way to defend God's righteousness. He writes:

> If I cannot hope for Thy mercies, who but Thou will have pity on me?
> Therefore, 'though Thou kill me, I shall hope in Thee' [Job 13:15],
> And if Thou search out my sin, I shall flee from Thee to Thee, and hide myself from Thy wrath in Thy shadow,
> I shall hold on to the skirts of Thy mercy until Thou hast pity on me. 'I will not let Thee go, except Thou bless me' [Gen. 32:27],
> Remember that of clay Thou didst make me, and with these afflictions didst Thou try me.
> Therefore do not visit my acts upon me … (*Keter Malkhut*, 38th stanza).[25]

Finally, I shall mention a few modern, secular uses of the Aqedah story (the binding of Isaac) from Genesis 22. While the modern reception of the Aqedah discards key norms of the Torah such as love of God and the honouring of the covenant, it is completely aware of the complexity of the text before transforming it into its anti-normative message. The Six-Day War of 1967 provoked criticism against the parent generation, which expected their sons and daughters to be prepared at all times to sacrifice themselves for its dream of a Jewish State. The dramatist Hanokh Levine had the dead Isaac address Abraham in the theatre production *Malkat haAmbatya* (The Queen of the Bath) from 1970. The dead Isaac says to his still living father: 'And don't say that you made a sac-

---

25   Quoted from Bernard Lewis' translation, cf. Gabirol 2003 (1961), 112. For more on Gabirol, cf. Schleicher 2006.

rifice, because the one who made a sacrifice is me'.[26] Here, Levine is using the Aqedah to challenge the norms of the parental generation, including a preparedness to send its own children off to war. The discursive positioning of Abraham as the hero, as we find it in the Torah, is deliberately undermined in an attempt to transform Jewish, secular normativity in the State of Israel to herald the primacy not of sacrifice – but of life.

The Six-Day War, however, brought an even more radical self-criticism upon the Israelis and their profiting at the cost of the Palestinians. The poet Yehuda Amichai also focussed on the character that had to be sacrificed for the sake of the Israeli state. Going one step further than Levine, however, the one to be sacrificed was not Isaac but the ram. In 'haGibor haAmiti shel haAqedah' (the true hero of the Aqedah) from 1971, Amichai writes:

The true hero of the binding is the ram
Who didn't know about the other people's conspiracy.
He sort of volunteered to die in Isaac's place.
I want to sing a song in his memory.
About the curly fleece and the human eyes.
About the horns that were so quiet in his living head.
And after he was slaughtered, they made shofars out of them
To sound the fanfare for their war
Or the fanfare of their coarse rejoicing.

I want to remember the last scene
Like a pretty picture in a tasteful fashion magazine:
The tanned, spoiled youth in his natty clothes
And by his side the angel in a long silk gown
At an official reception
And both of them with empty eyes
Looking at two empty places.
And behind them, in the colourful background, the ram,
Caught in the thicket before the slaughter.

And the thicket is his last friend.
The angel went home.
Isaac went home.
And Abraham and G-d have long since gone.

But the true hero of the binding
Is the ram.[27]

---

26 Quoted from Kartun-Blum 1995, 199.
27 Quoted from Kartun-Blum 1995, 195-196.

Similar to Levine's critical focus on the expectation of Isaac to accept victimhood, but within an American Diaspora context, the film *The Believer* by Henry Bean from 2001 deserves mentioning. In this film, which is a modern midrash on the Aqedah, a young Jewish man, Daniel Balint, becomes a Nazi as a way of protesting against the role of the passive victim that Jews have been given in the course of Western history, a role which has also been accepted to a certain extent as a central part of Jewish identity. In flashbacks into Daniel's early reaction to the Aqedah in the Torah classes of his Jewish school, the child cannot come to terms with God's tyrant demands on Abraham and God's traumatising of Isaac. Subsequently, he is expelled from the school, which initiates the process towards the ultimate heresy of becoming a Nazi, but also of sacrificing himself to put an end to Jewish victimhood once and for all. He achieves the latter by blowing himself up on the eve of Yom Kippur, an act which the religious Jews will understand as a kind of vicarious atonement on the part of his childhood congregation, which he was about to punish for its uncritical stance toward the Torah. However, instead of blowing up the congregation to make it atone for its blind acceptance of scripturally and culturally enforced victimhood, he chooses to give up his own life in his quest against ethnic victimisation. Again, the scriptural encouragement to accept victimhood if so required by God is refused, but a textual reading of the discourse with all its consequences takes place prior to this radical self-criticism of Jewish identity. *The Believer* exemplifies textual use despite the negative traits that it attributes to the face of the Torah.

Conclusion

This article concludes that the many possible meanings and infinite applicability of the Torah depend not only on its interpretative, textual use, but in particular on the manipulative, artefactual use of the Torah. After the fall of the Jerusalem Temple, various commentaries, accessories and ritual acts characterised, defined and revealed the Torah scroll as *the* holy object in Jewish tradition. As such the primary function of the projective artefactual use seems to be to create transitivity between the individual, the collective and the cultural on the one hand, and on the other hand these three and the holy sphere which lends authority to the social relations and current norms of beliefs and practices. In cases where the inherent encouragement of the Torah to exposit the text would make one expect to find interpretative textual use of scripture, one is surprised to witness that the need for transitivity and current relevance often leads to ignorance of the textual discourse. To a large extent it seems that the textual use of scripture is only to be found among the elite; i.e. rabbis engaged in halakhic studies, philosophers, poets and artists. In this context, textual use offers itself as a means to achieve a conscious dealing with the discourse of the Torah when psychological, social and cultural needs of the user invite advice from or rejection of this key normative text on how to think, behave and situate oneself with respect to the boundaries of Jewish tradition. In other words, reception and moderate transformation of religious normativity, sanctioned by scripture, requires only manipulative artefactual use of scripture; whereas significant change within the historical and cultural context requires radical reception and transformation of scripture-based normativity through a textual approach.

Bibliography

Assmann, Jan 2006. *Religion and Cultural Memory* (2000). Stanford: Stanford University Press.

Cohen, Shaye J.D. 2006. *From the Maccabees to the Mishnah* (2nd edn). Louisville: Westminister John Knox Press.

Elbogen, Ismar 1993. *Jewish Liturgy – A Comprehensive History* (1913). Philadelphia: Jewish Publication Society.

Gabirol, Solomon ibn 2003. *The Kingly Crown – Keter Malkhut* (trans. Bernard Lewis, 1961). Notre Dame: University of Notre Dame Press.

Halivni, David Weiss 1991. *Peshat and Derash – Plain and Applied Meaning in Rabbinic Exegesis.* Oxford: Oxford University Press.

Holdrege, Barbara 1989. 'The Bride of Israel: The Ontological Status of Scripture in the Rabbinic and Kabbalistic Traditions'. In: Levering (ed.), *Rethinking Scripture.* Albany: SUNY Press, 180-261.

Jacobs, Louis 2004. *Jewish Preaching – Homilies and Sermons.* London: Vallentine Mitchell.

Kartun-Blum, Ruth 1995. 'Isaac Rebound: The Aqedah as a Paradigm in Modern Israeli Poetry'. In: Wistrich & Ohana (eds.), *The Shaping of Israeli Identity – Myth, Memory and Trauma.* London: Frank Cass, 185-202.

Maimonides, Moses 1981. *Maimonides' Commentary on the Mishnah – Tractate Sanhedrin* (ed. Rosner). New York: Sepher-Hermon Press.

Malley, Brian 2004. *How the Bible Works – An Anthropological Study of Evangelical Biblicism.* Walnut Creek: AltaMira Press.

Neusner & Avery-Peck (eds.) 2001. *The Blackwell Reader in Judaism.* Oxford: Blackwell.

Ricoeur, Paul 1979. 'The "Sacred" Text and the Community'. In: W.D. Flaherty (ed.), *The Critical Study of Sacred Texts.* Berkeley: Berkeley Religious Studies Series, 271-276.

Ricoeur, Paul 2003. 'From Existentialism to the Philosophy of Language' (1975). *The Rule of Metaphor – The creation of meaning in language.* London: Routledge, 372-381.

Rod-Salomonsen, Børge & J. Winther 2001. *Jødedommen – Religiøse tekster gennem 2000 år,* vol. 1. Copenhagen: Spektrum.

Schleicher, Marianne 2006. 'Det andalusiske kulturmøde. Jødedom, kristendom og islam i Gabirols religiøse digtning'. In: Faber (ed.), *Religion. Tidsskrift for Religionslærerforeningen for Gymnasiet og HF,* #3, 14-25.

Smith, Jonathan Z. 1978. 'Sacred Persistence: Towards a Redescription of Canon'. In: Green (ed.) *Approaches to Ancient Judaism.* Missoula: Scholars Press, 11-28.

Stemberger, Günter 2000. 'The Foundation of Rabbinic Judaism, 70-640 CE'. In: Neusner & Avery-Peck (eds.), *The Blackwell Companion to Judaism.* London: Blackwell, 78-92.

Stern, David 1987. 'Midrash'. In: Cohen & Mendes-Flohr (eds.), *Contemporary Jewish Religious Thought.* New York: Charles Scribner's Sons, 613-620.

Stern, David 2003. 'On Canonization in Rabbinic Judaism'. In: Finkelberg & G. Stroumsa (eds.)
   Homer, the Bible, and Beyond – Literary and Religious Canons in the Ancient World. Leiden: Brill,
   227-252.

Stroumsa, Sarah 2003. 'Saadya and Jewish *kalam*'. In: Frank & Leaman (eds.), *The Cambridge
   Companion to Medieval Jewish Philosophy.* Cambridge: Cambridge University Press, 71-90.

Trautner-Kromann, Hanne 2001. 'Religiøse bevægelser i østeuropæisk jødedom'. In: Krag & Warburg
   (eds.), *Amol iz geven – jødisk kultur og historie i det gamle Østeuropa* (1985). Copenhagen:
   Forum, 201-214.

A THEOLOGY OF SCRIPTURAL PERFORMANCE
RECEPTION AND TRANSFORMATION
IN CHRISTIAN COMMUNITIES

Johannes Nissen

Bible reading as a transformative act

Biblical studies have been marked by a shift of attention from the relationship between author and text to the interaction between text and reader.[1] A new model of interpretation has emerged. It is based on the belief that deep insight and relevance lie neither in the original meaning of the Bible alone nor in the contemporary context, but in the to and fro of questions and answers between them. This model is that of a conversation. It brings with it a change in the understanding of New Testament hermeneutics. In the past, New Testament hermeneutics has been occupied predominantly with how texts serve to pass on *information*. Today the focus has shifted to the question of how texts might have a *transformative* role (Green 1995b, 413).

The relation between text and reader can be seen as a fusion between two horizons, between the world of the text and the world of the readers. In the fusion between the readers' world and the world of the text, both are transformed. When the readers enter the world of the text it transforms them by providing a new way of seeing and being, it offers them new possibilities. When the world of the readers is brought to the text it transforms the text by allowing a plurality of possible meanings not perceived in the past to be appropriated in the present by the readers; it offers the text a new way of speaking (West 1999, 44). Furthermore, by the very fact that we react to the text, we are transformed by the text. This is particularly clear in case of positive response to the text. We are informed, instructed, or taught by it. This is also clear when we are angered or infuriated by the text (Patte 1995, 97).

Traditionally, classical exegesis presupposed the existence of "objective", dispassionate readers, but this kind of neutrality has been called into serious question by the new methods. The "interested" reader has replaced the "objective reader". There are two

---

[1] In recent years a great number of methods have been used in biblical interpretation. One useful way of classifying the various methods is based on where the interpreter seeks to locate meaning: behind the text, in the text or in front of the text (Green 1995a, 6-9). The first approach – "behind the text" – emphasises the historical and sociological context of the Bible. The text is seen as a window into the intention of the author, into the history by which the materials collected by the author were formed or into the events reported by the text. The second approach – "in the text" – emphasises the literary and narrative content of the Bible. The text is seen as a cultural product or an artefact and as literature. The third approach – "in front of the text" – emphasises the role of the reader or the reading community. It is argued that different readers read differently. A crucial question is: "Does the reader discover the meaning or does he/she create the meaning?" The first option must be given preference. If meaning is not in some sense "there" in the text, how could texts ever challenge, inform, or transform their readers? How could the text ever criticise a dominant ideology? (Vanhoezer 1995, 317).

different models for reading: a moderate form ("reader reception") and a radical form ("reader-resistance"). In keeping with the first form, I give priority to a "hermeneutics of hearing" (Nissen 2006). According to this model we need to hear a voice other than our own or that of our community (Snodgrass 2003, 9). Yet, this is not to say that the text should be seen as a "meaning container". Rather, the text offers "potentialities of meaning" that can be actualised in a reading process that makes the text "meaningful" (Patte 1995, 94).

The Christian community as the embodiment of Scripture

The Christian hermeneutical task is not completed by the work of analysis and commentary; to interpret a text is to put it to work, to perform it in a way that is self-involving so that our interpretation involves our own commitments and risks.

One consequence of this hermeneutical guideline is that interpretation of the New Testament cannot be performed by isolated individuals; the embodiment of the Word happens in the body of Christ, the church. Christian hermeneutics is necessarily a communal activity (Fowl & Jones 1991). 'The performance of scripture', contends Lash, 'is the life of the church. It is no more possible for an isolated individual to perform *these* texts than it is for him to perform a Beethoven quartet or a Shakespearean tragedy' (Lash 1986, 43).

This communal aspect of embodying the Word is underlined by Paul in several passages, perhaps most impressively in 2 Cor 3:3: 'You are a letter of Christ… written not with ink but with the Spirit of the living God, not on tablets of stone but on the tablets of fleshy hearts.' Paul's statement illustrates the hermeneutical relation between text and community. The church itself, being transformed into the image of Christ (cf. 2 Cor 3:16.18), becomes a *living* metaphor for the power of God to which the text also bears witness. The metaphor reflects a dialectical process: the text shapes the community, and the community embodies the meaning of the text. 'Thus, there is a hermeneutical feedback loop that generates fresh readings of the New Testament as the community grows in maturity and as it confronts changing situations' (Hays 1997, 304).

The New Testament itself insists on the necessity of the embodiment of the Gospel. The sequence of the verbs in Romans 12:1-2 is interesting: '*Present* your bodies as living sacrifices… Be *transformed*.. that you may *discern* what is the will of God what is good and acceptable and perfect'. This passage indicates that the knowledge of the will of God *follows* the transformation of the Christian community. In order to conceive what the text means, we must see how it is embodied by the community. Thus, the most crucial hermeneutical task is the formation of communities that seek to live under the Word (Hays 1997, 306).

One common mistake is to think that reading mainly concerns extracting meaning-content "out of" Scripture by means of a process that bypasses the body altogether (with the possible exception of the eyes). The truth of the matter is that reading is 'not mere mental activity aroused by the eye moving across a page'. Rather it involves a full, complete, bodily engagement, and as such it is 'an unavoidably social and communal enterprise' (Mitchell 1999, 172; cf. Fodor 2006, 149).

Widespread notions of reading are largely disembodied and disembedded. They construe the reader as a solitary, silent individual before the printed page whose object is mentally to harvest the text's meaning or sense. When reading is viewed as a silent, mental, "inward" process, a private and thus hidden cognitive operation, it is not recognised as a practice that forms the identity (Fodor 2006, 153-154). Reading is never simply a cognitive decoding of written signs or following an argument; it is also – and perhaps even primarily – a means of forming, disciplining the emotions and offering a new orientation.

In recent years, bibliodramas have become a new way of embodying the Scripture. Bibliodrama intends to understand the Bible with body and soul, and with heart and mind. Tim Schramm asserts that the goal of our devotion to the Scripture, the aim of all human endeavours at interpreting biblical texts, should be – as Luther once said – to bring the Bible into our daily lives ('*die Bibel in das Leben ziehen*') and to transform written words into living words ('*Leseworte zu Lebensworten machen*') (Schramm 1992, 58). Walter Wink notes that practitioners of bibliodrama are trying not only to grasp what the Bible means but also to become the people that the Bible proclaims 'We are not just learning about the Bible but attempting to incarnate the God revealed by Jesus, who incarnated that God. We are not merely examining the doctrine of the Holy Spirit but opening our bodies, quite literally, to become the temples of the Holy Spirit within us' (Wink 1992, 128).

In the Christian tradition, reading is a communal speech act *par excellence*, a collective "performance" of the Bible. To the extent that Bible reading embodies itself in specific gestures, spaces, and habits, it is incarnational: reading "enfleshes" the Word, reading gives human form to the Word in space and time (Fodor 2006, 154). According to Carlos Mesters, the Bible must be read with the 'head', with the 'heart' and with the 'feet'. 'The feet are very important. The Bible was written as a product of a journey. It is only by following with our own feet the same journey that we can get to know all the meaning of the Bible for us'.[2]

The task of Christians is to *embody* Scripture in the various contexts in which they find themselves. Discerning *how* to go about embodying Scripture, however, is a complex matter. In part, the complexities are the result of distances between the contexts in which the Bible was originally written and read and the variety of contemporary contexts in which Christians read Scripture (Fowl & Jones 1991, 1).

Analogical imagination

Current work on the use of Scripture in Christian life often rests on presumptions that are problematic. In fact, casting the issue in terms of "use" suggests that Scripture

---

2   Carlos Mesters' paper *God's Project* is here quoted from Rowland & Corner 1990, 13.

is something out there waiting to be "used". All that is needed is the proper method which will (1) excavate the meaning of the Bible, (2) apply that meaning to this or that situation, and (3) identify how the meaning found in the Bible ought to be understood in relation to other possible sources of guidance (Fowl & Jones 1991, 4).[3]

Another way of combining Scripture and Christian life is the hermeneutics of analogy. However, there are also problems in this approach, in particular when it comes to the field of ethics. In the first place, it is difficult to see how the analogies between biblical situations and our own are to be controlled. Second, what is to be done when no biblical analogy is apparent? Are Christians bereft of guidance in the face of radically new challenges? Third, this approach seems to disrespect the autonomy and freedom of the agent.

To avoid the risks of a simple analogical model, one can argue that patterns and paradigms exercise a normative role through the analogical imagination, which seeks to act in new situations in ways that are faithful to the original pattern. William Spohn notes that in order to be both free and faithful, modern believers reason by analogy from the earlier interaction which is witnessed in the biblical text to a similar response to the challenges of their own time. Analogical thinking relies on imagination and on the ability to discern similarities and differences between one situation and another (Spohn 1995, 7). Similarly, Richard Hays says: 'The use of the New Testament in normative ethics requires *an integrative act of the imagination*, a discernment about how our lives, despite their historical dissimilarity to the lives narrated in the New Testament, might fitly answer to that narration and participate in the truth it tells' (Hays 1997, 298; emphasis in the original).[4]

Two historical situations are never totally analogous. However, it is possible to speak of a "dynamic analogy" between the text and the contemporary situation (Long 1989, 128). This means that no historical situation is repeated exactly, but a dynamic analogy results when we identify in some ways with characteristics or circumstances in the text and thus participate in the tensions and resolutions of the text.

The crucial question is: How are we to respond to our challenges in ways analogous to the responses that the first Christian communities made to their challenges? In order to answer this question we must take into consideration the discontinuity as well as the continuity between "then" and "now" (Nissen 2006, 95). I suggest a procedure that has three steps: listening, learning, and living. (1) The first task is *listening* carefully to

---

3   Joel Green characterises this approach as "interdisciplinarity as an import-export operation". According to this proposal, the gap between exegetical and systematic theological studies is negotiated by borrowing insights and/ or categories from one discipline for use in the other. In this instance the biblical scholar does not participate in the theological studies but imports what has already been analysed from one disciplinary system into the other (Green 2000, 37).

4   This way of conceiving interdisciplinarity assumes, according to Green, the status quo of theological and biblical studies. Instead he suggests a more organic approach to theological hermeneutics. He argues that the fundamental character of division between the biblical world and our own, or between biblical studies and theological studies, is not historical. 'It is theological. It has to do with a theological vision, the effect of which is our willingness – whether we are biblical scholars or theologians or some other species – to inhabit Scripture's own story' (Green 2000, 42; cf. Fowl & Jones 1991, 61).

the two texts: the "text" of the Bible and the "text" of life; (2) The second task is *learning*. From our listening to the biblical text and to our own context, we should learn to discern God's will in the present situation. (3) The *living* in front of the text. The task is not simply that of copying the example of Jesus, or mechanically repeating the words of Jesus. It is to live faithfully and responsibly in a new situation.

Thus, there is the double task of reading the text and reading the world (Fowl & Jones 1991, 36-49). On the one hand, the Bible as Scripture forms the life of Christian communities. Christians will need to learn to read biblical texts "over-against ourselves" rather than simply "for ourselves". We must be willing to be interrogated *by* Scripture in addition to interrogating it. On the other hand, there are readings of the world. The process of faithfully embodying an interpretation of Scripture presupposes that Christian communities have already analysed and diagnosed the contexts in which they find themselves.

The Bible as transformative narrative

In churches, the Bible is often "used" practically and ethically as a compendium of rules, as a prescriptive and proscriptive blueprint for pastoral practice and moral behaviour. In this context the word "used" points to the underlying assumption that Scripture is seen as a source book at our disposal rather than a means of God's grace through which we are formed and moulded (Colwell 2005, 212-213). But the Bible is not just a series of rules and propositions. Rather, it is a series of stories. Overwhelmingly, Scripture takes the form of narrative. The propositions and rules occurring in Scripture are rooted in and explicated by the narratives in which they occur (Colwell 2005, 216).

Many scholars recognise that story is a fundamental category in the Bible. A story creates a world before people's eyes and ears and invites them to recognise that they do or can live in that world (Goldingay 1995, 31). Historical criticism has difficulty tolerating this ambiguity and openness; it assumes that the author aimed at clarity and precision, and it brings all the resources of historical and linguistic scholarship to bear on elucidating the text's clear meaning. An audience-oriented approach to interpretation presupposes that ambiguity is inherent in a story, and asks what its openness does to the audience or the readers (Goldingay 1995, 40).

For most Christians throughout the greater part of history the Bible has been "heard" rather than "read". In part this was the outcome of illiteracy, but primarily it was simply due to the fact that before the printing press copies of the Bible were rare and precious. The availability of the Bible as an object of personal study promotes the idea that this is the proper nature and function of the Bible, as a resource of prescriptive rule. Conversely, a liturgical context for the hearing of Scripture promotes the recognition that the hearing of Scripture is itself a sacramental event, a means of grace through which something happens beyond the mere imparting of information. Scripture comes to us in the context of liturgy, not as a dead letter but as a vehicle for a living word (Colwell 2005, 218). When the Bible is read or heard in the context of the church's liturgy, we are addressed directly and immediately. The entire event of worship, prayer and confession functions as a means through which the congregation becomes part of the Christian story (Colwell 2005, 221).

The parables of Jesus belong to the most important stories in the New Testament. They are narratives in metaphoric form which refer to another realm beyond themselves. The parables have four characteristics: they are realistic, metaphorical, paradoxical or surprising, and open-ended. The ordinary expectations are subverted.[5] The reader can become caught by listening attentively to a parable. When this engagement occurs, we do not interpret parables so much as they interpret us (Spohn 1995, 90).

In most parables Jesus begins in people's everyday world of home and family, of work and worship, of sowing and harvest, of shepherding and labouring, of weddings and funerals, of Pharisees, tax farmers, priests, Levites, and Samaritans. He thus draws his hearers into his stories because they manifestly relate to their world. Near the end the parables turn surrealistic. Jesus moves the familiar world of his listeners to an unfamiliar, revolutionary world. The parables portray a realistic but strange world, one transformed by God's grace. 'They create a world before people's eyes and ears, a familiar world into which people cannot help but be drawn, but then challenge them as to whether they will live according to the logic of merit that is inherent in this familiar world, or go with God into a world that lives according to the illogic of grace' (Goldingay 1995, 80-81).

The performance of the text

The concept of performance has a significant potential for revitalising the interpretation of the New Testament. In this light, biblical interpretation is not primarily something archaeological where the relatively detached academic postpones the question of truth.[6] Rather, on the performance analogy, biblical interpretation is something practical, personal, communal and "political" (Barton 1999, 184).

According to Nicholas Lash, one of the closest analogies to biblical interpretation is the interpretation of a Beethoven score or a Shakespearean tragedy. The central act of the interpretation of a Beethoven score is the performance, which has to be a matter of more than technical accuracy. Instead it is a kind of *creative fidelity* that allows the musical score to come alive again in the present moment. Important also is the recognition that this is a social or communal activity involving not just conductor and orchestra, but an audience of listeners and critics as well. These analogies help establish Lash's

---

5   The element of reversal is an important aspect of many parables. So, for instance, in the parable of the workers in the vineyard (Matth 20:1-16), there is a collision between two worlds, between two sets of experiences, namely life as fairness versus life as grace. A similar collision can be detected in the parable of the prodigal son (Luke 15:11-32). To understand such parables is to be changed by them. It is to have our vision of the world reshaped by them (Nissen 2006, 97).

6   Barton 1999, 182 argues that inquiry into the meaning of the Bible is inadequate if it is not at the same time an inquiry into its truth, that is to say, an inquiry into whether or not creative fidelity to who and what the text is about makes human transformation possible.

main point that there are at least some texts that only begin to deliver their meaning in so far as they are "brought into play" through interpretive performance. The Bible is one such text. 'The fundamental form of the *Christian* interpretation of Scripture is the life, activity, and organisation of the believing community' (Lash 1986, 42).

The *dis*analogies with performance models of reading, however, are perhaps as important as the analogies. There are clearly significant differences between dramatic "enactment" or musical "performance" and "living a life" (Fodor 2006, 151). For even the most dedicated musician or actor, the interpretation of Beethoven or Shakespeare is a part-time activity. At this point the analogy with biblical texts does not apply. The interpretation of these texts is a full-time affair. 'The performance of scripture *is* the life of the church' (Lash 1986, 43). Another analogy may help. The fundamental form of the political interpretation of the American Constitution is the life, activity and organisation of American society. 'That society exists… as the *enactment* of its Constitution. Similarly, we might say that the scriptures are the "constitution" of the church' (p. 43).

The concept of performance is also used by N.T. Wright. To respond adequately to the Bible as Scripture we have to take its storied shape seriously. For Wright this includes taking the Bible *as a whole* as a story. The interpretation of the New Testament is compared with the improvisation of a lost fifth act of a Shakespearean play by skilled actors who have to immerse themselves in the first four acts in a way that enables them to develop and conclude the play in a way which can be recognised as being "right" and "fitting". The first four acts are the authority for the fifth act: they constrain the variety possible in it. Wright suggests that we should think analogously of the Bible as a drama in five acts, namely Creation, Fall, Israel, Jesus, the New Testament and the Church. The New Testament is the first scene in the fifth act, giving clues as to how the story is supposed to end. The church would thus live under the authority of the story and be responsible for offering an improvisation and performance of the final act with sensitivity and creativity (Wright 1992, 142; cf. Bartholomew 2005, 142-143).

David Rhoads in a similar way asserts that performing a text is like playing a musical composition. One of the most interesting aspects of performance is the experience of entering the world of the story. At every point, the storyteller uses imagination to re-create the story. You re-enact the world of the story in the space on the stage. The act of performing the whole narrative leads a person to be immersed in this world (Rhoads 1992, 103-104). Furthermore, the interaction between performer and audience is much more than communication. The audience participates in more ways than understanding. Words and stories do not just have denotations of meaning. They also have an impact on people (Rhoads 1992, 108).

The idea of performing the scriptures rests on the insight that we have to work analogically and dialectically between the past and the present. As Lash puts it: 'We do not *first* understand the past and *then* proceed to seek to understand the present. The relationship between the two dimensions of our quest for meaning and truth is dialectical; they mutually inform, enable, correct, and enlighten each other' (Lash 1979,

24-25).[7] It is not simply the question of the Christian communities reading biblical texts, but of actually performing them. Such performances require the development of well-informed character. We read and perform Scripture hoping that our lives will be transformed into the likeness of Christ. Such transformation takes place in and through the formation of a community of disciples (Fowl & Jones 1991, 62-63).

The whole idea of performing Scripture corresponds to seeing the New Testament as an "open text". To be sure, the canon is closed, but biblical texts are open for never-ending re-readings (Nissen 2003, 655). The New Testament is an open text because it points to a future which transcends the time in which the text came into existence. It is also "open" because it invites the readers to go into history and embody the text in their lives (cf. Barton 1999, 195-196).

Reception and transformation in the Christian worship

For Lash, the performative interpretation of Scripture finds its best illustration in the celebration of the eucharist and in the liturgy of the Word. In the eucharist, 'that interpretative performance in which all our life consists – all our suffering and care, compassion, celebration, struggle and obedience – is dramatically distilled, focussed, concentrated, rendered explicit'. In the liturgy of the Word, the story is told 'not so that it may merely be relished or remembered, but that it may be *performed* in the following of Christ' (Lash 1986, 46).

The heart of Christian formation lies in worship, through which the story of salvation is re-enacted in the modes of prayer, proclamation and sacrament. In worship, we receive identity and are morally formed. By encountering God we learn how to be disciples; we learn generosity by being treated generously. The two liturgical acts, baptism and the Lord's Supper, both had an important formative role for communal life, e.g. Romans 6; 1 Cor 11:17-34. Most important, however, was the Lord's Supper, because it was celebrated more frequently than baptism. As at Jesus' table there was an open invitation to overcome suspicions, divisions, and hostilities, so at the Eucharistic table Jew and Gentile, rich and poor, weak and strong come together and experience a new and challenging depth of community. The Eucharistic liturgy specifically ties memory and hope to our participation in the story of Jesus. This participation gives us new eyes to see the world and new energy to bear witness in it (Nissen 2006, 92-93).

Sometimes, however, Christians fail to receive the tradition in an appropriate manner, which means that they cannot benefit from the transformative function of the gospel. An early example of this is the celebration of the Lord's supper in 1 Cor 11:17-34 which reflects a collision between the new era and daily reality, between Paul's theological vision and the social consequences drawn from that vision. Paul's statement indicates that he had expected the Christians to act according to the vision with

---

7   Fowl and Jones (1991, 58-61) rightly note that we find examples of this thinking in the practice of some of the earliest Christians as reflected in Scripture. Two examples are Romans 6:1-11 and Philippians 1:27-2:18.

analogical imagination. The Corinthians should have acted faithfully to the tradition and creatively to the new situation. However, the rich members of the community disregarded the needs of the poor members, and so the sacrament became invalid. 'It is not the Lord's supper that you eat' (1 Cor 11:20).

Gordon Lathrop has argued that there is a parallel between the way in which the first Christians used their texts and traditions in the assemblies and the way in which we use our biblical texts today. The deep structure of liturgy is this very biblical pattern: the old is made to speak the new (Lathrop 1998, 24). Hearing the Bible, we are gathered into a story, we have a place for our sorrow to sink. At the same time, the liturgical vision is that these stories mediate an utterly new thing, beyond all texts. 'Juxtaposed to this assembly, the texts are understood by the liturgy to have been transformed to speak now the presence of God's grace. In this way, the texts are made to carry us, who have heard the text and been included in its evocations, into this very transformation: God's grace is present in our lives' (Lathrop 1998, 19).

Just as the hopes and symbols of Christians in the first century became materials that were transformed into ways of speaking of Christ, so our gatherings, actions, words and hopes are also drawn into the same transformation. 'Christian corporate worship is made up of chains of images: our gathering, our washing, our meal are held next to biblical stories, themselves read in reinterpretive chains, and this whole rebirth of images is itself biblical' (Lathrop 1998, 24).[8] However, this reading of old stories as of new realities is a complex undertaking. We are not Israelites, nor are we early Christians. We partake in the biblical stories, simply because we are human beings. We share the sorrow and hope that mark the human situations expressed in these texts (Lathrop 1998, 17).[9]

Through the liturgical reading of biblical texts, Christians become schooled and trained into a new way of seeing and being. Reading is the pivotal rite of dislocation – of re-orientation by disorientation – whereby one's identity becomes radically transposed. 'Faithfully reading the Scripture means permitting oneself to be cross-examined, challenged, and remade by the Scripture' (Fodor 2006, 149).

Christian worship, then, provides alternative ways of seeing reality. The same may be said more generally. Richard Hays notes that the world we know is reconfigured when we "read" it in counterpoint with the New Testament. The hermeneutical task is to relocate our contemporary experience on the map of the New Testament story. By telling us a story that overturns our conventional ways of seeing the world, the New Testament provides images and categories in the light of which the life of our community is interpreted (Hays 1997, 302).

---

8   'Old texts, old stories and songs are borrowed to speak of the world transformed. Old meal practices and old washing symbolism, our ritual structures, are shaped to speak of Jesus Christ' (Lathrop 1998, 26).

9   It should be noticed that the texts are not simply read, as in a lecture hall or even a theatre. They are received with reverence, yet they are criticised and transformed. They become the environment for the encounter with God. They become language for current singing (Lathrop 1998, 20).

Walter Brueggemann has recently underlined that the Bible, the tradition, and the long history of church practice constitute a particular, distinctive, clear, but flexible script according to which life in the world may be lived out differently. This scripting of life is seen as a *counterscripting*. It is an *alternative performance* of human life in the world, a performance that requires precisely the kind of imagination, courage, energy, and freedom for which this script vouches in peculiar ways (Brueggemann 2006, 46).

The problem of normativity in the interaction between Bible and community

Embodying and performing biblical texts does not imply that all that is written in the Bible should be adopted uncritically. The question, however, is where to locate the normativity in the interaction between text and community.[10] Basically there are two different approaches: a "hermeneutics of trust" and "a hermeneutics of suspicion" (Watson 1993, 10). Is it possible to construe the relation of the interpreter to the text in a way that escapes this antithesis of trust and suspicion? Can we combine the objective, distancing, critical approach to Scripture with the engaged, trusting, experiential approach?

The dialectic in the interpretive process can be seen in terms of three moments: fusion, distance and communion (Wink 1973, 19-80). It takes people from a fusion with Scripture that provides an "orientation", by way of a distancing from this heritage that can demystify it and thus enable it to be heard in its own terms, as they move towards the goal of communion, genuine dialogue between interpreter and text. As mentioned above, this is in line with the parables of Jesus: They begin from the hearer's familiar world and disorient them with God's unfamiliar world in order to lead them to a "reorientation".

A different way of seeing the reading process is proposed by Gerald West, who is one of the advocates for contextual Bible studies. He points to a two-fold critical reading (West 1999, 23 and 76). The first step is a critical reading of the Bible, the next step is a critical appropriation and "reading" of our own context. This means that there is no simple correspondence between the Bible and our own context. We cannot move simply from our biblical reading to a present application. The move from text to context is a critical, complex and cautious exercise.

The two ways differ as to the starting point of the reading process, but apart from this they both insist on the dialectic nature of the relation between text and interpreter. The traditional way of setting the Bible and the church against each other or one above the other in normativity fails to testify appropriately to the historical complexity (Nissen 2003, 656-657). The community of faith is the proper context in which the Bible is to be understood. In one sense this is not new. Form criticism already called attention

---

10   "Normativity" is here used in the same sense as "authority", which is the most common term in relation to the issue of the hermeneutical importance of the Bible (cf. Nissen 2003).

to the communities which preserved, shaped and generated the tradition. However, the active role of the community has been emphasised even more by new methods (sociological studies, contextual exegesis etc.). Thus there is a hermeneutical circle operating within the believing community.

There is a dialectic between "the text" of life (experience) and the text of Scripture, and this dialectic is the kernel of the interpretive enterprise.[11] The community of Christians formed and shaped the Christian canon. But the same canon in turn forms and shapes the community (Vogels 2000, 220). However, if the Bible represents the self-understanding of the community that produced it, it is by no means an idealised statement of Christian propaganda. Rather, the Bible, Old and New Testament alike, is a series of critiques of the very community that produced it (Actemeier 1980, 92).

The relationship between the text and the interpreter can be seen as a mutual challenge. Sandra Schneiders notes that 'for the dialogue between text and reader to be genuine, the text must maintain its identity, its "strangeness", which both gifts and challenges the reader. It must be allowed to say what it says, regardless of whether this is comfortable or assimilable to the reader' (Schneiders 1991, 171).

The normativity of the Bible cannot be based on some hypothetical "objective reading"; rather; it grows out of a living encounter with Scripture. The experience of the community cannot be discounted. It constitutes a vital part of the unending dialogue with God's living word.

At the same time there is a need for re-evaluation of normativity itself (cf. 'The Authority of Scripture' 1983, 113).[12] Normativity in the sense of "authority" is often seen as being inflexible and hierarchical. True authority can never be imposed; it only works when offered, chosen and freely accepted. When applied from above, vertically, it is oppressive, but when it happens horizontally, it expands – not in an exclusive way but inclusively. The Word became words: stories, dialogues, lives, action – flesh. The early Christian community was involved in the shaping of the text itself, "living the scriptures" by telling and living its story in changing circumstances.

The first Christian communities ventured to write the gospel anew. Today's communities must do the same. This is the precondition required for the realisation of true authority. When the community ventures to write the gospel anew, the Bible will remain a living reality, a source for continuing dialogue.

If the Bible is considered to be normative, the reader becomes the listener, seeking to enter into dialogue with the text, to enter personally in the story, to live it, to take part in it, to re-live it.[13] In this understanding, the embodiment of the text in the life

---

11   For further reflections on the interaction between biblical text and modern experiences, see Nissen 1997.

12   This publication is a result of the Amsterdam Consultation organised by the "Community of Women and Men in the Church" study – a special programme of the WCC located in the sub-unit on Faith and Order in cooperation with the sub-unit on "Women in Church and Society".

13   Cf. Vogels 2000, 223. The author also notes: 'As with any other text, the Bible has no authority in itself. The reader decides if and to what extent he or she will give it authority. But if the reader decides to take up the Bible, the rules of the game must be respected. This means respect of the communitarian authority of the Bible as canon and respect of the literary authority as a literary product' (p. 225).

of the readers is of great importance to its continued status as normative. Christians read and perform the text in the hope that their lives will be transformed. When this occurs, they as readers become disciples. A hermeneutics of hearing will include a hermeneutics of action, knowing that texts are the result of actions and are intended to produce action (Snodgrass 2003, 27). There is a move from the emphasis on the act of reading to a focus on the practices of Christian communities fostered by that reading.

Bibliography

Achtemeier, Paul 1980. *The Inspiration of Scripture. Problems and Proposals.* Philadelphia: Westminster Press.

'The Authority of Scripture in Light of New Experiences of Women'. 1983. In: W.H. Lazareth (ed.), *The Lord of Life.* Geneva: World Council of Churches, 101-115.

Bartholomew, Craig 2005. 'In Front of the Text: The Quest of Hermeneutics'. In: Paul Ballard & Stephen R. Holmes (eds.), *The Bible in Pastoral Practice. Readings in the Place and Function of Scripture in the Church.* London: Darton, Longman and Todd, 135-152.

Barton, Stephen 1999. 'New Testament as Performance'. *Scottish Journal of Theology* 52, 179-208.

Brueggemann, Walter 2006. *The Word That Redescribes the World. The Bible and Discipleship.* Minneapolis: Fortress Press.

Colwell, John 2005. 'The Church as ethical community'. In: Paul Ballard & Stephen R. Holmes (eds.), *The Bible in Pastoral Practice. Readings in the Place and Function of Scripture in the Church.* London: Darton, Longman & Todd, 212-224.

Fodor, Jim 2006 (2004). 'Reading the Scriptures: Rehearsing Identity, Practicing Character'. In: Stanley Hauerwas & Samuel Wells (eds.), *The Blackwell Companion to Christian Ethics*, Oxford: Blackwell, 141-155.

Fowl, Stephen E. & L. Gregory Jones 1991. *Reading in Communion. Scripture and Ethics in Christian Life.* London: SPCK.

Goldingay, John 1995. *Models for Interpretation of Scripture.* Grand Rapids: Eerdmans & Carlisle: The Paternoster Press.

Green, Joel B. 1995a. 'The Challenge of Hearing the New Testament'. In: J.B. Green (ed.), *Hearing the New Testament. Strategies for Interpretation.* Grand Rapids: Eerdmans & Carlisle: The Paternoster Press, 1-9.

Green, Joel B 1995b. 'The Practice of Reading the New Testament'. In: J.B. Green (ed.), *Hearing the New Testament. Strategies for Interpretation.* Grand Rapids: Eerdmans & Carlisle: The Paternoster Press, 411-427.

Green, Joel B. 2000. 'Scripture and Theology: Uniting the Two So Long Divided'. In: J.B. Green & M. Turner (eds.), *Between Two Horizons. Spanning New Testament Studies and Systematic Theology.* Grand Rapids: W.B. Eerdmans, 23-43.

Hays, Richard B. 1997. *The Moral Vision of the New Testament. A Contemporary Introduction to New Testament Ethics.* Edinburgh: T. & T. Clark.

Lash, Nicholas 1979. 'Incarnation and Imagination'. In: M.D. Goulder (ed.), *Incarnation and Myth. The Debate Continued.* London: SCM Press, 19-26.

Lash, Nicholas 1986. *Theology on the Way to Emmaus*. London: SCM Press.

Lathrop, Gordon W. 1998 (1993). *Holy Things. A Liturgical Theology*. Minneapolis: Fortress Press.

Long, Thomas 1989. *The Witness of Preaching*. Louisville: Westminster/John Knox Press.

Mitchell, Nathan D. 1999. 'Ritual as Reading'. In: J.M. Pierce & M. Downey (eds.), *Source and Summit Commemorating Josef A. Jungmann, SJ*. Collegeville, MN: The Liturgical Press, 161-181.

Nissen, Johannes 1997. 'Mødet mellem Bibelen og nutidens mennesker'. In: B. Thyssen (ed.), *Bibelbrug og livsoplysning. Bibeldidaktiske overvejelser*. Frederiksberg: Materialecentralen, 41-98.

Nissen, Johannes 2003. 'Scripture and Community in Dialogue. Hermeneutical Reflections on the Authority of the Bible'. In: J.-M. Auwers & H.J. de Jonge (eds.), *The Biblical Canons*. Leuven: Leuven University Press & Uitgeverij Peeters Leuven, 651-658.

Nissen Johannes 2006. 'Bible and Ethics. Moral Formation and Analogical Imagination'. In: Gaye W. Ortiz & Clara A.B. Joseph (eds.), *Theology and Literature. Rethinking Reader Responsibility*. New York: Palgrave Macmillan, 81-100.

Patte, Daniel 1995. *Ethics of Biblical Interpretation. A Re-evaluation*. Louisville: Westminster/ JohnKnox Press.

Rhoads, David 1992. 'Performing the Gospel of Mark'. In: B. Krondorfer (ed.), *Body and Bible. Interpreting and Experiencing Biblical Narratives*. Philadelphia: Trinity PressInternational, 102-119.

Rowland, Christopher & Max Corner 1990. *Liberating Exegesis. The Challenge of Liberation Theology to Biblical Studies*. London: SPCK.

Schneiders, Sandra 1991. *The Relevatory Text. Interpreting the New Testament as Sacred Scripture*. San Francisco: HarperCollins.

Schramm, Tim F. 1992. 'Bibliodrama in Action: Reenacting a New Testament Healing Story'. In: B. Krondorfer (ed.), *Body and Bible. Interpreting and Experiencing Biblical Narratives*. Philadelphia: Trinity Press International, 57-84.

Snodgrass, Klyne 2003. 'Reading to Hear: A Hermeneutics of Hearing'. *Horizons in Biblical Theology*, 34, 1-32.

Spohn, William C. 1995. *What are they Saying about Scripture and Ethics* (Revised and expanded edition). New York/Mahwah, NJ: Paulist Press.

Vanhoezer, Kevin J. 1995. 'The Reader in New Testament Interpretation'. In: J.B. Green (ed.), *Hearing the New Testament. Strategies for Interpretation*. Grand Rapids: Eerdmans & Carlisle: The Paternoster Press, 301-328.

Vogels, Walter 2000. 'The Role of Reader in Biblical Authority'. *Theology Digest*, 47, 219-225.

Watson, Francis 1993. 'Introduction: The Open Text'. In: F. Watson (ed.), *The Open Text. New Directions for Biblical Studies*. London: SCM Press, 1-12.

West, Gerald O. 1999. *Contextual Bible Study*. Pietermaritzburg: Cluster Publications.

Wink, Walter 1973. *The Bible in Human Transformation*. Philadelphia: Fortress Press.

Wink, Walter 1992. 'Bible Study and Movement for Human Transformation'. In: B. Krondorfer (ed.), *Body and Bible. Interpreting and Experiencing Biblical Narratives*. Philadelphia: Trinity Press International, 120-132.

Wright, N.T. 1992. *The New Testament and the People of God*. Minneapolis: Fortress Press.

RESPONDING TO GOD

RECEPTION AND TRANSFORMATION IN CHRISTIAN HYMNS[1]

Kirsten Nielsen

The Danish *folkekirke* is an evangelical-Lutheran church. At church services texts are read from both the Old and the New Testament, while the sermon occupies a central position. It could nevertheless be justifiably claimed that the most characteristic feature of the Danish *folkekirke* service is hymn singing. At morning service at least 5 hymns are sung, and whenever you enter a Danish church you immediately notice a shelf full of hymn books. There is no corresponding shelf of Bibles. The hymn book is intended for congregational singing – 'To give voice to the congregation's *current response* to God's address', as a Danish hymnologist has put it (Jens Lyster 1991, 32).

On 29th July 2002 Her Majesty Queen Margrethe II authorised a new hymn book for use in services in the Danish Lutheran Church. Just as the Bible is an authoritative text whose many books have been selected and canonised by the early Christian Church, so is the Danish hymn book authorised by the highest authority in the Danish Lutheran Church. Both the Bible and the hymn book thereby acquire a *normative function* for the congregation's interpretation and practice of life.

If we are to define further the relationship between the two textual collections, it is important to emphasise that the hymns have come into being in a dialogue with the biblical message as the congregation's *current response* and in recognition of the normative function of the Bible. The hymn writers respond to the biblical message in a way which carries both reception and transformation of the Bible's way of speaking about God. They are themselves dependent on the norm which the Bible sets, but are nevertheless able to create new understanding in their hymns. The aim of this article is therefore to show partly what the biblical norm comprises, and partly how the hymn writers relate to this norm in their reception and transformation of the biblical way of speaking about God.

The Bible as intertext for the Danish hymn book (DDS)

As we take a closer look in the following at the link between the Bible and the Danish hymn book, the focus will be on the relationship between the biblical images of God and the images of God in the hymns.[2] In this context we shall examine the concept of

---

1   This article has been translated by Edward Broadbridge.
2   A deeper analysis of the use of images of God in the Bible and recent Danish hymns is to be found in Kirsten Nielsen 2007, on which this article builds.

intertext, a term for which I am indebted to Julia Kristeva's theory of *intertextuality* (see Marianne Schleicher 2007). Kristeva regards the reading of texts as a dialogue between various voices: the author, the receiver and the contexts in which they respectively find themselves (past and present). The meeting between the many voices in the text she calls intertextuality. If we apply this to a study of recent Danish hymns, the situation is as follows: Via the hymn the reader enters into dialogue with the writer and his/her contexts as well as with his own. Both the writer's and the reader's context consists of many different experiences, but to a greater or lesser degree both have the Bible and its reception history as their common context. For this reason the Bible serves as an important intertext for the hymn. When I refer below to the Bible as intertext, I am suggesting primarily that by re-creating a specific story from the Bible or by using one of its significant expressions the hymn writer wishes to bring the biblical narratives and themes into the reader's consciousness. The reader's task is to follow the author's intention by recognising the *markers* which the author employs to indicate the biblical intertext (see further Kirsten Nielsen 2000). However, the reader's role is not limited solely to following the author's intention; in many cases the reader may well call to mind biblical intertexts that the author has not intended.

The great precursors

Those hymn writers whose work appears for the first time in the new Danish hymn book are following in a long tradition, beginning with the Psalms of David and continuing through four centuries of Danish hymn writing. In his poetics, *The Anxiety of Influence: A Theory of Poetry*, the literary critic Harold Bloom distinguishes between strong and weak poets and their various ways of relating to their great precursors. The weak borrow their precursors' feelings and compose on top of them, so to speak; whereas the strong poets he characterises as 'major figures with the persistence to wrestle with their strong precursors, even to the death' (Bloom 1973, 5). Bloom's interest gathers around the strong poets' struggle against their great precursors and the 'patricide' they must commit in order to create their own text and thereby create themselves as artists. Their patricide therefore consists of a creative misreading of their precursors' work.

Continuing this line of thought, it might be said that the New Testament has come into being in a struggle with the Old Testament, whereby the message concerning Christ leads to a new interpretation and thus to a victory over parts of the Old Testament. Correspondingly, in the tradition of Christian hymn writing a struggle is waged between various voices. In a less dramatic formulation we might say that all hymn writers enter into a tradition to which they must relate – not only by endorsement but also by rejection. If the poet is to create something new, it is not enough to repeat the precursors' work. The hymn writer can choose to rework a biblical text in a clear continuation of the biblical writer's line of thought. But nearly all reception will also include transformation. Let us look at an example of how such a transformation can take place in one of the new Danish hymns.

Reception and transformation in a Danish hymn

The Danish hymn writer Holger Lissner wrote a hymn in 1972 which begins with the words, *Cain, Where is Your Brother?* (DDS 698). The name Cain is a clear marker, and to understand the hymn we must follow the marker and include as intertext the biblical narrative of Cain's murder of his brother Abel in Gen 4:1-16. In a literal translation the first four verses read:

Cain, where is your brother?
You don't really think
you can hide from me, do you?
Surely you know
how he suffered
when you thrust him away?
Look, here is your brother!

Cain, where is your brother?
You don't really think
I'm deaf and blind, do you?
There is blood
on your foot,
and your bread tastes of it.
Look, that is your brother!

Cain, where is your brother?
You don't really think
you're free, now that he's dead, do you?
You can walk to –
but never reach –
the place where he isn't anyway.
Look, there is your brother!

Cain, where is your brother?
You don't really think
he doesn't need you, do you?
So give
him your life –
which you yourself have from me.
Look, he is your brother!

If we do not know the sequence of events in the Old Testament intertext, the hymn remains somewhat cryptic. Who is asking this question of Cain? Nowhere in the hymn does it say it is God. And to what is the questioner referring when he asks after Cain's brother? The reader must supplement the text with the required knowledge of the Old Testament story. In this case the story is relatively well-known, so most churchgoers will be able to identify the speaker as God and the brother as the murdered Abel. But precisely because they have interpreted the hymn on the background of the Old Testament story, the last verse of the hymn comes as a surprise. For here Holger Lissner introduces a quite different intertext:

Cain, where is your brother?
You don't really believe
I don't love you, do you?
Just look up.
On my body
are the gash and the nail-holes.
Cain, I am your brother!

By including this new intertext Holger Lissner presents an innovative interpretation of the original. The story of Cain and Abel is not only exposed to reception but also to transformation through the introduction of the New Testament intertext. The questioner is no longer the Old Testament God; now it is Jesus who takes up the question, though again without this being stated. It is not until the first two questions have been asked yet again that the reader realises that the intertext is new. The words, 'gash and the nail-holes', serve as new markers, pointing to Christ's crucifixion and death for the sake of mankind. However, because the intertext is different, there is also a marked transformation of roles in relation to the Old Testament narrative. Jesus is not only the speaker in v. 5; in the very last line of the hymn he reveals that it is he himself who is the murdered brother. This dramatic role change also implies that Cain is no longer the biblical character but is in fact the present reader – for whom Jesus has died. The God of the Old Testament who appears in Gen 4 and the first four verses of the hymn to be a prosecutor against the criminal now changes roles. He puts on a human figure and becomes the reader's brother. Through this change of role the writer opens the way for a different ending from the Old Testament – an ending in which justice is done and Cain is punished by having to leave the arable land. In Holger Lissner's hymn justice is tempered with mercy, in that Jesus as the brother of all mankind bears the punishment himself by dying on the cross. The hymn tells the story of salvation without actually saying so. The reader is left to include both the Old and the New Testament intertexts.

Imagery in the Bible and in the hymns

Since this article concentrates on images of God in recent Danish hymns, it is essential to clarify what is meant by *imagery* (see also Kirsten Nielsen 1989, 65). In this context I distinguish between two forms of imagery: *metaphors* and *metonymies*.

It is characteristic of a *metaphor* that it functions through an interplay (dialogue) between two different statements or contexts. When the psalmist calls God 'my rock' in Ps 18:3, he is claiming that something that is true of a rock is also true of God. Not everything, of course. There are points of similarity between a rock and God, but there is not total identity. Similarity presupposes that there are also differences. It then becomes the reader's task to select which meaning potentials are relevant for speaking about God in this way, and which are not. The rock contains a number of meaning potentials. Taken literally, all of them are valid, but when used metaphorically, it is left to the reader to choose which meanings are relevant. When God is called "my rock", it is valid to think of the rock as a stable and safe place to stay when the enemy threatens. But it is irrelevant whether, for instance, the rock is made of granite or whether it is a black or a red rock. Out of this interplay between what is normally true of rocks and what is normally said about God, new meaning is created.

My use of *metonymy* can be explained as follows. In Ps 18:3 the psalmist refers to God by not only using various metaphors: 'rock, fortress, mountain, shield, horn of salvation and stronghold', but by also including a depiction of how nature reacts to God's appearance – with dark clouds heavy with rain, thunder and lightning, Ps 18:8-16. These natural phenomena are consequential in that they say something characteristic about the Old Testament God by pointing to him as the actual cause of the stormy weather. So when I speak of *metonymic relations* in the following, it is most often these causal relations, with God regarded as the source of earthly phenomena, to which I am referring.

This characteristic in modern Danish hymn writing involving the inclusion of a whole range of biblical intertexts and various types of imagery means that the hymns are open to interpretation. They invite dialogue with the reader, and thus allow the reader to contribute a number of supplementary statements based on the intertextuality of which the reader is a part. For theological reasons it is important to insist that a single statement is never adequate to express who or what God is; instead the language of open dialogue is required.

The prohibition against imagery in Ex 20:4-6 (see also Deut 5:8-10) is the only one of the Ten Commandments linked to the threat of punishment in case of disobedience. Historically this commandment had to do with the statues of gods, but if it is to be validated as a norm today, it requires a more comprehensive interpretation. The commandment prohibits any attempt to reduce God to anything that mankind can embrace and manipulate, including the use of language. Nor must any such language set defining limits to God. According to the biblical norm no human conception or speech concerning God must exhaust His being, and it is precisely this that is respected through the use of multiple images.

Summarising, we can say that my theoretical basis is in line with the scholarship that emphasises the multiple meanings of language and imagery and the interlacing of the individual text in an intertextual network. This entails old texts receiving new meaning in a new context. The approach nevertheless raises the question: How can texts that are so open to interpretation serve as normative texts? And if so, what then is 'normative' in relation to, respectively, the Bible and biblically based hymns?

Selected biblical images of God and their application in recent hymns: God as a person

One important premise for hymn writing is the image of God as a person. The poet must expect that God can hear his words and react to them. This is particularly true of biblical psalms, where personal metaphors are dominant, though not absolute (cf. Kirsten Nielsen 2002). That God may resemble a person is clear from the three classic psalm genres: Prayer psalms (lamentations), Thanksgiving psalms and Hymns. Prayer psalms seek to move God to change the plight in which the psalmist finds himself. Psalms of thanksgiving are the logical consequence of God's intervention. And the Hymn, through its praise of God's great works, seeks to maintain the close connection between the psalmist/congregation and God. Thus the psalmist expects that God can not only see and hear what happens on earth but also has the will and the power to intervene. A being that is capable of this we normally regard as a person.

The three classic psalm genres are found again in the Danish hymn book, just as most of the hymns are formed as an address to God as a person. A glance at the Contents page reveals many hymns beginning with 'You'. Hymn writers can also begin by calling upon: God, Lord, Lord God, Lord Jesus, Jesus, or Holy Spirit! And such a direct address is of course found in abundance throughout the individual hymns. The new hymn writers thus follow a *biblical norm* which for the majority is so natural that we hardly think of it as a norm.

The fact that the personal image is such a matter of course may entail that the non-personal metaphors are perceived as metaphors, while the personal metaphors are regarded more or less as literal. In a Christian context, where the incarnation is a central dogma, it is perhaps even more natural to identify the personal and the divine. For this very reason it is important to consider whether the new hymn writers also follow the biblical norm by using personal metaphors (such as God as father) *as well as* non-personal metaphors (such as God as sun). In this context we shall examine how hymn writers employ nature as an image of God, such as God as sun or light. There are two possibilities here, if we are to follow the biblical norm when speaking of God. From nature the hymn writer can draw on various non-personal metaphors for God, but they may also include nature in the form of metonymic relations, where God is understood as the source and cause of all nature.

The role of nature: light

In a hymn from 1998 on the resurrection of Christ (*DDS* 239), the poet Sten Kaalø begins the first verse by describing the entombment of Jesus:

In that night of silent screams
the stone of Hell was set
like a devilish denial
after the pain of Friday.
Under the torn cloud
God died, in the city of hope,
after the pain of Friday.

Night and the torn cloud are not merely images used to create an atmosphere here. Night is an expression of God's absence; and therefore it marks out a metonymic relation to the absent God, who through his passivity is the cause of the darkness. The cloud over the dying Christ is torn, for nothing can be whole when God dies and the stage is left to the devil. In the following three verses the emptiness and abandonment of the world are depicted. Satan's perfidy has surrounded Jesus' grave, and 'dark was the Paschal garden', until 'death burst apart and Christ rose up / to the light of dawn.' The Danish word for the light of dawn, *morgenrøde* (lit. morning-red) is the final word in verse 4, and serves as a cue for the profusion of light with which the hymn closes in verse 5:

The lighted room of the third day
breaks through the sorrow,
the heavenly ground of Paradise
shines on Easter morning.
Sparks like a sun-sheaf, young,
blazes round the whole earth,
shines on Easter morning.

The shining Easter sun is a familiar motif in Danish hymn writing, but Sten Kaaløs's version of it is nevertheless original. Here the event becomes a room, a space into which the congregation can enter and be illuminated. The image of the sun as a sheaf in which each straw is a sun's ray has no precedence either in the Bible or in the Danish hymn book. In the biblical depictions of the resurrection there is of course some mention of light. It is the break of day, and according to Mt 28:3 the angel's appearance is 'like lightning and his clothes white as snow'. In Mk 16:2 the sun has already risen when the women arrive at the grave, where there is a young man dressed in white. In Lk 24:4 and Jn 20:12 there are respectively two young men in radiant clothing and two angels in white clothes.

Seen in relation to the biblical intertexts there is a marked transformation in this Easter hymn. It is no longer the radiant angels who proclaim that Christ is risen: it is the sun shining and sparkling which thus witnesses the resurrection. The hymn is set to be sung on Easter Day in a climate in which winter is characterised by darkness and rain. The sun, and not least the sun in spring, therefore plays a decisive role for the view of life in the country. The sun is seen as a sign of the victory of life over death. It is Danish nature which becomes the intertext for the poet in his reworking of the message of biblical texts. Through this a transformation takes place by which Christ's resurrection becomes the cause of the sunlight.

It is not an innovation in the Danish hymn tradition to link sunlight with the resurrection. Thus N.F.S. Grundtvig begins a hymn from 1846 (*DDS* 234) with the lines:

Like the morning-red of the spring sun
Jesus rose up from the womb of the earth
with life and light as well…

If we compare the old Grundtvig hymn with the new one by Kaalø, we can see that where the former compares the resurrection to a sunrise, the latter chooses to use sun and light to express a metonymic relation: the resurrection makes itself known in the form of a spring morning, to which we all respond. The light is not a metaphor for Jesus but a consequence of his returning to life. The resurrection is thus actualised for the congregation, as it experiences the sunrise on Easter morning over the Danish countryside. And everyone who rises with the Easter dawn and goes outside can in this way receive the message of Easter.

Finally, there is a classic place in the Bible that may have contributed to the two hymn writers' use of the sun in connection with Christ's resurrection, or one at least which the reader might be able to include as intertext when interpreting the hymn. This is Zacharias' hymn of praise, where the father of John the Baptist speaks of how 'the sunrise from on high will visit us' (Lk 1:78) – though where Zacharias is referring to Jesus' entry into the world, the Danish hymn tradition is concerned with his resurrection. It can sometimes be difficult to determine whether it is the hymn writers' own experience of nature they are writing about, or whether they are simply drawing on the biblical motifs, because these natural phenomena are common human property.

In the biblical tradition the star of Bethlehem is an example of a light phenomenon which signifies a metonymic relation between God and the events of Christmas night. In 1977 the hymn writer Johannes Johansen wrote a carol in which this light is the central motif – *It was a night like no other* (*DDS* 98). The hymn contains a number of biblical intertexts, but the most significant is the opening verses from the prologue to the Gospel of John, where Christ is depicted as the Word and the light in Jn 1:1-5. Light and darkness confront each other in the prologue, but the light is stronger and drives out the darkness. This contrast also characterises Johannes Johansen's carol, in which the first verse describes the night which was like no other:

It was a night like no other,
for all creation held its breath
and watched angels by the thousand wander

the earth by the light of the stars.
This night was a blaze of light in time,
it has shone through the generations ever since
the time God Himself became the light of mankind.

In verse 2 the stars move towards Bethlehem, and we hear of the shepherds that 'in the image of God they could not but shine / at the time God Himself became the light of mankind.' In the subsequent verses we again meet the motif of light: in verse 3 the child is able to see the pearl shining even in 'the most wretched man or woman', while in the last line of verse 4 the link between Jesus and the light is underlined: 'he is God, he is the light of mankind.' And he who was the light also becomes the Word in the fifth and final verse. We have thus returned to John's prologue, but in the meantime the poet has moved from the past into the present:

It is a word like no other,
it can topple even the tyrant of death,
it is the light by which we must wander
through the darkness to the land of the morning.
This word was a blaze of light in time,
it has shone through the generations ever since,
it is God, it is the light of mankind.

Johannes Johansen includes two central intertexts in this carol: the story of the shepherds in the field and the child coming into the world, Lk 2:1-20, and John's interpretation of Jesus as the Word and the light. Light and dark are used as images; but there is no attempt to describe the darkness as being like a December night in Denmark. The intertext here is not our own experience but the gospel of Jesus Christ – which is why it is a night like no other!!

The motif of light which in verse one is linked to angels is a break with everyday life. It is a quite extraordinary light, linking the earthly night with the heavenly world and thereby creating a metonymic relation between God and the world. Moreover the light is employed as a metaphor to interpret the child's identity: it is God Himself who is becoming the light of mankind. In a number of modern Christmas carols poets emphasise the humanity of Jesus. The child is recognisable as one of our own, a baby lying in his mother's embrace. The incarnation becomes very real. However, in Johannes Johansen's carol it is the divine origin which is underlined. We hear nothing of the child-mother relationship. It is very much the image of light which carries the carol's message and interprets the child's significance. And yet the choice of light in contrast to the dark is extremely easy for Danes to understand, celebrating Christmas as we do at the darkest time of the year.

Danish flowers and biblical hawthorn hedges

The hymn writer Lisbeth Smedegaard Andersen includes many images from nature in her hymns. In the first verse of *Summer Hymn in Liturgical Colours* (Lisbeth Smedegaard Andersen 1993, 30) she depicts the joy of early summer, with the sun shining and nature in bloom. In verse 2 she finds examples of plants in the Danish countryside and mentions the hawthorn hedge along with death as a sign that the negative has been overcome:

For life is no longer enclosed
by death and the hawthorn hedge;
but the daisy and the wall fern
grow prolifically in every chink.
Even the splendour of the devil's dandelion
takes root in God's creative power
and the soil in my garden.

It is not a coincidence that it is the hawthorn hedge which is linked to death. Here the biblical intertext plays a role, more precisely Gen 3:18-19, where Adam is banished from Paradise to a land which God has cursed and which is therefore full of thorns and thistles. This negative image of nature is taken from the biblical intertext, whereas the positive image of nature is clearly taken from Denmark. And yet it is still possible to understand the hawthorn hedges as negative images without including the Old Testament intertext. Partly our understanding is helped by the parallel drawn between death and the hedge of thorns, and partly the thorns in the hedge are seen as more characteristic of the hawthorn than its beautiful flowers.

The use of images from nature has the advantage that the poets can exploit common experiences. In a country like Denmark, where the climate and the seasons change noticeably, the countryside and the weather are very much part of everyday life and a perennial subject of conversation. So when the poets draw on images from nature, they can exploit our knowledge of light and darkness, and of the difference between summer and winter, spring and autumn. The flowers and trees, the birds and animals of nature are similarly shared experiences, and no specialist knowledge is required to imagine the kingdom of God as an eternal summer after a long, cold winter. Such a use of imagery also invites us to realise that the kingdom is not reserved for the few but for the many.

Experiences of nature and historical events

It is characteristic of modern Danish hymn writers to regard the love of God as unbounded: the gospel is for everyone. Images of God as the father of *all* and images of nature *shared* and linking us to the creator are therefore widespread. But this also means that recent hymns are not concerned at all with historical events – such as Denmark's liberation from the Nazi occupation in May 1945. Under the influence of those times the poet Mads Nielsen wrote the song called *A Lark Took Off*. It soon became known and loved as a liberation song and is still to be found in the *Folk High School Song-book* (*Højskolesangbogen*) from 2006 (no. 514), the classic Danish songbook for use in schools and at public meetings. In the first two verses Mads Nielsen portrays the joy of experiencing a free Denmark in spring with the church bells ringing, but in verse 3 he remembers those who died in the struggle and asks God to comfort those who are suffering severe loss. In the fourth and final verse he interprets the allied victory as God's intervention:

But you who topple the kingdoms of the proud
and release prisoners from bolts and bonds,
our hearts' thanks flies up to meet you,
our fate is in your strong hand.
Now it is spring and Denmark is free,
bless it, Lord, from the sound to the dunes.

Mads Nielsen dares to interpret Hitler's defeat as a result of God's intervention for the benefit of a small country. God appears here as the real reason for the defeat, thus giving rise to a metonymic relation between God and the world. Mads Nielsen is following in the tradition of other Danish patriotic songs in which the sense is given that God is watching over Denmark, or as one of these songs ends: 'There is yet a God above / who rules for Denmark's cause' (*Højskolesangbogen* 2006, no. 362). With this in mind, and in the light of the role that history plays in the Bible, it is striking that an event such as the end of the Second World War has not given rise to any new hymns. The few hymns which *are* to be found under the title Patriotic Songs (nos. 707-711 in the Danish hymn book) were all written considerably earlier. It is not the violent God of history whom the new hymn writers address, but rather the loving, caring God who embraces the whole world. When they refer to His intervention in the world it is solely in the form of Christ and the sending out of the Holy Spirit. It is not Danish national history which occupies them, but the basic Christian story that links all Christians, though by omitting the historical aspect the new hymn writers break with the biblical norm, which speaks of God as both the God of creation and the God of history.

The language of the Bible and the language of philosophy

The more recent psalms included in the new Danish hymn book are authorised for use at morning and evening service. Their way of speaking to and about God is a model for how Christians can address Him. It is therefore no surprise that even though they do not just repeat biblical thought but carry out transformations, there will always be a close connection between the language of the Bible and the language of the hymn book. This is seen in the reworking of central biblical images, but even the phenomenon of speaking of God in the form of metaphors and metonymies has also had a normative effect in relation to the hymn book. It is true that there are many examples of new hymn writers composing in imagery and ideas that do not have the Bible as intertext. Yet time and again such non-biblical formulations cannot stand alone when it is the Christian God to whom the hymn is addressed.

One of the new hymn writers, Lars Busk Sørensen, has written a short book entitled: *To God. Reflections on the Concept of God. A Ring of Poems (Til Gud. Refleksioner over Gudsbegrebet. En digtkreds).* This is not a collection of hymns, even though the dedication 'To God' is reminiscent of the genre. In contrast to the requirements of a hymn, his poems are not metrical either, so they are not for congregational singing. Nor is the designation 'Reflections' normally used in connection with hymns, being better known from the language of philosophy. It is precisely this combination of words associated with the hymn writing genre and words that mark the philosophical universe of the modern world which is characteristic of the poems in the collection. A good example of this is the poem *You are the one who is,* (*Du er den der er*, Lars Busk Sørensen 2004, 7).

You are the one who is,
the causeless being
who gives my being meaning,
the eternally inevitable
in whom all wisdom grows
and all questions wither.

The known starry skies
cannot contain you,
any more than my metaphors can,
and yet your entire fullness
is in the smallest grass-blade.

You are the word God,
the subject of the sentence
who is always still standing,
when the conversation falls silent.

You are the necessary word
I rejoice at the spring sun,
when life embraces me
with my beloved's arms.

You are the father-name
I whisper to the stars' coldness,

when the emptiness crowds in on me,
the name which also today
prevents my consciousness from
dissolving in the great nothing.

Your place and your purpose
I do not know.
I only know that you are.

Despite the philosophical use of language, there is no doubt that the Bible is among the intertexts for these verses. 'You are the one who is' may at first glance appear a purely philosophical formulation, but the expression plays on the name of God in the Old Testament, Yahweh, which can be rendered: 'I am the one I am' or just 'I am', Ex 3:14. It also reminds us of the various 'I-am statements' in the Gospel of John: 'I am the good shepherd', Jn 10:11, or 'I am the way and the truth and the life', Jn 14:6. In the Bible these words are expressions of self-revelation by God and Jesus, but in Lars Busk Sørensen's poem they are a confession to the God to which the ring of poems is addressed. It is thus no abstract concept of God to which the poet is relating, it is the God of the Bible.

The idea that God is the one in whom all wisdom grows acquires a special meaning if we include the Old Testament story of the Garden of Eden and the Tree of Knowledge as an intertext. In Gen 3 the Tree of Knowledge is the forbidden tree which man must not eat of. In Lars Busk Sørensen's confession to God, on the other hand, wisdom is depicted as positive, for the perspective is turned around: Here it is a question of *God's* wisdom, in the face of which all questions should wither and die. The biblical account of the Fall lies behind the wording, but in the praise of God all reference to man's Fall is omitted.

Down through the poem the poet tries to come closer to who and what God is. But neither heaven (cf. Solomon's temple prayer in 1 Kings 8:27) nor language can contain God. However much the poet employs metaphors and thus linguistic forms that are open to interpretation, these are inadequate. The word 'metaphor' belongs to linguistic science, whereas the references to heaven are taken from the biblical intertext. There is also a biblical intertext which can deepen the assertion that the fullness of God can be contained in even the smallest blade of grass. The very choice of 'blade of grass' surprises. For in the Bible grass is an image of man's ephemerality (cf. Ps 103:15-16; Isa 40:6-8). But by choosing 'grass' the poet can indirectly put words to the incarnation: that God Himself became man at a particular point in history and lived under human conditions. God is thereby not only the Old Testament God, but also He who came in human form and thus had to die as a man.

Lars Busk Sørensen says that the word 'God' is the subject of the sentence, the controlling element, not the controlled. Even in silence the word 'God' is present. He is the very pre-condition whom the poet addresses when he is gripped by the joy of life. When he feels the infinity of space and all its coldness, it is the name of God the father that he whispers. It is not the everyday word for a father which he sets up against emptiness and nothingness; it is the solemn and archaic word for a father which is still used in the Danish Bible as a designation for God. It is this relation between God the Father and the child which prevents consciousness from dissolving into nothingness.

In the first verse, God is the place of growth for wisdom; in the last verse the poet confesses his own lack of insight. Concerning God all he knows is that 'you are'. The poem closes with an apparently formal definition of God's existence. This resembles philosophy's way of defining things; but the poet does not describe God in the third person, he uses the second person. Moreover, the Old Testament intertext that lies behind the introductory words, 'You are the one who is', says more than the fact *that* a God exists. For it is the God of whom the Bible speaks in imperfect words and inadequate metaphors. The God who is the subject and not the object. It is the God who revealed Himself to Moses in the name: 'I am'.

Reception and transformation may also appear in such a combination of two language types that are often kept apart: the biblical and the philosophical. The technique reminds us of the one that lies behind the use of metaphors, where two contexts that are normally not linked interplay with one another. For precisely by connecting the hitherto unconnected it is possible to say something new. When two parallel lines, against all expectation, nevertheless cross, something unexpected occurs.

The poem was written some 10 years after the publication of the new hymn book and was therefore never considered for inclusion by the commission. But if one requires of a hymn that it should have the Bible as a decisive intertext and should be the current response of the congregation, this poem can be defined as a hymn. The fact that its metrical complexity makes it unsuitable for congregational hymn singing is another matter.

Biblical normativity as theological challenge

In this treatment of a number of hymns and poems we have seen how the Bible serves as an intertext for recent hymns, as well as how hymn writers have been able not only to rework biblical texts but also to undertake transformations so that the way in which God is spoken of is not only repetition but also innovative. The Bible has thus served as the central intertext for the hymn book, and the hymn writers have allowed the Bible to be normative for the way in which they compose. But this has not prevented the poets from breaking with the norm, for instance by omitting images of the God of history and thereby reducing the number of images of God. We have seen how biblical images of God are re-employed in recent hymn writing partly as metaphors and partly as metonymic relations. As regards both content and form, the Bible has served as a normative text. But we have also noted that the biblical norm which the hymn writers have taken over, and which they themselves pass on to the reader, can be described in a few words as: *multiplicity, interpretation and innovation.* Both the biblical writers and the hymn writers speak of God with the help of many different images, and even though the Bible is limited by its covers, the hymn writers demonstrate that it is still possible to create new images. Often this happens through a combination of biblical formulations, but it can also happen by combining biblical and non-biblical expressions.

The concept of normativity is often linked to simplicity and unambiguity. As a legal concept it presumes that we can clearly distinguish what meets the norm and what falls outside it. The canonisation of the Bible limited the number of normative texts, but not the possibility of various interpretations. As an authorised hymnal, the Danish hymn book is limited to a certain number of hymns. But it is not exactly the same hymns that are found in the hymn books which have been authorised for use in the Danish Lutheran church over the years. In contrast to the individual books of the Bible, the hymns in the hymn book can be replaced. And because the hymn books are regularly renewed, more flexibility is available which ensures the continued relevance of the authorised hymns and their interpretation of the biblical message.

The theological challenge therefore lies in the two most important authoritative texts of the Danish Lutheran Church, the Bible and the hymn book, representing the norm of *multiplicity, interpretation and innovation*. The two books maintain a norm which is in good agreement with the Old Testament prohibition against imagery. For the norm which the prohibition on imagery asserted must be defined for the church's way of speaking about God as follows: 'You must not make any fixed, limited image of God'. To live up to the biblical norm it must therefore be required of the theologian and the hymn writer alike that their reading of the biblical message takes place not only as a repetition of the biblical words, but also as a reception and transformation of them.

Bibliography

Andersen, Lisbeth Smedegaard 1993. *Klædt i støv. Salmer og digte*. Herning: Poul Kristensens Forlag.

Bloom, Harold 1973. *The Anxiety of Influence: A Theory of Poetry*. Oxford: Oxford University Press.

Den Danske Salmebog 2002 (*The Danish Hymn Book*). Copenhagen: Det Kgl. Vajsenhus' Forlag.

Højskolesangbogen 2006 (*The High School Songbook*). Udgivet af Folkehøjskolernes Forening i Danmark (18th edition). Copenhagen: FFDs Forlag.

Lyster, Jens 1991. 'Hvad er en salme?'. In: *Haderslev Stiftsbog 1991*, 30-48.

Nielsen, Kirsten 1989. *There is Hope for a Tree. The Tree as Metaphor in Isaiah*. Sheffield: JSOT Press.

Nielsen, Kirsten 2000. 'Intertextuality and Hebrew Bible'. In: A. Lemaire & M. Sæbø (eds.), *Congress Volume Oslo 1998*. Leiden – Boston – Köln: E.J. Brill, 17-31.

Nielsen, Kirsten 2002. 'The Variety of Metaphors about God in the Psalter: Deconstruction and Reconstruction?'. *Scandinavian Journal of the Old Testament* 16, 151-159.

Nielsen, Kirsten 2007. *Der flammer en ild. Gudsbilleder i nyere danske salmer*. Copenhagen: Forlaget Aros.

Schleicher, Marianne 2007. *Intertextuality in the Tales of Rabbi Nahman of Bratslav. A Close Reading of Sippurey Ma'asiyot*. Leiden: Brill.

Sørensen, Lars Busk 2004. *Til Gud. Refleksioner over gudsbegrebet. En digtkreds*. Frederiksberg: Forlaget Alfa.

ABOUT THE AUTHORS

Kirsten M. Andersen, MA (Theology) (1992). Lecturer at the Department for Teacher Training in Silkeborg, University College Via, Denmark. Has published various articles on the subject of religious education and in the field of literature and theology.

David Bugge, MA (Theology) (2000), PhD (2004). Associate Research Professor at the Department of Systematic Theology, Aarhus University, Denmark. Several publications on literature & theology, ethics, and the philosophy of religion.

Iben Damgaard, MA (Theology) (2002), PhD (2005). Assistant Professor in Ethics and Philosophy of Religion at the Department of Systematic Theology, Aarhus University, Denmark. Her PhD dissertation is entitled: *Mulighedens Spejl: Forestilling, fortælling og selvforhold hos Kierkegaard og Ricoeur.* Her published articles deal mainly with Kierkegaard. She is co-editor of *Subjectivity and Transcendence*, Mohr Siebeck 2007.

Laura Feldt, MA (2004), PhD scholar studying fantasy and religion in the Hebrew Bible and ancient Mesopotamian literature at the Department of the Study of Religion, Aarhus University, Denmark. Has published various articles on monstrosity, fantasy, and ancient Near Eastern religious literature.

Maria Louise Odgaard Møller, MA (Theology) (2005), PhD scholar (2007-) at the Department of Systematic Theology, Aarhus University, Denmark.

Kirsten Nielsen, MA (1970), Lic.Theol (1976) and Dr.Theol (1985). Professor in the Old Testament at the Department of the Old and New Testament, Aarhus University, Denmark. Has published *There is Hope for a Tree. The Tree as Metaphor in Isaiah* (Sheffield: JSOT Press 1989), *Satan – the Prodigal Son? A Family Problem in the Bible* (Sheffield: Sheffield Academic Press 1998), and various articles on metaphors and Old Testament theology. In her latest book she analyses images of God in modern Danish hymns, *Der flammer en ild. Gudsbilleder i nyere danske salmer* (A Fire is Blazing. Images of God in Modern Danish Hymns), (Frederiksberg: Aros Forlag 2007).

Marie Vejrup Nielsen, MA (2003), PhD (2007). Assistant Professor in Modern Christianity at the Department of the Study of Religion, Aarhus University, Denmark. See http://person.au.dk/da/mvn@teo for a full list of publications and activities.

Jakob Nissen, MA (Theology) (2004). Vicar in the Evangelical-Lutheran Church of Denmark (2005).

Johannes Nissen. Associate Professor of New Testament Exegesis and Practical Theology at Aarhus University, Denmark. Has published a number of books and articles, especially on the Bible and ethics, the New Testament and mission, hermeneutics, and practical theological issues. His recent publications include *New Testament and Mission: Historical and Hermeneutical Perspectives* (Peter Lang, 1999, 2007, 4th. ed.), *Bibel og etik: Konkrete og principielle problemstillinger* (Aarhus University Press, 2003), *Bibel og økumeni: Essays om enhed og mangfoldighed* (Aros forlag, 2006), *Diakoni og menneskesyn* (Aros forlag, 2008).

Marianne Schleicher, MA (1998), PhD (2003). Assistant Professor in Jewish Studies at the Department of the Study of Religion, Aarhus University, Denmark. In 2007 she published *Intertextuality in the Tales of Rabbi Nahman of Bratslav. A Close Reading of Sippurey Ma'asiyot* (Leiden: Brill, 666 pages) on Rabbi Nahman's complex use of scripture.